Exploring Elementary
Mathematics

Exploring Elementary
Mathematics

MERVIN L. KEEDY

LESLIE A. DWIGHT

CHARLES W. NELSON

JOHN SCHLUEP

PAUL A. ANDERSON

Holt, Rinehart and Winston, Inc.
New York, Toronto, London, Sydney

Contents

Copyright © 1970
Holt, Rinehart and Winston, Inc.
All Rights Reserved/Printed in the United States of America
ISBN: 0-03-081143-0
123456789   071   98765

CHAPTER ONE

Numbers and Numerals

USING NUMBERS

1. The people in the picture at the left are at a basketball game.

   a. Are there a few people? many people?

   b. Do the words many and few give us exact answers?

2. For an exact answer we think of a number.

   a. Are more than 50 people at the game? more than 100? more than 500? How would you find the exact number?

   b. Name the exact number of basketballs.

3. We count to find the number of members in a group. The number tells how many.

   a. How many girls are in the group?

   b. How many boys are cheerleaders?

   c. How many girls have shakers?

   d. How many girls have no hats?

4. John has a ball. He is sixth in line. Words like sixth, first and second tell which one.

   a. Bill is the boy with the bat. What number in line is he?

   b. In what place is the boy with the book?

   c. Which boy is wearing glasses?

   d. Which boy is petting the dog?

EXERCISES

Read each sentence. Is the number used to tell *how many* or *which one?*

1. Ray is drinking his second milk shake.

2. Sue is reading page 67.

3. There are 127 people at the game.

4. John lives at 462 Shadow Lane.

5. These words often tell how many: one, two, three. Continue the list to twenty-two.

6. Words like first, second, and third tell which one. Continue the list to thirteenth.

NUMERALS

The pyramid is 9999∩∩∩II feet tall. The building was built in MDCCCXCII. The symbols MDCCCXII and 9999∩∩∩II are numerals. A numeral is a symbol used to name a number.

1. Long ago people made a single tally mark, | to stand for one. They wrote ||| to name three. What number is named by these marks?

   a. |||||||||||

   b. ||||||||||||||||||||

   c. What would happen if 2,568 were named with tally marks?

2. John kept score for the arithmetic contest.

   Boys ̶I̶I̶I̶I ̶I̶I̶I̶I II   Girls ̶I̶I̶I̶I ̶I̶I̶I̶I

   a. How did John make his tally marks easier to read?

   b. What was the score?

   c. How would John name the number 30?

3. Read the final score.

   Boys ̶I̶I̶I̶I ̶I̶I̶I̶I ̶I̶I̶I̶I ̶I̶I̶I̶I ̶I̶I̶I̶I ̶I̶I̶I̶I ̶I̶I̶I̶I II

   Girls ̶I̶I̶I̶I ̶I̶I̶I̶I ̶I̶I̶I̶I ̶I̶I̶I̶I ̶I̶I̶I̶I ̶I̶I̶I̶I ̶I̶I̶I̶I ̶I̶I̶I̶I

3

EGYPTIAN NUMERALS

The Egyptians of long ago used these numerals.

Egyptian Numeral	Our Numeral	Word Names
|	1	one
∩	10	ten
၆	100	one hundred
⚒	1,000	one thousand
⟋	10,000	ten thousand
⟋	100,000	one hundred thousand
⚎	1,000,000	one million

1. They could name a number several ways.

Our Numeral	Egyptian Numeral	Meaning
12	∩|| or |∩|	10 + 1 + 1 or 1 + 10 + 1
35	∩∩∩||||| or ∩|∩|∩|||	10 + 10 + 10 + 1 + 1 + 1 + 1 + 1 or 10 + 1 + 10 + 1 + 10 + 1 + 1 + 1
212	၆၆∩|| or ၆∩၆||	100 + 100 + 10 + 1 + 1 or 100 + 10 + 100 + 1 + 1
1,203	⚒၆၆||| or ၆၆⚒|||	1000 + 100 + 100 + 1 + 1 + 1 or 100 + 100 + 1000 + 1 + 1 + 1

a. How do we find the meaning of Egyptian numerals?

b. Does the order of the numerals matter?

c. Write another Egyptian numeral for 212.

2. Write two Egyptian numerals for 897.

4

3. A name for 1,324 is 𐦀999∩∩IIII . Write another Egyptian numeral for 1,324.

4. Kathy said it was easier to write an Egyptian numeral for 2,568 than to use John's tally system. Why?

EXERCISES

Write our numerals for these.

1. ∩∩∩II

2. ∩I∩I∩

3. ∩∩∩IIII

4. ⌐𐦀9∩I

5. ∩∩II

6. ∩∩∩IIIII

Write Egyptian numerals for these numbers.

7. 38

8. 56

9. 121

10. 131

11. 232

12. 1,000

13. A pyramid is 9I9I9I9II feet tall. Write our numeral for the height of the pyramid.

14. An Egyptian traveled 9∩I miles. Write our numeral to tell how far he traveled.

UNEXPLORED TERRITORY

1. The ∩ is the Egyptian numeral for ten. How many strokes name ten?

$$IIIIIIIIII = ∩$$

2. For each, write another Egyptian numeral.

a. ∩∩∩∩∩∩∩∩∩∩

b. 9999999999

ROMAN NUMERALS

The Romans used this way of naming numbers.

Roman Numeral	Our Numeral
I	1
V	5
X	10
L	50
C	100
D	500
M	1,000

1. The Romans combined symbols like this.

    III means 1 + 1 + 1 or 3
    VI means 5 + 1 or 6
    XXXI means 10 + 10 + 10 + 1 or 31
    CLV means 100 + 50 + 5 or 155

2. Copy and complete.

    a. XXVI means 10 + ___ + ___ + 1 or ___

    b. CI means ___ + 1 or ___

    c. DCX means ___ + 100 + ___ or ___

    d. MLV means ___ + ___ + ___ or 1,055

    e. LXXV means ___ + ___ + ___ + ___
       or ___.

3. The Romans used six shortcuts.

    IV means 5 — 1 or 4
    IX means 10 — 1 or 9
    XL means 50 — 10 or 40
    XC means 100 — 10 or 90
    CD means 500 — 100 or 400
    CM means 1,000 — 100 or 900

6

4. We can combine symbols and use the short-cuts.
   a. L IV means 50 + 4 or 54
   b. What does M CM L IX mean?
5. Copy and complete.
   a. XIII means 10 + 1 + 1 + 1 or ___
   b. LXIV means ___ + 10 + ___ or ___
   c. CCXV means ___ + ___ + ___ + ___
      or 215
   d. CMLI means ___ + 50 + ___ or ___
   e. MCDIX means 1,000 + ___ + ___ or ___

EXERCISES

Write our numerals for these.

1. XI	**2.** XXXIII	**3.** IX
4. XXIV	**5.** LV	**6.** DCL
7. XLV	**8.** XCVIII	**9.** CDII
10. MCMLXX	**11.** LVII	**12.** LXVIII

Write Roman numerals for these.

13. ten	**14.** five	**15.** six
16. twelve	**17.** three	**18.** eight
19. 24	**20.** 32	**21.** 17

UNEXPLORED TERRITORY

Add. For each, write a Roman numeral.

1. V + III	**2.** III + II	**3.** X + I
4. VI + III	**5.** II + IV	**6.** VI + V

OUR NUMERALS

1. The number of members in each set can be named with one symbol.

How many members are in the set named by the symbol 7? by the symbol 3? by the symbol 0?

We use ten symbols when writing numerals:

0, 1, 2, 3, 4, 5, 6, 7, 8, 9

We call them **digit symbols**. The numbers they name are sometimes called **digits**.

2. The number of this set cannot be named by a single digit symbol.

   a. John might name it this way. ╫╫ ╫╫ ‖
      This means 5 + 5 + 2.

   b. The Egyptians might have named it this way. ∩‖
      This means ___ + 1 + 1.

   c. The Romans wrote XII.
      This means ___ + 1 + 1.

   d. We name it with the numeral 12.

3. In our system we think of grouping by tens.

    a. There are ___ groups of ten and ___ ones.

    b. A numeral for the number of this set is 23.
The numeral 23 means ___ tens + 3 ones.
It also means 20 + ___.

EXERCISES

Copy and complete.

1.	1 ten + 5 ones	10 + 5	15
2.	2 tens + 1	20 + ___	21
3.	___ tens + 7	30 + 7	___
4.	6 tens + 9	___	69
5.	8 tens + 4 ones	___	___

Write our numeral for each.

  6. 5 tens + 3 ones   **7.** 3 tens + 4 ones

  8. 4 tens + 3   **9.** 9 tens + 0

10. 50 + 1   **11.** 20 + 2

Copy and complete.

12. 96 = ___ tens + ___ ones

13. 87 = ___ tens + ___ ones

14. 36 = 30 + ___   **15.** 48 = ___ + 8

STANDARD AND EXPANDED NUMERALS

1. How many members are in this set? We call 27 a *standard numeral*.

2. The numeral 27 means 2 *tens* + 7 *ones*.

    a. We can name 2 tens as 2 × 10.
    Rename: 5 tens, 8 tens, 1 ten.

    b. We can name 7 ones as 7 × 1.
    Rename: 5 ones, 6 ones, 9 ones.

    c. Here are names for twenty-seven:
    2 tens + 7 ones, (2 × 10) + (7 × 1).
    They are *expanded numerals* for 27.

3. Copy and complete.

Standard Numeral	Expanded Numeral
a. 68	(6 × 10) + (8 × ___)
b. 33	(3 × ___) + (3 × 1)
c. 93	___ + ___
d. ___	(9 × 10) + (9 × 1)
e. 49	___ + ___

4. 76 means 7 ___ plus 6 ___.
   67 means 6 ___ plus 7 ___.
   Why is the order of the symbols important?

5. Study the numeral 83. Which digit symbol names the number of ones? the number of tens?

Numbers can be named in different ways.
   Standard numeral: 23
   Expanded numerals: 2 tens + 3 ones
                            20 + 3
                            $(2 \times 10) + (3 \times 1)$

Write expanded numerals.

Example $67 = (6 \times 10) + (7 \times 1)$

1. 4 tens   **2.** 3 ones   **3.** 9 tens

4. 6 ones   **5.** 5 tens   **6.** 1 one

7. 35   **8.** 97   **9.** 21

Write standard numerals.

10. $(8 \times 10) + (6 \times 1)$ **11.** $(8 \times 10) + (8 \times 1)$

12. $(1 \times 10) + (0 \times 1)$ **13.** $(4 \times 10) + (8 \times 1)$

14. 30 + 4   **15.** 80 + 8

16. 6 tens + 4 ones   **17.** 7 tens + 0 ones

18. 9 tens + 1 one   **19.** 2 tens + 3 ones

20. 5 ones + 8 tens   **21.** 8 tens + 3 ones

22. What is the largest number you can name using two digit symbols?

23. What is the smallest number you can name using two digit symbols?

TENS AND HUNDREDS

1. Each box holds ten blocks. We call it a tens-box.

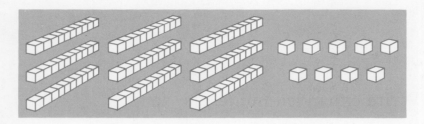

   a. How many tens-boxes are there?

   b. How many single blocks are there?

   c. There are 9 tens + 9 ones. Write the standard numeral.

2. **a.** If we put one more block with the 99 blocks, can we group again?

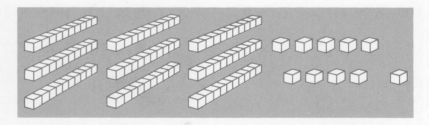

   b. How many tens-boxes will we have?

3. We group the 10 tens to make 1 hundred.

$$10 \text{ tens} = 100$$

4. We can rename 300 as 3×100. Rename:

   a. 600   **b.** 200   **c.** 900

5. This place-value chart shows the meaning of the numeral 463.

Hundreds	Tens	Ones
4	6	3
4 × 100	6 × 10	3 × 1

The 4 names the number of hundreds.
What does the 6 name? the 3?

6. An expanded numeral for 234 is

$$(2 \times 100) + (3 \times 10) + (4 \times 1).$$

Write expanded numerals.

a. 47   **b.** 986   **c.** 777   **d.** 320

7. Study the picture below.

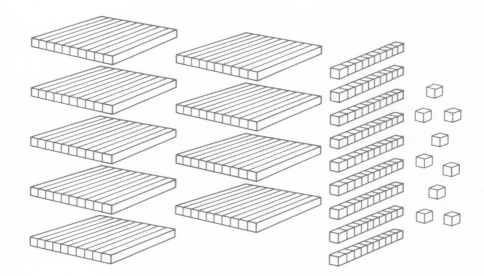

a. How many hundreds-boxes are there?

b. How many tens-boxes are there?

c. How many single blocks are there?

8. If we put one more block with the 999 blocks, we regroup. We get 10 hundreds, or ____.

> Ten ones make 1 ten or 10.
> $10 \times 1 = 10$
> Ten tens make 1 hundred or 100.
> $10 \times 10 = 100$
> Ten hundreds make 1 thousand or 1,000.
> $10 \times 100 = 1,000$

Write standard numerals.

1. 1 hundred + 6 tens + 5 ones

2. $(2 \times 100) + (3 \times 10) + (8 \times 1)$

3. 3 hundreds + 8 tens + 0 ones

4. $(8 \times 100) + (0 \times 10) + (8 \times 1)$

5. $(1 \times 100) + (3 \times 10) + (0 \times 1)$

6. Nine hundred sixty-three

7. Nine hundred sixty

Copy and complete.

8. 768 means ____ hundreds + ____ tens + ____ ones

9. 909 means ____ hundreds + ____ tens + ____ ones

Write expanded numerals.

10. 368   **11.** 999   **12.** 207   **13.** 370

14

THOUSANDS

1. Look at the numeral 2,345. In which place is the 5? 4? 3? 2?

2. Study the place-value chart.

Thousands	Hundreds	Tens	Ones
4	8	3	5
4 × 1,000	8 × 100	3 × 10	5 × 1

The standard numeral 4,835 means ___ thousands + ___ hundreds + ___ tens + ___ ones.

3. We can name 4,835 as 4,000 + 800 + 30 + 5. Copy and complete.

   a. 9,627 = 9,000 + ___ + ___ + ___
   b. 3,942 = ___ + ___ + ___ + ___

4. An expanded numeral for 4,835 is (4 × 1,000) + (8 × 100) + (3 × 10) + (5 × 1). Write expanded numerals.

   a. 6,734   b. 3,921   c. 9,135   d. 2,031

5. The standard numeral for (3 × 1,000) + (9 × 100) + (4 × 10) + (8 × 1) is 3,948.

   Write the standard numerals.

   a. (8 × 1,000) + (9 × 100) + (7 × 10) + (6 × 1)

   b. (7 × 1,000) + (3 × 100) + (0 × 10) + (4 × 1)

Write the standard numerals.

1. 3 thousands + 6 hundreds + 4 tens + 7 ones

2. $(9 \times 1{,}000) + (8 \times 100) + (0 \times 10) + (3 \times 1)$

3. 2 thousands + 0 hundreds + 1 ten + 0 ones

4. 6 thousands + 5 hundreds + 0 tens + 8 ones

5. $(8 \times 1{,}000) + (0 \times 100) + (0 \times 10) + (0 \times 1)$

6. Six thousand, four hundred eighty-two

7. $(3 \times 1{,}000) + (4 \times 100) + (8 \times 10) + (9 \times 1)$

8. Seven thousand, eighty-four

Copy and complete.

9. $1{,}492 = 1{,}000 + \underline{\quad} + 90 + 2$

10. $9{,}063$ means $\underline{\quad}$ thousands + $\underline{\quad}$ hundreds + $\underline{\quad}$ tens + $\underline{\quad}$ ones

Write expanded numerals.

Example 3,498 means $(3 \times 1{,}000) + (4 \times 100) + (9 \times 10) + (8 \times 1)$

11. 1,246

12. 1,084

13. 9,999

14. 3,000

15. What is the largest number you can name using three digit symbols?

16. What is the largest number you can name using four digit symbols?

THE ABACUS

An abacus may be used to show numbers.

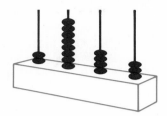

1. The wire on the right shows 3 ones. What do the beads on the other wires mean?

2. The abacus above shows $(2 \times 1,000) + (8 \times 100) + (4 \times 10) + (3 \times 1)$. Write the standard numeral.

3. Write an expanded numeral and the standard numeral for each number shown.

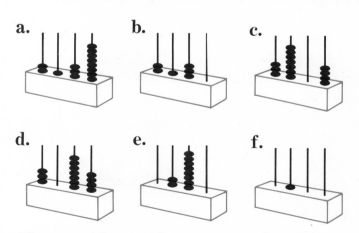

a.   b.   c.

d.   e.   f.

4. Show each number on an abacus.
    a. 9,487   b. 9,407   c. 8,008   d. 3,048

5. Can you place more than 9 beads on a wire? Why?

17

NAMING LARGER NUMBERS

We know 1,000 = 10 × 100. In the numeral 1,000 the 1 is in the *thousands* place.

1. Read the numeral on this place-value chart.

1,000	100	10	1
1	3	4	9

2. The next place is the *ten thousands* place. Read the numeral.

10,000	1,000	100	10	1
1	3	4	9	2

3. The next place is the *hundred thousands*. Read the numeral.

100,000	10,000	1,000	100	10	1
1	3	4	9	2	0

4. The digit symbols in 134,920 are grouped in *periods*. Commas are used to separate the periods.

Thousands	Ones
134	920

   a. In what period is 134?

   b. In what period is 920?

5. Commas help us read numerals. Separate these numerals into periods.

   a. 284947   **b.** 4132   **c.** 81927

   d. 56001   **e.** 340751   **f.** 925380

6. Study this expanded numeral.
   34,128 means $30,000 + 4,000 + 100 + 20 + 8$
   Write this kind of expanded numeral for:

   a. 92,476   **b.** 439,149   **c.** 90,321

7. This is another kind of expanded numeral.
   28,269 is $(2 \times 10,000) + (8 \times 1,000)$
   $\qquad\qquad + (2 \times 100) + (6 \times 10) + (9 \times 1)$
   Write expanded numerals.

   a. 42,076   **b.** 276,463   **c.** 903,413

8. How many thousands are in each?

   a. 1,413   **b.** 93,413   **c.** 930,413

EXERCISES

1. Make a place-value chart for 326,047.

Write standard numerals.

2. Fourteen thousand, two hundred twenty-six

3. Four hundred thousand, twenty-six

In 659,074 which digit tells the number of:

4. thousands   5. tens   6. ten thousands

In which period are the underlined symbols?

7. 232,<u>128</u>   8. <u>78</u>,128   9. 720,<u>136</u>

Write two expanded numerals for each.

10. 22,198   11. 807,456   12. 13,706

13. What is the largest number you can name using five digit symbols?

MILLIONS

1. Let us think of still larger numbers.

We write:	We say:
1,000	One thousand
10,000	Ten thousand
100,000	One hundred thousand
1,000,000	One million

If you put a million of these books end to end, they would reach about 150 miles.

2. Study this chart. In which place is 7? 4? 8? In which period is 956?

Millions			Thousands			Ones		
Hundreds	Tens	Ones	Hundreds	Tens	Ones	Hundreds	Tens	Ones
8	4	7	1	2	3	9	5	6

We say: Eight hundred forty-seven million, one hundred twenty-three thousand, nine hundred fifty-six.

3. Read: 578,136,414. In what place is each of these digit symbols?

    a. 5   **b.** 3   **c.** 8   **d.** 6   **e.** 7

4. How many millions are named in each?

    a. 7,126,453   **b.** 800,404,901

    c. 27,384,986   **d.** 904,186,431

5. In 543,724,273 what does the 5 mean?

6. The numeral 43,124,876 means:

4 × 10 million	or	40,000,000
3 × 1 million	or	3,000,000
1 × 100 thousand	or	100,000
2 × 10 thousand	or	20,000
4 × 1 thousand	or	4,000
8 × 1 hundred	or	800
7 × ten	or	70
6 × one	or	6
		43,124,876

Show what the numeral 9,486,273 means.

7. Read the numerals in Item 4.

EXERCISES

Write standard numerals.

1. Eight million

2. Eighty million

3. Eight hundred million, eight

4. Two hundred forty-three million,
six hundred sixty-six thousand,
four hundred twenty-one.

In each numeral, one digit symbol is underlined.
What does it mean? Which period is it in?

Example   476,289,349 ⟶ (4 × 100,000,000)
millions period

5. 286,493,129

6. 387,126,418

7. 286,493,129

8. 129,310,460

9. 286,493,129

10. 900,000,000

READING A TABLE

RECENT POPULATION OF COUNTRIES OF THE WORLD	
Japan	99,920,000
France	49,890,000
Sweden	7,869,000
India	511,115,000
United States	200,064,000
Liechtenstein	20,000
U.S.S.R.	235,543,000

1. What was the population of each of these countries?

   a. Japan   **b.** United States   **c.** Sweden

   d. France   **e.** U.S.S.R.   **f.** India

2. Which country had the most people?

3. Which country had the fewest people?

4. List the countries above in order of their population, from the smallest to the largest.

Let's Practice

Write standard numerals.

1. $(7 \times 1,000) + (3 \times 100) + (4 \times 10) + (9 \times 1)$

2. $(3 \times 10,000) + (4 \times 1)$

3. $(5 \times 1,000,000) + (6 \times 100)$

4. $50,000 + 8,000 + 700 + 90 + 0$

5. $3,000,000 + 30,000 + 30 + 3$

READING NUMERALS

1. A toy-maker sold 4,732,740 toys in one year. Mike's dog license has the numeral 4732740. When a numeral is used in this way, we read each digit symbol: "four, seven, three, two, seven, four, zero." Read these numerals this way:

   a. 6492864   **b.** 7426882   **c.** 4326907

2. Read 8,891,321 and 8891321.

3. How would a telephone operator read the numeral 473-2740? the numeral 473-2741?

4. Bill called 688-9200. He said, "six, eight, eight, nine, two hundred." Read these telephone numbers.

   a. 724-8937   **b.** 764-4300   **c.** 736-5000

5. Read these sentences.

   a. Columbus came to America in 1492.

   b. Jack has 1,492 stamps in his collection.

   c. Mr. White's phone number was 1492.

6. The numeral 5,600 may be read "five thousand, six hundred" or "fifty-six hundred." Read this sentence in two ways: The distance between two cities by air is about 2,500 miles.

BOYS 68
GIRLS 65

COMPARING NUMBERS

1. Who is ahead? How do you know?

We know:	*We write:*
68 is greater than 65	68 > 65
65 is less than 68	65 < 68

Which sentences are true?

a. 384 > 382   **b.** 1840 > 1845   **c.** 92 < 98

2. We can compare the number of tens, hundreds, or thousands. We know:

746 > 726   since 4 tens > 2 tens;
1846 > 1746 since 8 hundreds > 7 hundreds;
4189 < 5189 since 4 thousands < 5 thousands.

EXERCISES

Make each sentence true. Use > or <.

1. 97 ≡ 87   **2.** 86 ≡ 46

3. 486 ≡ 949   **4.** 3,847 ≡ 3,947

5. 4,986 ≡ 9,486   **6.** 12,874 ≡ 12,873

7. 692,483 ≡ 682,483   **8.** 874,198 ≡ 875,198

9. 746 ≡ 748   **10.** 5,416 ≡ 5,461

11. 130 ≡ 103   **12.** 148,748 ≡ 149,743

ROUNDING NUMBERS

1. Jim guessed that he had 30 marbles. He counted them. He had 27. Was his guess a good one?

2. Sometimes we do not need an exact answer. We know: 38 > 30 and 38 < 40. Is 38 nearer to 30 or to 40?

3. We know: 183 > 180 and 183 < 190. Is 183 nearer to 180 or to 190?

4. Is 281 nearer to 280 or to 290?

When we choose the **nearest** ten, we say we have rounded to the nearest ten. We round 281 to 280. We round 186 to 190.

5. Round to the nearest ten.

   a. 432   **b.** 59   **c.** 436   **d.** 162

6. Is 35 nearer to 30 or to 40?

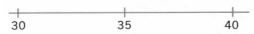

We agree that a number halfway between two tens is rounded up to the greater ten.

7. Round to the nearest ten.

   a. 85   **b.** 135   **c.** 105   **d.** 195

   e. 355   **f.** 5   **g.** 678   **h.** 295

8. We know: 513 > 500 and 513 < 600. Is 513 nearer to 500 or to 600?

9. Is 1,785 nearer to 1,800 or to 1,700?

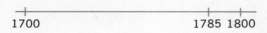

10. The number 386 is nearer to 400 than to 300. When we round 386 to the nearest *hundred*, we get 400.
Round to the nearest hundred.

   a. 831   **b.** 1,894   **c.** 1,831

11. Consider 750. Since 750 is halfway between 700 and 800, we agree to round up.
Round 550 to the nearest hundred.

EXERCISES

Round to the nearest 10.

  1. 18   **2.** 391   **3.** 1,281   **4.** 94,287

  5. 95   **6.** 486   **7.** 32,436   **8.** 949

Round to the nearest 100.

  9. 344   **10.** 1,236

11. 384,032   **12.** 38,212

13. 354   **14.** 1,250

15. 384,199   **16.** 284,150

17. 284,163   **18.** 785,307

ANOTHER LOOK AT GROUPING

We use different words to describe groupings.
   A *decade* is a group of ten.
   A *score* is a group of twenty.
   A *century* is a group of one hundred.

1. Jack has lived for a decade. How old is he?

2. His father has lived 4 decades. How old is he?

3. When Abraham Lincoln spoke at Gettysburg, he said "4 score and 7 years ago." How many years was this? Think: 4 twenties + 7.

4. How many years are in a century?

5. How many decades are in a century?

6. In the ancient Roman army a group of 100 soldiers was called a century. How many men were in 3 centuries? in 6 centuries?

UNEXPLORED TERRITORY

Columbus came to America in 1492. We say 1492 was in the 15th century. The year 1592 was in the 16th century.

Santo Domingo

1. In what century was the year 1892?

2. In what century was the year 234?

3. In what century was the year 56?

4. In what century were you born?

MONEY

1. What amount is named?
   Read each numeral.
   - **a.** $.05
   - **b.** $14.47
   - **c.** $134.86
   - **d.** $1.47
   - **e.** 5¢
   - **f.** 147¢

2. Six cents may be named in two ways, $.06 and 6¢. What other amounts of money are named two ways in Item 1?

3. Name these in two ways.
   - **a.** Twelve cents
   - **b.** One cent
   - **c.** Ten cents
   - **d.** Four cents

4. In $3.47, why do we write a point between 3 and 4?

5. $4.76 rounded to the nearest dollar is $5.00. Round these to the nearest dollar.
   - **a.** $6.28
   - **b.** $9.82
   - **c.** $1.59

EXERCISES

Name these amounts of money in two ways.

1. One dollar and eighty-five cents

2. Two dollars and six cents

3. Forty-nine cents   4. Nine cents

Write words for these.

5. $3.45   6. $20.08   7. 283¢

8. 531¢   9. $.45   10. $1.06

28

CHAPTER REVIEW

Does the number tell *how many* or *which one?*

1. There are 486 pages in the book.

2. John has read to page 49.

3. Harold lives at 53 Hudson Street.

Write expanded numerals.

4. $37 = \underline{} + 7$

5. $494 = \underline{} + 90 + \underline{}$

6. $3920 = \underline{} + 900 + \underline{} + \underline{}$

7. 438 means $\underline{}$ hundreds $+$ $\underline{}$ tens
$+ \underline{}$ ones

An expanded numeral for 494 is
$$(4 \times 100) + (9 \times 10) + (4 \times 1).$$

Write expanded numerals.

8. 3,498   9. 124,309   10. 8,287,040

Numerals like 938 and 40 are standard numerals. Write standard numerals.

11. $(3 \times 1,000,000) + (4 \times 10,000) + (5 \times 10)$

12. $300,000 + 2,000 + 40 + 2$

13. Five hundred ninety-eight thousand, three hundred four.

What number is named?

14. IV   15. XLV   16. LVIII   17. XC

Tell what the 7 means in each numeral.

18. 973,284   **19.** 807,392,863   **20.** 117

Make each sentence true. Use >, <, or =.

21. 139 ≡ 140   **22.** 2486 ≡ 2486

23. 12,394 ≡ 12,593   **24.** 396,287 ≡ 346,287

25. Look at the numeral 874,236,184. In what period are the symbols 874? the symbols 236?

Use commas to separate each numeral into periods.

26. 2743921   **27.** 1874728   **28.** 284947621

Round to the nearest ten.

29. 68   **30.** 91   **31.** 735   **32.** 428

Round to the nearest hundred.

33. 892   **34.** 348   **35.** 350   **36.** 994

Name these amounts of money with numerals.

37. Ten dollars and fifteen cents

38. Twenty-five dollars and nine cents

Terms You Should Know

number	periods
numeral	Roman numerals
digit symbol	expanded numeral
standard numeral	Egyptian numerals
rounding numbers	is less than
is greater than	abacus
digit	

CHAPTER TEST

Copy and complete.

1. $86 = \underline{\hspace{1cm}}$ tens $+ \underline{\hspace{1cm}}$ ones

2. $947 = \underline{\hspace{1cm}}$ hundreds $+ \underline{\hspace{1cm}}$ tens $+ \underline{\hspace{1cm}}$ ones

3. $197 = 100 + \underline{\hspace{1cm}} + 7$

4. $3,842 = \underline{\hspace{1cm}} + 800 + 40 + \underline{\hspace{1cm}}$

Write expanded numerals.

Example $827 = (8 \times 100) + (2 \times 10)$
$+ (7 \times 1)$

5. 78   6. 789,426   7. 2,700,001

Write standard numerals.

8. $(6 \times 10) + (9 \times 1)$

9. $1,000 + 900 + 30 + 6$

10. $3,000,000 + 3,000 + 300$

Use $>$ or $<$. Make each sentence true.

11. $97 \equiv 79$ 12. $4,826 \equiv 8,462$ 13. $602 \equiv 206$

Round to the nearest 100.

14. 497   15. 746   16. 1,350

Round to the nearest 10.

17. 53   18. 67   19. 35   20. 14

Write standard numerals.

21. XII   22. IV   23. VI   24. XX

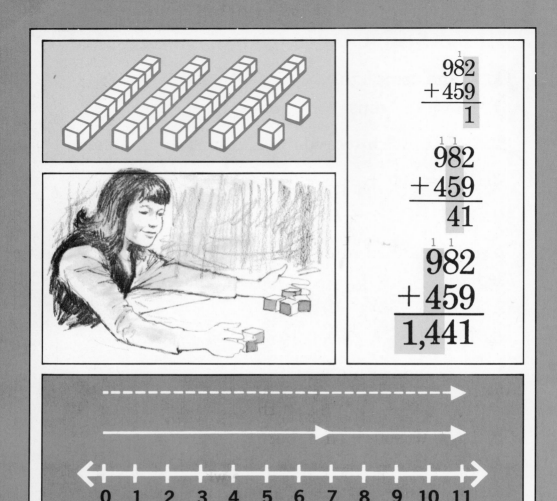

CHAPTER TWO

Addition

WHOLE NUMBERS

1. Count the objects in the first set below.

    a. What was the first number you named in counting?

    b. Did you name a number for each object?

> These numbers are the **counting numbers:**
> $$1, 2, 3, 4, 5, 6, 7, 8, \ldots$$
> The dots show that the pattern goes on without end.

2. **a.** How many members are in the second set above? We call this the empty set.

    b. What is the number of the empty set?

> These numbers are called the **whole numbers:**
> $$0, 1, 2, 3, 4, 5, 6, 7, 8, \ldots$$

3. What is the difference between the whole numbers and the counting numbers? Are the counting numbers in the set of whole numbers?

4. **a.** What is the smallest whole number?

    b. What do you think is the greatest whole number? Name the whole number that is one greater than this number.

    c. Is there a greatest whole number?

THE NUMBER LINE

We can show the order of numbers.

LET'S EXPLORE

1. This is a picture of a line. Some points are marked on it.

Is the distance between the points the same?

2. We can name some of the points.

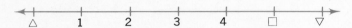

a. What numeral should replace the □?

b. What numeral should replace the ▽?

c. What do you notice about the numbers named as we go to the right?

d. Where does 0 belong?

3. Sometimes we show only part of a number line.

a. What numeral should replace the △?

b. What numeral should replace the □?

c. How many whole numbers are between 65 and 69? between 62 and 63?

4. For each, what number is one greater?

   a. 35   b. 6,350   c. 4,809   d. 25,799

1. Draw a number line. Mark 15 points. Name the points, starting with zero.

Copy the parts of the number lines below. Replace the frames with the correct numerals.

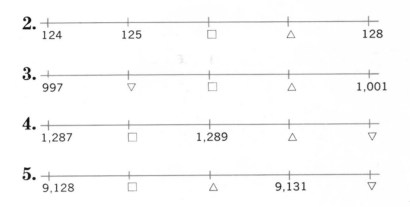

2. 124 125 □ △ 128

3. 997 ▽ □ △ 1,001

4. 1,287 □ 1,289 △ ▽

5. 9,128 □ △ 9,131 ▽

6. How many whole numbers are between 0 and 1? between 10 and 11?

For each, what number is one greater?

7. 69	**8.** 1,287	**9.** 3,876	**10.** 98,609
11. 80,001	**12.** 1,179	**13.** 264,004	**14.** 999
15. 46,274	**16.** 3,103	**17.** 732,880	**18.** 0

For each, what number is one less?

19. 396	**20.** 2,846	**21.** 1,001	**22.** 80,030
23. 89,029	**24.** 7,530	**25.** 999,999	**26.** 70
27. 63,401	**28.** 5,287	**29.** 100,004	**30.** 1

ADDITION

1. a. How many members are in each set?

b. Think of combining the sets. To find the number of members in all we can add 5 and 3.

$$5 + 3 = \underline{\quad}$$

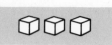

c. The numbers 5 and 3 are addends. What is the sum?

2. We can also use the number line to picture addition. This shows $3 + 4 = 7$.

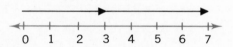

a. Name the addends.

b. Name the sum.

3. What addition is shown?

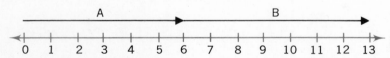

a. What addend does arrow A represent?

b. What addend does arrow B represent?

4. Draw a number line to show each addition.

a. $3 + 7 = \square$ **b.** $4 + 9 = \square$

c. $7 + 8 = \square$ **d.** $6 + 5 = \square$

5. Name the addends in Items 4a-4d.

NUMBER SENTENCES

We use sentences in our language. A sentence about numbers is a number sentence.

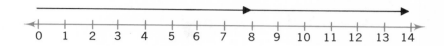

1. We call $8 + 6 = 14$ a number sentence.

   a. Is it a true sentence?

   b. Is the number sentence $6 + 8 = 14$ true?

   c. Is the sentence $8 + 6 = 19$ true?

2. Look at the number sentence $9 + 4 = \square$. We cannot tell if it is true or false until we replace the $\square$ with a numeral.

   a. Replace the $\square$ to make it true.

   b. Replace the $\square$ to make it false.

3. Which sentences are true?

   a. $3 + 7 = 10$ b. $9 > 3 + 4$ c. $8 + 7 = \square$

   d. $5 + 7 = 11$ e. $3 + \square = 9$ f. $6 < 3 + 8$

A number sentence with $=$ is an **equation.**

4. Which of these are equations?

   a. $2 + 8 = 10$ b. $3 > 1 + 1$ c. $12 = 8 + 4$

5. Let's see if the equation $5 + 7 = 12$ is true.

   a. What number is named on the left of $=$?

   b. What number is named on the right of $=$?

In a true equation the same number is named on both sides of =.

6. **a.** Is the equation $4 + 2 = 6$ true?

   b. Is the equation $3 + 5 = 9$ true? Why?

Copy the number sentences that are equations.

1. $6 + 3 = 9$ 2. $0 + 2 = 3$

3. $2 + 8 = 4 + 6$ 4. $6 + 0 = 0 + 6$

5. $2 + 3 < 9$ 6. $3 + 5 > 2 + 4$

7. $16 = 8 + 8$ 8. $13 + 0 = 13$

Copy the true equations.

9. $4 + 7 = 11$ 10. $6 + 8 = 7 + 5$

11. $9 = 3 + 5$ 12. $4 + 11 = 7 + 8$

13. $\triangle = 9 + 5$ 14. $0 + 12 = 3 + 9$

Make these equations true.

15. $3 + 2 = \square$ 16. $6 + 9 = \square$

17. $\square = 6 + 5$ 18. $\square + 8 = 10$

19. $9 + 0 = \square$ 20. $\square + 9 = 11$

21. $3 + 2 = 1 + \square$ 22. $4 + \square = 5 + 7$

23. $4 + \square = 9 + 8$ 24. $3 + 9 = 2 + \square$

25. $7 + \square = 8 + 5$ 26. $6 + \square = 7 + 8$

THE COMMUTATIVE PROPERTY

If we change the order of addends, does the sum change?

1. We know $8 + 6 = 14$ because $8 + 6$ and 14 are names for the same number.

   a. Make $6 + 8 = \square$ a true sentence.

   b. Does $8 + 6 = 6 + 8$? Why?

2. Study the number line.

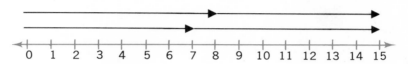

   a. Does $8 + 7 = 7 + 8$? Think: $8 + 7 = \square$, $7 + 8 = \square$.

   b. Did changing the order of the addends change the sum? Does $6 + 3 = 3 + 6$?

3. Consider the sentence $\square + \triangle = \triangle + \square$.

   a. Replace each $\square$ with 6.

   b. Replace each $\triangle$ with 4.

   c. Is the sentence true?

4. Consider the sentence $\square + \triangle = \triangle + \square$.

   a. Replace each $\square$ with the same numeral.

   b. Replace each $\triangle$ with the same numeral.

   c. Is the sentence true?

   d. Is $\square + \triangle = \triangle + \square$ always true?

5. a. Since $12+13=25$, we know $13+12=\square$. Why?

    b. Since $88+16=104$, we know $16+88=\square$. Why?

> If we change the order of addends, we do not change the sum. This is the **commutative property of addition.**

EXERCISES

Copy and complete.

1. $8 + 3 = 11$, so $3 + 8 = \square$

2. $3 + 9 = 12$, so $9 + 3 = \square$

3. $\square + 4 = 13$, so $4 + \square = 13$

4. $\square + 5 = 9$, so $5 + \square = 9$

Copy the sentences which show the commutative property of addition.

5. $8+8 = 5+8$ 6. $17+16 = 16+17$

7. $18+15 = 15+18$ 8. $343+864 = 864+343$

9. $8+13 = 18+3$ 10. $10+5 = 8+7$

Let's Practice

Name these amounts of money in two ways.

1. Eight cents   2. Fifty-three cents

3. Three dollars and four cents

4. Twenty dollars and sixteen cents

REVIEWING ADDITION FACTS

1. Mrs. Allen asked her pupils to make the equation $\square + \triangle = 8$ true. Jack wrote the sentence $7 + 1 = 8$. Is it true?
Does $1 + 7 = 8$? Why?

2. George wrote these true equations for $\square + \triangle = 8$ on the board.

$$0 + 8 = 8 \qquad 6 + 2 = 8 \qquad 5 + 3 = 8$$

Write other true equations for $\square + \triangle = 8$.

3. Use names for whole numbers. Write true equations for $\square + \triangle = 17$.

4. **a.** When zero is added to a given number, what is the sum?

   b. Write a true sentence for $\square + 0 = \triangle$.

EXERCISES

Write true equations. Use whole numbers.

1. $\square + \triangle = 1$
2. $\square + \triangle = 2$
3. $\square + \triangle = 3$
4. $\square + \triangle = 4$
5. $\square + \triangle = 5$
6. $\square + \triangle = 6$
7. $\square + \triangle = 7$
8. $\square + \triangle = 9$
9. $\square + \triangle = 10$

Make each sentence true. Replace $\square$ with 2, 3, 4, 5, 6, 7, 8, and 9.

10. $\square + \triangle = 11$
11. $\square + \triangle = 12$
12. $\square + \triangle = 13$
13. $\square + \triangle = 14$
14. $\square + \triangle = 15$
15. $\square + \triangle = 16$

PROBLEM SOLVING

We can use number sentences to help us solve problems.

1. Al had 7 marbles. He won 5 more marbles. How many does he have now?

   a. What facts do we know?

   b. What do we want to find?

   c. These number sentences fit the story.

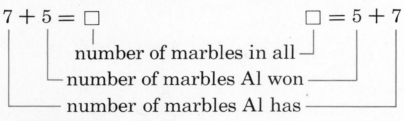

$$7 + 5 = \square \qquad\qquad \square = 5 + 7$$

number of marbles in all
number of marbles Al won
number of marbles Al has

Make the sentence $7 + 5 = \square$ true.

2. Write number sentences that fit these stories. Make them true.

   a. One week Mike ate 5 peaches and 4 pears. How many pieces of fruit did he eat in all?

   b. Ellen found 4 small shells and 9 large shells on the beach. How many shells did she find?

   c. Scott put 8 dimes into his bank on Monday. He put 5 nickels in on Friday. How many coins did he put into the bank in all?

3. Mary has ☐ pencils. Sue has △ pencils. Together they have 10 pencils. How many does each girl have?

    a. We can write the sentence $☐ + △ = 10$.

    b. Make the sentence true.

    c. Find as many answers as you can.

4. The same number of children are in each of 2 rows. There are 12 children altogether. How many children are in each row?

    a. Make the sentence $☐ + ☐ = 12$ true.

    b. How many answers do you find?

EXERCISES

Write number sentences for these stories. Make the sentences true.

1. Joan got 9 problems right on one test and 8 problems right on another test. How many did she get right altogether?

2. Jerry caught 6 fish. His dad caught 8. How many fish did both catch?

3. Jack has ☐ books. Jean has △ books. They have 11 books altogether. How many books might each child have?

4. If Jack has one more book than Jean, how many books does each have?

5. There are 9 guppies and 4 goldfish in the fishtank. How many fish are there in the tank in all?

GROUPING—THE ASSOCIATIVE PROPERTY

1. When adding three or more numbers, we add two numbers at a time.
   Consider $5 + 7 + 3$.
   We can add 5 and 7 first, or we can add 7 and 3 first.

   $5 + 7 + 3$
   $5 + 7 + 3$

2. Parentheses ( ) are used to show grouping. We add the numbers named inside the parentheses first. Add.

   a. $(5 + 7) + 3$
   $\underline{} + 3$
   $\underline{}$

   b. $5 + (7 + 3)$
   $5 + \underline{}$
   $\underline{}$

   c. Compare the sums you found in item a and item b. What do you discover?

   d. Make this sentence true.
   $(5 + 7) + 3 = 5 + (\triangle + 3)$

3. Look at $(\triangle + \triangledown) + \square = \triangle + (\triangledown + \square)$.

   a. Replace each $\triangle$ with 3, each $\triangledown$ with 4, and each $\square$ with 5.

   b. Add. What do you find?

   c. Choose 3 other numbers to replace the frames. Add.

> We can change the grouping of addends and get the same sum. This is called the **associative property of addition.**

44

4. Suppose that you do not remember the sum of 7 and 8, but you know that $7 + 7 = 14$. How can you find the sum $7 + 8$?

$$7 + 8 = 7 + (7 + 1)$$
$$= (7 + 7) + 1$$
$$= \underline{} + 1$$
$$= \underline{}$$

5. Sometimes we can rename and then regroup to get 10. Copy and complete.

a. $9 + 8 = 9 + (1 + 7)$
$ = (9 + 1) + 7$
$ = \underline{} + 7$
$ = \underline{}$

b. $9 + 8 = (7 + 2) + 8$
$ = 7 + (2 + 8)$
$ = \underline{} + \underline{}$
$ = \underline{}$

EXERCISES

Which grouping is more helpful in finding the sum?

1. $(6 + 9) + 1$ or $6 + (9 + 1)$

2. $(3 + 7) + 8$ or $3 + (7 + 8)$

3. $4 + (6 + 8)$ or $(4 + 6) + 8$

4. $15 + (5 + 12)$ or $(15 + 5) + 12$

5. $(96 + 8) + 12$ or $96 + (8 + 12)$

Rename one addend and use the associative property to find the sum.

6. $8 + 4$

7. $7 + 6$

8. $9 + 7$

9. $9 + 9$

10. $7 + 8$

11. $9 + 4$

12. $7 + 5$

13. $8 + 5$

14. $8 + 6$

45

ADDING ONES TO TENS AND ONES

1. Add 13 and 4.

$$13 + 4 = (10 + 3) + 4$$
$$= 10 + (3 + 4)$$
$$= 10 + \underline{}$$
$$= \underline{}$$

a. How is 13 renamed?

b. What property of addition is used?

c. Copy and complete the addition.

2. Copy and complete item a. Explain item b.

a. $25 + 4 = 20 + 5 + 4$
$= 20 + \underline{}$
$= \underline{}$

b. 25
$\underline{+\ 4}$
29

3. Add. Look for a pattern.

a.
5	15	25	45
+4	+4	+4	+4

b.
6	16	26	56
+2	+2	+2	+2

EXERCISES

Add.

1. 14
$\underline{+2}$

2. 16
$\underline{+3}$

3. 36
$\underline{+2}$

4. 24
$\underline{+5}$

5. 25
$\underline{+2}$

6. 26
$\underline{+3}$

7. 52
$\underline{+4}$

8. 73
$\underline{+4}$

9. 63
$\underline{+4}$

10. 18
$\underline{+1}$

11. 15
$\underline{+2}$

12. 13
$\underline{+5}$

ADDITION

1. If $4 + 3 = 7$, what is $40 + 30$? $400 + 300$?

2. Find these sums.

   a. 6 tens
   $+3$ tens

   b. 4 hundreds
   $+4$ hundreds

   c. 6 thousands
   $+1$ thousand

   d. 60
   $+30$

   e. 800
   $+100$

   f. 4,000
   $+3,000$

3. We can use our knowledge of numerals when we add. Find the sums.

   a. 24 $20+4$
   $+35$ $30+5$
   $\overline{\hspace{1cm}}$ $50+9$
   $\overline{\hspace{1cm}}$

   b. 463 $400+60+3$
   $+215$ $200+10+5$
   $\overline{\hspace{1cm}}$ $600+70+8$
   $\overline{\hspace{1cm}}$

4. Add. Copy and complete.

   a. 36 $30 + \underline{\hspace{0.7cm}}$
   $+53$ $\underline{\hspace{0.7cm}} + 3$

   b. 147 $100 + \underline{\hspace{0.7cm}} + 7$
   $+252$ $\underline{\hspace{0.7cm}} + 50 + 2$

5. Explain each step.

   347
   $+231$
   $\overline{8}$

   347
   $+231$
   $\overline{78}$

   347
   $+231$
   $\overline{578}$

6. We can use what we know about the order of addends to check addition.

   43
   $+24$
   $\overline{67}$

   24
   $+43$
   $\overline{67}$

Add 38 and 21. Check.

Add and check.

1.	40 +50	**2.**	70 +6	**3.**	47 +21	**4.**	36 +142
5.	600 +300	**6.**	500 +50	**7.**	312 +425	**8.**	540 +425
9.	8,124 +342	**10.**	6,312 +2,487	**11.**	7,432 +524	**12.**	8,932 +1,054

Write a number sentence that fits each story. Make the sentence true.

13. Miss Harker's class has 31 pupils. Mr. O'Hearn's class has 28 pupils. How many pupils are in the two classes?

14. Gerald traveled 432 miles by bus and 121 miles by train. How far did he go?

15. There are 20 teachers, 2 secretaries, 1 principal, and 2 custodians at school. How many adults work at the school?

16. One state had 41 representatives. Another had 38 representatives. How many representatives did both states have?

17. a. On their trip, David and Luke drove 3,456 miles. They drove 3,201 miles to return. How many miles did they drive in all?

b. Ben flew 4,382 miles by plane and drove 5,207 miles by car. How many miles did he travel?

RENAMING

1. Add 8 tens and 4 tens.

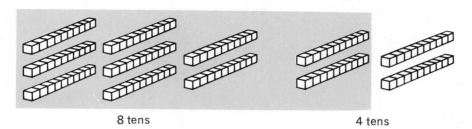

8 tens   4 tens

    a. 10 tens = 1 hundred

    b. 12 tens = 1 hundred + ___ tens

2. Rename 13 hundreds.

    a. 10 hundreds = 1 thousand

    b. 13 hundreds = 1 thousand
                                      + ___ hundreds

Copy and complete.

3. 8 tens + 6 tens = ___ hundred + ___ tens

4. 9 ones + 4 ones = 1 ___ + 3 ones

5. 6 tens + 7 tens = 1 ___ + 3 tens

6. 14 hundreds = ___ thousand
                                      + ___ hundreds

UNEXPLORED TERRITORY

1. The sum of three numbers is 18. All addends are the same. What is each addend?

2. The sum of two numbers is 18. The difference is 6. What are the two addends?

EXTENDING ADDITION

1. Add. Do you see a pattern?

   a. $5 + 7$
   $15 + 7$
   $25 + 7$
   $85 + 7$

   b. $9 + 8$
   $19 + 8$
   $29 + 8$
   $59 + 8$

2. Consider $28 + 54$. The 70 and 12 are partial sums. Copy and complete.

   $$\begin{array}{r} 28 \\ +54 \\ \hline \end{array}$$

   $20 + 8$
   $\underline{50 + 4}$
   $70 + 12$
   $70 + (10 + \underline{})$
   $(70 + 10) + \underline{}$
   $\underline{} + \underline{}$
   $\underline{}$

3. We can show partial sums in a column.

   $$\begin{array}{r} 28 \\ +54 \\ \hline 12 \\ 70 \\ \hline 82 \end{array}$$

   $(8+4)$
   $(20 + 50)$

   Add 47 and 35. Show partial sums.

4. Here is a shorter form.

   $$\begin{array}{r} {}^{1} \\ 68 \\ +26 \\ \hline 4 \end{array}$$

   Add ones: $8 + 6 = \underline{}$
   $14 = 1$ ten $+ 4$ ones
   Record 4 ones. Remember 1 ten.

   $$\begin{array}{r} {}^{1} \\ 68 \\ +26 \\ \hline 94 \end{array}$$

   Add tens.
   $(1$ ten $+ 6$ tens$) + 2$ tens $= \underline{}$ tens

5. Add. Use the short form.

	a.	b.	c.	d.
	19	67	36	59
	+36	+19	+48	+23

EXERCISES

Add.

1. 27
+6

2. 47
+7

3. 38
+9

4. 38
+29

5. 38
+19

6. 18
+69

7. 64
+16

8. 49
+28

9. 68
+27

10. 36
+29

11. 71
+15

12. 28
+65

13. 98
+3

14. 57
+34

15. 25
+37

16. 48
+36

Solve each of these problems.

17. There are 53 girls and 38 boys in the fourth grade at Hamlin School. How many children are in the fourth grade?

18. a. Mr. Bowers was on a car trip. He used 19 gallons of gas for the first 250 miles and 18 gallons for the next 240 miles. How many gallons of gas did he use?

b. Mr. Bowers used 39 gallons of gas for the next 500 miles. How much gas did he use on the whole trip?

19. Bret read 49 pages in a magazine and 27 pages in a book. How many pages did he read in all?

ADDING LARGER NUMBERS

1. The Chan family drove 365 miles one day and 227 miles the next day. How far did they drive? Complete the short form.

Partial Sums

```
  365
+227
   12
   80
  500
  592
```

Short Form

```
  365
+227
```

2. We often regroup the tens. Explain each step.

Expanded Form

```
692     600 +  90 + 2
274     200 +  70 + 4
966     800 + 160 + 6
        800 + (100 + 60) + 6
        (800 + 100) + 60 + 6
        900 + 60 + 6
        966
```

Partial Sums

```
692
274
  6
160
800
966
```

3. Add. Use the partial-sums form.

    a. 173 + 486   **b.** 440 + 398   **c.** 56 + 81

4. We often need to regroup ones and tens when we add. Explain each step.

a.
$$\begin{array}{r} \overset{1}{2\,5\,6} \\ 4\,6\,9 \\ \hline 5 \end{array}$$
Add ones: $6 + 9 = 15$
$15 = 1$ ten + _____ ones

b.
$$\begin{array}{r} \overset{1\;1}{2\,5\,6} \\ 4\,6\,9 \\ \hline 2\,5 \end{array}$$
Add tens.
$(1$ ten $+ 5$ tens$) + 6$ tens
$=$ _____ tens
12 tens $= 1$ hundred $+ 2$ tens

c.
$$\begin{array}{r} \overset{1\;1}{2\,5\,6} \\ 4\,6\,9 \\ \hline 7\,2\,5 \end{array}$$
Add hundreds.
$(1$ hundred $+ 2$ hundred$) +$
4 hundreds $=$ _____ hundreds

5. Use the short form. Check.

a. $\begin{array}{r} 259 \\ +182 \\ \hline \end{array}$ **b.** $\begin{array}{r} 776 \\ +124 \\ \hline \end{array}$ **c.** $\begin{array}{r} 846 \\ +98 \\ \hline \end{array}$ **d.** $\begin{array}{r} 97 \\ +9 \\ \hline \end{array}$

EXERCISES

Add.

1. $\begin{array}{r} 298 \\ +315 \\ \hline \end{array}$ **2.** $\begin{array}{r} 569 \\ +185 \\ \hline \end{array}$ **3.** $\begin{array}{r} 147 \\ +258 \\ \hline \end{array}$ **4.** $\begin{array}{r} 176 \\ +786 \\ \hline \end{array}$

5. $\begin{array}{r} 686 \\ +289 \\ \hline \end{array}$ **6.** $\begin{array}{r} 534 \\ +398 \\ \hline \end{array}$ **7.** $\begin{array}{r} 645 \\ +167 \\ \hline \end{array}$ **8.** $\begin{array}{r} 97 \\ +7 \\ \hline \end{array}$

9. $\begin{array}{r} 85 \\ +27 \\ \hline \end{array}$ **10.** $\begin{array}{r} 236 \\ +567 \\ \hline \end{array}$ **11.** $\begin{array}{r} 354 \\ +389 \\ \hline \end{array}$ **12.** $\begin{array}{r} 268 \\ +695 \\ \hline \end{array}$

13. $\begin{array}{r} 129 \\ +95 \\ \hline \end{array}$ **14.** $\begin{array}{r} 469 \\ +368 \\ \hline \end{array}$ **15.** $\begin{array}{r} 96 \\ +8 \\ \hline \end{array}$ **16.** $\begin{array}{r} 183 \\ +249 \\ \hline \end{array}$

THOUSANDS

1. Let's add thousands. Explain each step.

```
   1            1 1           1 1 1         1 1 1
 4,9 8 2       4,9 8 2       4,9 8 2       4,9 8 2
+3,4 5 9      +3,4 5 9      +3,4 5 9      +3,4 5 9
       1          4 1          4 4 1       8,4 4 1
```

a. How many times did you regroup?

b. Add 4,982 and 3,459 using the partial sums form.

2. Add. Use the short form. Check.

a. 8,329	**b.** 921	**c.** 4,876	**d.** 9,999
+1,486	+299	+9,829	+9,999

EXERCISES

Add.

1. 1,473	**2.** 3,209	**3.** 1,678	**4.** 5,928
+2,179	+4,584	+246	+95
5. 647	**6.** 237	**7.** 4,953	**8.** 7,894
+584	+785	+7,458	+2,247
9. 998	**10.** 985	**11.** 635	**12.** 421
+2	+437	+897	+889
13. 738	**14.** 9,842	**15.** 3,652	**16.** 3,421
+682	+4,369	+6,798	+6,579
17. 7,364	**18.** 6,846	**19.** 2,648	**20.** 8,567
+9,678	+5,376	+7,873	+2,896
21. 3,548	**22.** 2,908	**23.** 4,692	**24.** 5,285
+6,452	+3,497	+7,759	+8,857

EXTENDING ADDITION

1. Alice and John were playing with their dart game. Alice found her score this way. Explain each step.

8 ⟶ 10 ⟶ 16 ⟶ 21
2   6   5
6   5
<u>5</u>

2. She checked her work by thinking of these additions.

8   8   8 ⟶ 21
2   2 ⟶ 13
6 ⟶ 11
<u>5</u>

   a. What was the sum when Alice added down?

   b. What was the sum when she added up?

3. How did John group the addends?

6   6 ⟶ 10 ⟶ 20 ⟶ 21
3   4   1
4   3 ⟶ 10
7   7   1
<u>1</u>   1

4. Copy and add.

a. 7	**b.** 17	**c.** 125	**d.** 1,321
5	29	231	7,219
9	30	891	1,821
8	48	90	4,321

EXERCISES

Copy and find the sums. Change the order and grouping to check your work.

Example	8		8	
	7	$(8 + 2) + 7$	7	$(8 + 7) + 2$
	2		2	
	17		17	

1. 1	**2.** 7	**3.** 4	**4.** 8
5	6	6	3
9	3	8	2

Copy. Make each sentence true.

5. $9 + 7 + 8 + 2 = \square$ **6.** $2 + 7 + 3 + 5 = \square$

7. $4 + 9 + 1 + 5 = \square$ **8.** $9 + 3 + 6 + 9 = \square$

Add.

9. 14	**10.** 48	**11.** 83	**12.** 5,915
24	52	91	4,286
34	64	18	6,872
	76	24	3,368

13. 48	**14.** 10	**15.** 16	**16.** 3,193
67	9	7	107
85	13	103	42
8	31		1,451

PROBLEM SOLVING

A calorie is a measure of food energy. Here are some foods and the calories they have.

Food	Calories
milk (1 cup)	160
eggs (1 each)	74
hamburger (3 ounces)	245
sirloin steak (3 ounces)	330
chicken (3 ounces)	130
green beans (1 cup)	30
lettuce (1 head)	30
potatoes (1 cup, mashed)	185
apple (1)	70
bread (1 slice)	60
cereal (1 cup)	100

1. John ate one cup of cereal, one egg and drank one cup of milk. How many calories were in John's breakfast?

2. For lunch John ate one hamburger, two pieces of bread, one cup of mashed potatoes, and drank one cup of milk. How many calories were in John's lunch?

3. John ate 3 ounces of steak, one cup of green beans, and an apple for dinner. How many calories did John get from dinner?

4. What was John's total number of calories for the day?

5. Make a menu for yourself for breakfast, and dinner. How many calories would meal? for the whole day?

DO YOU REMEMBER?

Show the meaning of the 5 in each numeral.

Example 384,521 5 × 100 or 500

1. 714,560 **2.** 650,489 **3.** 485,286

Make each sentence true. Use >, <, or =.

4. 897 ≡ 879 **5.** 4,871 ≡ 4,881

6. 4 + 8 ≡ 8 + 4 **7.** 9 + 6 ≡ 8 + 7

8. 4 + 6 ≡ 8 + 8 **9.** 984 ≡ 984 + 0

Copy and complete.

10. 25 tens = ___ hundreds + ___ tens

11. 16 tens = ___ hundred + ___ tens

12. 7 tens + 4 tens = ___ hundred + ___ ten

Add.

13.	**14.**	**15.**	**16.**
43	37	126	268
+26	+28	+391	+563

Add. Look for pairs of numbers whose sum is ten.

17.	**18.**	**19.**	**20.**
3	1	6	2
4	2	5	7
7	8	6	3
6	3	5	6
2	4	1	8

21. 6 + 6 + 7 + 3 + 4 = □

22. 8 + 9 + 2 + 1 + 3 + 4 = □

23. 7 + 2 + 7 + 3 + 8 + 6

58

ESTIMATING

1. Bill has saved 80 cents. He wants to buy a whistle that costs 29 cents and a ball that costs 59 cents. We can estimate to find out if Bill saved enough money.

   a. Round 29 and 59 to the nearest 10. What is 30 + 60?

   b. Is 90 greater than or less than 80?

   c. Has Bill saved enough money?

   d. Find the exact cost.

   e. How much more money does he need to save?

2. Estimate the sum of 311 and 379.

   a. Round each addend to the nearest 100. Think: 300 + ___.

   b. What is your estimate?

   c. Find the exact sum.

3. Round each addend to the nearest ten. Estimate the sum.

a.	b.	c.	d.
45	52	89	63
+27	+77	+19	+21

4. Find the exact sums for Items 3a-3d.

5. Round each addend to the nearest hundred. Estimate the sum.

a.	b.	c.	d.
421	301	450	592
+294	+321	+679	+211

6. Find the exact sums for Items 5a-5d.

WORKING WITH MONEY

We have a system for recording amounts of money.

$ 3 . 2 5 —— Cents

L——— Tens of cents (dimes)

————— Hundreds of cents (dollars)

1. Jerry's mother bought 2 shirts. One cost $3.78 and the other cost $4.64. What was the cost of both shirts? Explain each step in the addition.

$$
\begin{array}{r}
\overset{1}{}\$3.78 \\
+4.64 \\
\hline
2
\end{array}
\qquad
\begin{array}{r}
\overset{1\;1}{}\$3.78 \\
+4.64 \\
\hline
.42
\end{array}
\qquad
\begin{array}{r}
\overset{1\;1}{}\$3.78 \\
+4.64 \\
\hline
\$8.42
\end{array}
$$

2. Mrs. Dorn bought a belt for $5.95 and a hat for $8.19. Estimate the total cost. $5.95 is about $6.00 and $8.19 is about $8.00. What is 6 + 8?

3. Pat paid $3.82 for a scarf and $5.26 for a hat. Estimate the amount of money Pat spent in all.

EXERCISES

Estimate. Find the exact sum.

	1.	2.	3.	4.
	$2.19 +3.47	$9.64 +8.09	$7.95 +4.82	$4.87 +7.78

	5.	6.	7.	8.
	$.06 +.04	$.19 +.93	$12.87 +42.38	$64.93 +97.68

	9.	10.	11.	12.
	$.73 +.28	$3.89 +6.72	$26.46 +52.95	$304.98 +84.19

BOY'S BICYCLE	$38.26
GIRL'S BICYCLE	$36.29
EXTRAS	
HORN	$2.78
SPEEDOMETER	$3.98
REFLECTOR	$.87
MUD FLAPS	$1.59
HAND GRIPS	$1.98

Solve each problem.

13. Mr. Louis bought a boy's bike with a speedometer. What was the total cost?

14. Mae's aunt bought a girl's bike with a horn and a reflector. What was the cost?

15. James bought a boy's bike with all the extra parts. What was the total cost?

16. Alice bought a girl's bike with all the extra parts. What was the total cost?

17. Mrs. Ross bought one girl's bike and one boy's bike with no extra parts. What was the total cost of the 2 bikes?

18. Mr. Vik bought 2 boy's bikes. Each had all the extra parts. Find the total cost.

19. Peter bought a horn and mud flaps for his bicycle. What was his total bill?

20. Donald bought his brother a horn, speedometer, and special handgrips for his bicycle. How much did he spend?

DO YOU REMEMBER?

Add.

1. 626 +37	**2.** 547 +236	**3.** 639 +355	**4.** 432 +149
5. 542 +76	**6.** 693 +274	**7.** 385 +572	**8.** 243 +95
9. 962 +835	**10.** 723 +564	**11.** 827 +632	**12.** 721 +943
13. 88 +64	**14.** 76 +47	**15.** 96 +47	**16.** 84 +96
17. 849 +86	**18.** 396 +39	**19.** 787 +89	**20.** 344 +98
21. 268 +459	**22.** 347 +486	**23.** 537 +394	**24.** 677 +285
25. 539 +628	**26.** 644 +839	**27.** 739 +338	**28.** 648 +492
29. 873 +645	**30.** 694 +733	**31.** 796 +842	**32.** 695 +421
33. 694 +536	**34.** 398 +899	**35.** 528 +897	**36.** 934 +978
37. 1,482 +8,999	**38.** 7,643 +9,878	**39.** 3,493 +3,943	**40.** 7,890 +4,329
41. 6,309 +4,711	**42.** 3,658 +9,677	**43.** 7,968 +5,543	**44.** 2,989 +8,706

CHAPTER REVIEW

Consider these number sentences.

$$8 + 7 = 15 \qquad 9 > 5 + 2 \qquad 16 = 4 + 11$$
$$19 + 12 = 20 + 11 \qquad\qquad 6 + 4 < 8 + 6$$

1. Which are true?

2. Which are false?

3. Which sentences are equations?

4. Name the addends in $8 + 7 = 15$.

5. Name the sum in $15 = 8 + 7$.

Copy and make each sentence true.

6. $4 + 8 = \square$

7. $14 = \square + 5$

8. $9 + 4 + 3 = \square$

9. $2 + 4 + 6 + 8 = \square$

10. $\square = 3 + 9 + 4$

11. $3 + 9 = \square + 2$

What property is shown in each sentence?

12. $7 + 6 = 6 + 7$

13. $(3 + 2) + 9 = 3 + (2 + 9)$

14. $947 + 286 = 286 + 947$

15. $24 + (35 + 65) = (24 + 35) + 65$

16. Copy and complete.

$$15 + 3 = (10 + 5) + \underline{}$$
$$= 10 + (5 + \underline{})$$
$$= 10 + \underline{}$$
$$= \underline{}$$

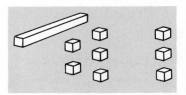

Copy and complete.

17. 13 ones = ___ ten + 3 ones

18. 49 tens = ___ hundreds + ___ tens

19. 17 hundreds = ___ thousand
                            + ___ hundreds

Round each addend to the nearest ten.
Estimate each sum.

20. $47 + 25$ 21. $21 + 49$ 22. $32 + 57$

23.-25. Find the exact sums for Exercises 20-22.

Round each addend to the nearest hundred.
Estimate each sum.

26. $420 + 598$ 27. $450 + 799$ 28. $659 + 349$

29.-31. Find the exact sums for Exercises 26-28.

Add.

32. 6,943
    +985

33. 2,476
    +3,894

34. 5,847
    +6,939

35. 4,967
    +8,385

36. 41
     288
    +65

37. 4,806
     149
    +67

Terms You Should Know

equation	whole numbers
addend	number sentence
number line	sum
commutative property of addition	
associative property of addition	

CHAPTER TEST

Rename.

1. 73 = ___ tens + 3 ones   **2.** 56 = ___ + 6

Add.

3.   455
  +313

4.   807
  +194

5.   468
  +237

6. 8,126
  +6,571

7.   379
  +488

8. $9.67
  +9.29

9.   889
  +78

10. $3.01
  +22.99

11. 8
   9
   4
   7

12. $.28
   .37
   .49
   .29

13. 398
  276
  498
  347

14. $18.24
  29.87
  33.49
  98.00

Solve each problem.

15. Jerald's mother bought some new clothes. She bought shoes for $10.87; socks for $1.98; trousers for $4.99; a shirt for $3.86. How much did the clothes cost?

16. The city placed a traffic counter on 7th Street. The number of cars that passed was as follows: Monday, 236; Tuesday, 387; Wednesday, 297; Thursday, 430; Friday, 968; Saturday, 1,287; Sunday, 104. How many cars passed during the whole week?

17. Bill shines shoes during the summer. One week he earned $8.65 and another week he earned $12.75. How much money did Bill earn?

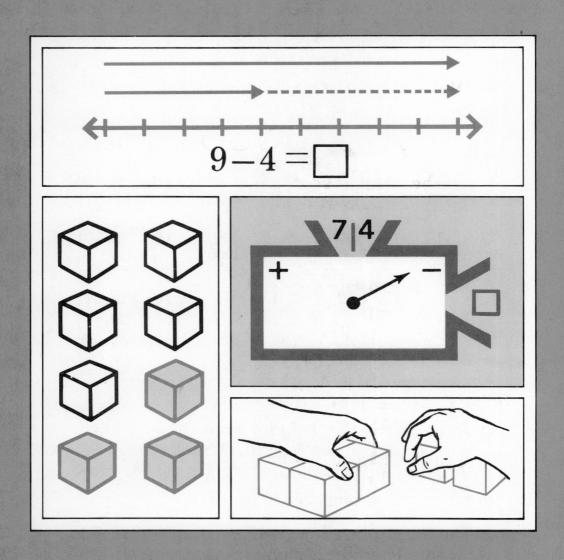

CHAPTER THREE

Subtraction

SUBTRACTION

1. Al has 6 marbles. How many more does he need to have 14 marbles?

  a. The number sentence $6 + \square = 14$ fits the story. Make it true.

  b. The number sentence $14 - 6 = \square$ also fits the story. Make it true.

2. Find the missing addends.

  a. $6 + \square = 11$ b. $\square + 6 = 9$ c. $\square + 5 = 12$
  d. $\square + 5 = 11$ e. $\square + 7 = 9$ f. $3 + \square = 9$

3. Make these equations true. Look for pattern.

  a. $\square + 6 = 11$ b. $5 + \square = 11$ c. $\square + 6 = 14$
     $11 - 6 = \square$ $11 - 5 = \square$ $14 - 6 = \square$

4. The sentences $\square + 6 = 15$ and $15 - 6 = \square$ are called *related sentences*. Write a related subtraction sentence for each.

  a. $\square + 9 = 10$ b. $\square + 5 = 7$ c. $5 + \square = 7$

When we subtract, we find a *difference*.

Difference	*Missing addend*
$15 - 6 = \square$	$\square + 6 = 15$

5. Find the differences or missing addends.

  a. $\square + 8 = 16$ b. $\square + 9 = 15$ c. $\square + 7 = 12$
     $16 - 8 = \square$ $15 - 9 = \square$ $12 - 7 = \square$

6. We can show the missing addend on a number line.

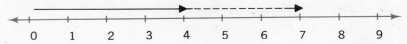

a. Show $5 + \triangle = 9$ and $9 - 5 = \triangle$ on a number line.

b. What does this show about a missing addend and a difference?

7. An addition sentence can have two related subtraction sentences.

$$8 + 6 = 14 \qquad 14 - 8 = 6 \qquad 14 - 6 = 8$$

Write two subtraction sentences for each.

a. $7+6=13$ b. $4+9=13$ c. $14+0=14$

8. Write a related subtraction sentence for $3 + 3 = 6$.

EXERCISES

Find each missing addend.

1. $\square + 8 = 16$ 2. $4 + \square = 8$ 3. $\square + 6 = 12$

Find each difference.

4. $4 - 3$ 5. $10 - 9$ 6. $11 - 9$ 7. $14 - 9$

Write two related subtraction sentences for each.

8. $9+5=14$ 9. $3+8=11$ 10. $9+6=15$

Solve the problem.

11. There are 3 boys in the Smith family. There are 7 children in all. How many girls are there?

REVIEWING SUBTRACTION FACTS

1. Use the numbers 0, 1, 2, 3, 4, 5, 6, 7, 8, 9, 10 to make the sentence □ − △ = 1 true.

   a. Use 10 for □ and make the sentence true.

   b. Find more numbers to make □ − △ = 1 true. Copy and complete the table.

□	10	9	8	7	6	5	4	3	2	1
△	9	8								
□ − △ = 1	1									

2. Make a table for □ − △ = 3. Use the numbers 0 through 12. Start by replacing the □ with 12.

EXERCISES

Use the given numbers to make each sentence true. Make a table for each.

1. □ − △ = 2   0 through 11

2. □ − △ = 4   0 through 13

3. □ − △ = 5   0 through 14

4. □ − △ = 6   0 through 15

5. □ − △ = 7   0 through 16

6. □ − △ = 8   0 through 17

7. □ − △ = 9   0 through 18

8. □ − △ = 0   0 through 9

AN OPERATION MACHINE

1. This is an operation machine. The numbers 8 and 6 are placed in the machine. The dial is set at +. What is the result?

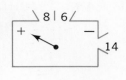

2. The numbers 8 and 6 are placed in the machine. The dial is set at —. What is the result?

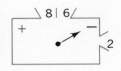

3. When we add or subtract two numbers, the result is a third number. Addition and subtraction are *operations* on numbers.

$$8 + 6 = 14 \qquad 8 - 6 = 2$$

EXERCISES

Look at the numerals and the setting of each machine. What is the result?

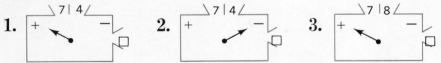

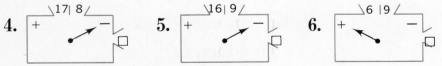

Find each missing number.

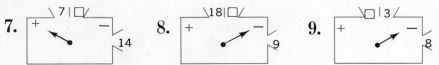

70

DO YOU REMEMBER?

Make each sentence true.

1. $9-8=\square$ 2. $13-7=\square$ 3. $4+8=\square$

4. $6+\square=18$ 5. $16-9=\square$ 6. $17-\square=9$

Find each missing number.

7. [diagram: $+$ $\square$ 1 $-$ 9]   8. [diagram: $+$ $\square$ 2 $-$ 9]   9. [diagram: $+$ $\square$ 6 $-$ 14]

Find each sum or difference.

10.	18	11.	9	12.	8	13.	8
	-9		$+9$		-7		$+7$

14.	14	15.	37	16.	12	17.	$10.84
	-8		$+26$		-8		$+13.96$

Add.

18.	487	19.	$ .06	20.	$12.41	21.	2,801
	394		7.23		.26		937
	203		.95		5.73		4,629

UNEXPLORED TERRITORY

Write an addition sentence to match the facts.

1. The sum of two addends is 14.

2. The sum of three addends is 26.

3. The sum of four addends is 19. None of the addends can be 0, 1, or 2.

4. The sum of four addends is five more than 18.

MORE SUBTRACTION

1. Try these subtractions.

   a.   7 tens   b.   90
         −3 tens   −50

   c.   6 hundreds   d.   900
         −4 hundreds   −100

   e.   9 thousands   f.   8,000
         −2 thousands   −2,000

2. Subtract. Explain the expanded forms.

   a.   48   40 + 8   b.   584   500 + 80 + 4
        −25   20 + 5   −132   100 + 30 + 2
               20 + 3   400 + 50 + 2

3. Subtract. Copy and complete.

   a.   49   40 + ___   b.   896   800 + 90 + 6
        −36   ___ + 6   −435   400 + ___ + ___

4. Explain each step in this short method.

   ```
     789        789         789
    −543       −543        −543
   ─────      ─────       ─────
       6         46         246
   ```

5. Subtract. Use the short method.

   a.   48   b.   97   c.   485   d.   376
        −35   −36   −231   −34

6. We check subtraction by using addition.

   48 − 35 = 13   because   13 + 35 = 48

   ```
      48              13
     −35             +35
    ─────          ─────
      13              48
   ```

7. Subtract and check.

a.	**b.**	**c.**	**d.**
876	479	6,348	7,488
−875	−307	−1,247	−307

EXERCISES

Subtract and check.

1.	**2.**	**3.**	**4.**
38	49	50	900
−6	−7	−40	−500

5.	**6.**	**7.**	**8.**
98	57	69	974
−47	−43	−32	−43

9.	**10.**	**11.**	**12.**
193	968	897	8,473
−82	−342	−456	−3,251

Solve each problem.

13. Oscar traveled 435 miles by bus and 121 miles by train. He traveled 1,984 miles by plane.

   a. How far did he travel by land?

   b. How much farther did he travel by air than by land?

14. Harold rode a train 236 miles. He rode a bus 427 miles. How many miles did he travel altogether?

15. The stairway to the lookout tower has 289 steps. Larry has climbed 148 steps. How many more does he have to climb?

SEQUENCES AND PATTERNS

1. Study this list.

　　　　3, 4, 6, 9, 13, 18, 24, ____

a. What number should come after 24? Missing addends can help us.

　　3+___=4,　　4+___=6,　　6+___=9

b. Subtraction can help us find the pattern.

　　24−18=___,　18−13=___,　13−9=___

c. What is the pattern in the above list?

2. Name the missing numbers in these sequences.

a. 4, 9, 14, 19, ____, ____, ____

b. 19, 16, 13, ____, 7, ____, 1

c. 30, 21, ____, 3

d. 3, 5, 6, 8, 9, ____, ____, ____

Let's Practice

When we subtract, we often need to rename.
Rename the hundreds and tens.

1. $460 = 400 + \square$
　　　$= 300 + \triangle$

2. $840 = \square + 40$
　　　$= \triangle + 140$

3. $843 = 800 + \square + 3$
　　　$= 700 + \triangle + 3$

4. $962 = \square + 60 + 2$
　　　$= \triangle + 160 + 2$

Rename the hundreds, tens, and ones.

5. $822 = 800 + \square + 2$
　　　$= 800 + \triangle + 12$
　　　$= 700 + 110 + 12$

6. $422 = 400 + 20 + \triangle$
　　　$= 400 + \square + 12$
　　　$= 300 + \triangledown + 12$

74

EXTENDING SUBTRACTION

1. Subtract. Do you see a pattern?

   a. $13 - 8$
      $23 - 8$
      $33 - 8$
      $93 - 8$

   b. $17 - 9$
      $27 - 9$
      $37 - 9$
      $57 - 9$

2. We can name numbers in different ways. Copy and complete.

   a. $37 = 30 + 7$
      $= (20 + 10) + 7$
      $= 20 + (10 + 7)$
      $= 20 + \square$

   b. $482 = 400 + 80 + 2$
      $= 400 + (70 + 10) + 2$
      $= 400 + 70 + \triangle$

3. We rename to subtract 19 from 43. How is 43 renamed? Explain each step.

$$
\begin{array}{ccc}
43 & 40 + 3 & 30 + 13 \\
-19 & 10 + 9 & 10 + 9 \\
\hline
 & & 20 + 4
\end{array}
$$

4. Consider $43 - 19$ again. How did we show that 43 is renamed?

$$
\begin{array}{r}
\overset{3\ 13}{4\,3} \\
-1\,9 \\
\hline
4
\end{array}
\qquad\qquad
\begin{array}{r}
\overset{3\ 13}{4\,3} \\
-1\,9 \\
\hline
2\,4
\end{array}
$$

Subtract ones.
$13 - 9 = \underline{}$

Subtract tens.
3 tens − 1 ten
$= \underline{}$ tens

5. Subtract. Use expanded numerals and then use the short form.

| **a.** | 54
−27 | **b.** | 30
−19 | **c.** | 192
−38 | **d.** | 468
−136 |

Subtract.

1.	55 −17	**2.**	90 −35	**3.**	147 −28	**4.**	360 −122
5.	86 −78	**6.**	43 −29	**7.**	854 −717	**8.**	168 −9
9.	54 −7	**10.**	624 −19	**11.**	872 −745	**12.**	184 −78

Solve each problem.

13. There are 78 children in the lunchroom. There are 39 boys. How many girls are there?

14. All of the 121 fourth graders were in the gym. Mr. Harold's class of 32 children left. How many children remained in the gym?

15. A group of 152 children went to the gym to see a movie. There were 148 chairs. How many more chairs were needed for the children?

SUBTRACTING LARGER NUMBERS

1. We sometimes rename in the tens place. Explain each step in this subtraction. Write the standard numeral for the difference.

$$
\begin{array}{r}
958 \\
-173 \\
\end{array}
\qquad
\begin{array}{r}
900 + 50 + 8 \\
100 + 70 + 3 \\
\end{array}
\qquad
\begin{array}{r}
800 + 150 + 8 \\
100 + 70 + 3 \\
\hline
700 + 80 + 5 \\
\end{array}
$$

2. Complete each step in this short form.

   a.
   $$
   \begin{array}{r}
   958 \\
   -173 \\
   \hline
   5 \\
   \end{array}
   $$
   Subtract ones.
   $8 - 3 =$ ___

   b.
   $$
   \begin{array}{r}
   {}^{8}{}^{15} \\
   \cancel{9}\,\cancel{5}\,8 \\
   -1\,7\,3 \\
   \hline
   8\,5 \\
   \end{array}
   $$
   Is there a whole number for the difference 5 tens − 7 tens?
   Rename $900 + 50 + 8$
   as $800 + 150 + 8$
   15 tens − 7 tens = ___ tens

   c.
   $$
   \begin{array}{r}
   {}^{8}{}^{15} \\
   \cancel{9}\,\cancel{5}\,8 \\
   -1\,7\,3 \\
   \hline
   7\,8\,5 \\
   \end{array}
   $$
   Subtract the hundreds.
   8 hundreds − 1 hundred
   = ___ hundreds

3. Use the short form to subtract.

   a.
   $$
   \begin{array}{r}
   839 \\
   -263 \\
   \end{array}
   $$
   b.
   $$
   \begin{array}{r}
   482 \\
   -390 \\
   \end{array}
   $$
   c.
   $$
   \begin{array}{r}
   958 \\
   -83 \\
   \end{array}
   $$
   d.
   $$
   \begin{array}{r}
   703 \\
   -592 \\
   \end{array}
   $$

4. Sometimes we rename twice.

   a. $421 = 400 + 10 +$ ___
   $421 = 300 +$ ___ $+ 11$

   b. $384 = 300 +$ ___ $+ 14$
   $384 = 200 +$ ___ $+ 14$

5. Consider 834 − 596. Explain the renaming in this form. Find the difference.

$$800 + 30 + 4 \qquad 800 + 20 + 14 \qquad 700 + 120 + 14$$
$$\underline{500 + 90 + 6} \qquad \underline{500 + 90 + \ \ 6} \qquad \underline{500 + \ \ 90 + \ \ 6}$$

6. Study each step in the short form.

a. $\begin{array}{r} 834 \\ -596 \\ \hline \end{array}$ Is there a whole number answer for 4 − 6?
Rename 30 + 4 as 20 + 14.

b. $\begin{array}{r} {}^{2\ 14}\!\!\!\!\!\!\! \\ 834 \\ -596 \\ \hline 8 \end{array}$ Subtract the ones.
14 − 6 = ___

c. $\begin{array}{r} {}^{2\ 14}\!\!\!\!\!\!\! \\ 834 \\ -596 \\ \hline 8 \end{array}$ Is there a whole number answer for 2 tens − 9 tens?
Rename 800 + 20 as 700 + 120.

d. $\begin{array}{r} {}^{7\ 12\ 14}\!\!\!\!\!\!\!\!\!\! \\ 834 \\ -596 \\ \hline 38 \end{array}$ Subtract the tens.
12 tens − 9 tens = ___ tens

e. $\begin{array}{r} {}^{7\ 12\ 14}\!\!\!\!\!\!\!\!\!\! \\ 834 \\ -596 \\ \hline 238 \end{array}$ Subtract the hundreds.
7 hundreds − 5 hundreds
= ___ hundreds

7. Try these subtractions. Check.

a. 784 − 596   **b.** 117 − 98   **c.** 107 − 98

8. Subtract thousands. Explain any renaming.

$$\begin{array}{r} 8,347 \\ -6,172 \\ \hline 5 \end{array} \qquad \begin{array}{r} {}^{2\ 14} \\ 8,347 \\ -6,172 \\ \hline 75 \end{array} \qquad \begin{array}{r} {}^{2\ 14} \\ 8,347 \\ -6,172 \\ \hline 175 \end{array} \qquad \begin{array}{r} {}^{2\ 14} \\ 8,347 \\ -6,172 \\ \hline 2,175 \end{array}$$

Copy and subtract.

1.	886 −367	2.	993 −264	3.	919 −764	4.	538 −116
5.	240 −68	6.	618 −447	7.	513 −119	8.	911 −824
9.	730 −92	10.	731 −498	11.	439 −193	12.	748 −631
13.	1,963 −1,356	14.	3,821 −2,939	15.	1,654 − 782	16.	1,143 − 567
17.	2,117 − 438	18.	4,967 −1,385	19.	7,439 −2,954	20.	6,327 −3,799
21.	3,648 − 58	22.	5,303 −1,745	23.	5,146 −2,388	24.	8,347 −6,172

Solve each problem.

25. The first single-rotor helicopter was flown in 1940. How many years ago was that?

26. Radio commercial broadcasting began in 1920. Regular television commercial broadcasting began in 1939. How many years after radio did television broadcasting begin?

27. How much greater than 1,158 is 1,169?

28. Leroy read a book for 45 minutes and finger-painted for 26 minutes. How much more time did he spend reading than finger-painting?

ZEROS IN SUBTRACTION

1. There were 405 people swimming in the pool on Monday and 291 on Tuesday. How many more people were swimming on Monday?

$$
\begin{array}{r}
400 + 0 + 5 \\
200 + 90 + 1 \\
\hline
\end{array}
\qquad
\begin{array}{r}
300 + 100 + 5 \\
200 + 90 + 1 \\
\hline
\end{array}
\qquad
\begin{array}{r}
\overset{3\ 10}{4\cancel{0}5} \\
291 \\
\hline
\end{array}
$$

   a. How is 405 renamed?

   b. Explain the short form.

2. Subtract.

   a. $\begin{array}{r} 807 \\ -194 \\ \hline \end{array}$
   b. $\begin{array}{r} 302 \\ -151 \\ \hline \end{array}$
   c. $\begin{array}{r} 706 \\ -661 \\ \hline \end{array}$
   d. $\begin{array}{r} 108 \\ -92 \\ \hline \end{array}$

3. Subtract 189 from 806.

$$
\begin{array}{r}
800 + 0 + 6 \\
100 + 80 + 9 \\
\hline
\end{array}
\qquad
\begin{array}{r}
700 + 100 + 6 \\
100 + 80 + 9 \\
\hline
\end{array}
\qquad
\begin{array}{r}
700 + 90 + 16 \\
100 + 80 + 9 \\
\hline
\end{array}
$$

4. How is 806 renamed in this short form?

$$
\begin{array}{r}
806 \\
-189 \\
\hline
\end{array}
\qquad
\begin{array}{r}
\overset{7\ 10}{8\cancel{0}6} \\
-189 \\
\hline
\end{array}
\qquad
\begin{array}{r}
\overset{9}{\overset{7\ \cancel{10}\ 16}{\cancel{8}\cancel{0}\cancel{6}}} \\
-189 \\
\hline
617 \\
\end{array}
$$

5. Subtract. Use both forms.

   a. $\begin{array}{r} 804 \\ -428 \\ \hline \end{array}$ **b.** $\begin{array}{r} 902 \\ -728 \\ \hline \end{array}$ **c.** $\begin{array}{r} 107 \\ -98 \\ \hline \end{array}$ **d.** $\begin{array}{r} 102 \\ -8 \\ \hline \end{array}$

6. We can rename in other ways to help us subtract. Copy and complete.

   a. 800 = ___ tens

   b. 1,000 = ___ tens

   c. 806 = 80 tens + 6

   = 79 tens + ___

   d. 4,005 = 400 tens + 5

   = ___ tens + 15

7. Consider 800 − 189. Explain each step.

   $\begin{array}{r} 800 \\ -189 \\ \hline \end{array}$ $\begin{array}{r} 80 \text{ tens} + 0 \text{ ones} \\ 18 \text{ tens} + 9 \text{ ones} \\ \hline \end{array}$ $\begin{array}{r} 79 \text{ tens} + 10 \text{ ones} \\ 18 \text{ tens} + 9 \text{ ones} \\ \hline 61 \text{ tens} + 1 \text{ one} \end{array}$

8. This is a shorter form. Explain how 800 is renamed.

   $\begin{array}{r} 800 \\ -189 \\ \hline \end{array}$ $\begin{array}{r} \overset{7\ 9\ 10}{800} \\ -189 \\ \hline \end{array}$ $\begin{array}{r} \overset{7\ 9\ 10}{800} \\ -189 \\ \hline 611 \end{array}$

9. Subtract. Use the methods in Items 7 and 8.

   a. $\begin{array}{r} 406 \\ -158 \\ \hline \end{array}$ **b.** $\begin{array}{r} 300 \\ -138 \\ \hline \end{array}$ **c.** $\begin{array}{r} 600 \\ -386 \\ \hline \end{array}$ **d.** $\begin{array}{r} 203 \\ -46 \\ \hline \end{array}$

10. How is 6,005 renamed? Find the difference.

   $\begin{array}{r} 6,005 \\ -1,388 \\ \hline \end{array}$ $\begin{array}{r} \overset{5\ 9\ 9\ 15}{6,005} \\ -1,388 \\ \hline \end{array}$

11. How is 3,000 renamed? Find the difference.

$$\begin{array}{r} 3{,}0\,0\,0 \\ -1{,}2\,8\,8 \end{array} \qquad \begin{array}{r} {}^{2\ 9\ 9\ 10}\\ \cancel{3}{,}\cancel{0}\cancel{0}\cancel{0} \\ -1{,}2\,8\,8 \end{array}$$

12. Subtract. Check.

a. $\begin{array}{r} 4{,}003 \\ -1{,}294 \end{array}$ **b.** $\begin{array}{r} 8{,}001 \\ -4{,}876 \end{array}$ **c.** $\begin{array}{r} 6{,}000 \\ -4{,}987 \end{array}$ **d.** $\begin{array}{r} 4{,}000 \\ -2{,}804 \end{array}$

EXERCISES

Subtract. Check each answer.

1. $\begin{array}{r} 607 \\ -332 \end{array}$ **2.** $\begin{array}{r} 704 \\ -449 \end{array}$ **3.** $\begin{array}{r} 802 \\ -117 \end{array}$ **4.** $\begin{array}{r} 608 \\ -132 \end{array}$

5. $\begin{array}{r} 8{,}004 \\ -1{,}987 \end{array}$ **6.** $\begin{array}{r} 5{,}073 \\ -2{,}186 \end{array}$ **7.** $\begin{array}{r} 9{,}000 \\ -3{,}682 \end{array}$ **8.** $\begin{array}{r} 3{,}002 \\ -874 \end{array}$

9. $\begin{array}{r} 4{,}000 \\ -1{,}986 \end{array}$ **10.** $\begin{array}{r} 4{,}001 \\ -204 \end{array}$ **11.** $\begin{array}{r} 6{,}040 \\ -1{,}738 \end{array}$ **12.** $\begin{array}{r} 1{,}000 \\ -999 \end{array}$

Solve each problem.

13. Columbus came to America in 1492. The Pilgrims came to America in 1620. How many years after Columbus did they come?

14. The first safety bicycle with both wheels the same size was invented in 1880. How long ago was that?

15. In Alaska, Mt. McKinley is 20,320 feet high. The highest point of Mt. Everest, in India, is 29,028 feet. What is the difference in their heights?

DO YOU REMEMBER?

Find each sum or difference.

1. 54 +36	**2.** 73 −9	**3.** 70 +62	**4.** 54 −27
5. 540 −36	**6.** 713 +69	**7.** $7.02 −.64	**8.** 487 +298
9. 409 −38	**10.** 7,000 −1,238	**11.** 7,004 −3,469	**12.** $80.13 +24.63
13. 1,841 +3,386	**14.** 5,847 +6,939	**15.** 65,034 −1,287	**16.** 14,983 −217

Add.

17. 248 +197	**18.** 1,247 +389	**19.** 7,894 +9,999	**20.** 8,888 +7,777
21. 8 7 6 5	**22.** 18 17 28 37	**23.** $.38 .19 .40 .05	**24.** $1.49 3.49 2.97 3.48

UNEXPLORED TERRITORY

Supply the missing symbols. Use what you know about checking subtraction.

1. 3?4 −186 138	**2.** 4,967 − 3?5 4,582	**3.** ?43 − 89 854	**4.** 5,324 −1,?45 3,579
5. 2,?03 − 947 1,056	**6.** 3,648 − ?8 3,59?	**7.** 9,?3? − 189 9,249	**8.** 67,5?2 −?5,?7? 51,869

USING RELATED SENTENCES

1. Mrs. Day made doughnuts and gave 9 of them to Mrs. Williams. She had 23 doughnuts left. How many doughnuts did Mrs. Day make?

   a. Does the sentence $\square - 9 = 23$ fit the story?

   b. Write a related addition sentence.

   c. Solve the sentence $23 + 9 = \square$ to find how many doughnuts Mrs. Day made.

2. Jerry has some mystery books. Bill has 17 books. The boys have 36 books altogether. How many books does Jerry have?

   a. These sentences fit the story.
   $$\square + 17 = 36 \quad \text{or} \quad 17 + \square = 36$$

   b. Write a related subtraction sentence.

3. Make each pair of related sentences true.

   a. $\square - 19 = 36$
   $36 + 19 = \square$

   b. $7 + \triangle = 51$
   $51 - 7 = \triangle$

   c. $\triangle + 39 = 52$
   $52 - 39 = \triangle$

   d. $32 = 76 - \triangle$
   $\triangle = 76 - 32$

Make each sentence true. Use what you know about related sentences to help you.

1. $762 + \triangle = 789$ 2. $86 + \triangle = 92$

3. $\triangle + 76 = 103$ 4. $\square - 149 = 328$

5. $520 = 670 - \triangle$ 6. $\square - 17 = 89$

7. $\triangle + 428 = 759$ 8. $115 = \square - 720$

Solve each problem.

9. There are 125 children in a swimming pool. There is room for 500 children. How many more children can enter the pool?

10. There were 2,636 tickets on sale for a football game. Only 2,321 tickets were sold. How many tickets were not sold?

11. Robert has some tickets for the school play. Mike has 19 tickets. The boys have 55 tickets altogether. How many tickets does Robert have?

12. Jeff and Bill are traveling 325 miles. They have gone 175 miles. How many miles do they have left to go?

13. The shelf has 10 books. It holds 18. How many more books are needed to fill the shelf?

14. The first airplane with a motor was flown by Orville and Wilbur Wright in 1903. About how many years ago was that?

ESTIMATING DIFFERENCES

1. Mary has 80 cents. She spends 39 cents. Estimate how much money she has left.

   a. Round 39 to the nearest ten.
   Think: 80 — 40. Estimate the difference.

   b. Find the exact difference.

2. Mickey had 325 pictures of football players. He gave away 189 pictures. About how many does he have left?

   a. Round 325 and 189 to the nearest hundred.
   Think: 300 — 200. Estimate the difference.

   b. Find the exact difference.

3. Mrs. Nelson has $10.00. She wants to buy a sweater for $5.00 and a scarf for $2.98. Does she have enough money? Explain.

EXERCISES

Round to the nearest ten. Then estimate the difference.

1.	72	2.	63	3.	91	4.	45
	—48		—55		—19		—19

Round to the nearest hundred. Estimate.

5.	550	6.	794	7.	649	8.	880
	—121		—108		—345		—460

9. Find the exact differences in Exercises 1–8.

10. Miss Cole had $15.00. She bought a sweater for $5.98 and a skirt for $7.98. About how much money does Miss Cole have left?

USING MONEY

1. Ron's brother has $7.34. If he buys a record that costs $4.95, how much money will he have left? Explain each step.

$$
\begin{array}{r}
\overset{2\ 14}{\$7.3\cancel{4}} \\
-\ 4.9\,5 \\
\hline
9
\end{array}
\qquad
\begin{array}{r}
\overset{6\ 12\ 14}{\$\cancel{7}.\cancel{3}\cancel{4}} \\
-\ 4.9\,5 \\
\hline
.3\,9
\end{array}
\qquad
\begin{array}{r}
\overset{6\ 12\ 14}{\$\cancel{7}.\cancel{3}\cancel{4}} \\
-\ 4.9\,5 \\
\hline
\$2.3\,9
\end{array}
$$

2. Bill bought a set of paints for 79¢. He gave the clerk $1.00. When the clerk counted out the change, she said, "79 cents for the paints, 80 cents, 90 cents, one dollar." What coins did Bill get in change?

3. Pretend that you are a clerk. Tell more than one way to make change.

Cost of Item	Amount Received
a. 32 cents	50 cents
b. $4.24	$5.00
c. $8.89	$10.00
d. $1.45	$5.00
e. $.75	$1.00

Subtract.

1. $3.98
    −2.67

2. $3.27
    −1.09

3. $9.32
    −4.68

4. $8.47
    −3.88

5. $8.95
    −6.49

6. $2.97
    −1.46

7. $8.00
    −3.99

8. $10.00
    −7.36

9. $24.82
    −17.93

10. $68.47
    −19.00

11. $27.43
    −7.29

12. $104.23
    −94.23

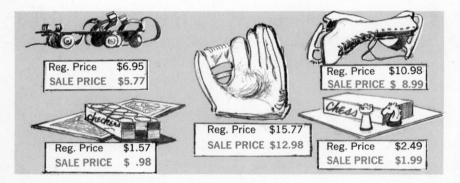

Reg. Price $6.95
SALE PRICE $5.77

Reg. Price $10.98
SALE PRICE $ 8.99

Reg. Price $1.57
SALE PRICE $ .98

Reg. Price $15.77
SALE PRICE $12.98

Reg. Price $2.49
SALE PRICE $1.99

Solve each problem.

13. How much can John save on a pair of roller skates while they are on sale?

14. Which gift has the greatest difference between the regular price and the sale price?

15. Joan has $10. She must buy three different gifts. Which three can she buy? How much would she still have left from the $10?

16. Larry has $20 to spend on gifts. How much would he have left if he bought the baseball glove? Can he also buy the skates?

DO YOU REMEMBER?

Subtract.

1. 26
   −5

2. 57
   −7

3. 39
   −28

4. 73
   −21

5. 47
   −9

6. 61
   −8

7. 73
   −7

8. 60
   −3

9. 83
   −55

10. 94
    −48

11. 40
    −25

12. 90
    −18

13. 460
    −48

14. 581
    −79

15. 784
    −369

16. 872
    −735

17. 958
    −73

18. 139
    −52

19. 609
    −78

20. 147
    −92

21. 829
    −263

22. 704
    −592

23. 782
    −490

24. 248
    −182

25. 342
    −75

26. 156
    −77

27. 118
    −99

28. 111
    −72

29. 9,832
    −1,643

30. 9,721
    −7,594

31. 8,660
    −4,469

32. 6,213
    −5,176

33. 1,703
    −445

34. 7,608
    −489

35. 9,405
    −2,157

36. 107
    −98

37. 600
    −159

38. 6,000
    −2,849

39. 7,000
    −5,986

40. 900
    −178

Make each sentence true.

41. $\square + 69 = 84$

42. $500 - \square = 129$

CHAPTER REVIEW

Write two related subtraction sentences for each addition sentence.

1. $5+4=9$ **2.** $25+42=67$ **3.** $49+51=100$

Write a related subtraction sentence for each sentence. Make both sentences true.

4. $4+\triangle=12$ **5.** $9+\triangle=18$ **6.** $7+\triangle=15$

We often need to rename when we subtract. Copy and complete each number sentence.

7. $\begin{array}{r} 43 \\ -28 \\ \hline \end{array}$ **a.** $43 = \underline{\quad}$ tens $+$ 13 ones
   b. $43 - 28 = \underline{\quad}$

8. $\begin{array}{r} 400 \\ -123 \\ \hline \end{array}$ **a.** $400 = \underline{\quad}$ hundreds $+$ 9 tens $+$ 10 ones
   b. $400 = 39$ tens $+ \underline{\quad}$ ones
   c. $400 - 123 = \underline{\quad}$

9. $\begin{array}{r} 423 \\ -178 \\ \hline \end{array}$ **a.** $423 = 3$ hundreds $+ \underline{\quad}$ tens $+$ 13 ones
   b. $423 = 300 + \underline{\quad} + 13$

Subtract.

10. $\begin{array}{r} 117 \\ -9 \\ \hline \end{array}$ **11.** $\begin{array}{r} 112 \\ -98 \\ \hline \end{array}$ **12.** $\begin{array}{r} 5{,}002 \\ -4{,}934 \\ \hline \end{array}$ **13.** $\begin{array}{r} 9{,}123 \\ -1{,}789 \\ \hline \end{array}$

Terms You Should Know

missing addend   operation
subtraction   difference
related sentences   estimate

CHAPTER TEST

Subtract.

1.	99 −76	2.	$.52 −.48	3.	60 −19	4.	98 −88
5.	436 −428	6.	4,360 −4,283	7.	$7.31 −1.37	8.	6,741 −1,476
9.	$41.34 −38.71	10.	7,683 −1,234	11.	9,000 −8,466	12.	8,006 −4,040

Find the missing number.

13. $4,976 - \square = 1,982$ 14. $3,498 - \square = 1,000$

15. $\square - 1,986 = 6,941$ 16. $\square - 3,492 = 10,000$

17. Round to the nearest ten. Estimate the difference: $.65 − $.32.

Solve each problem.

18. The Amazon River in South America is about 3,912 miles long. The Mississippi River is about 2,348 miles long. How much longer is the Amazon River?

19. The first building known as a "skyscraper" was 10 stories high. The Empire State Building in New York City is 102 stories high. How many stories higher than the first skyscraper is it?

20. World's Fairs were held in New York in 1939 and in 1964. How many years were between the fairs in New York?

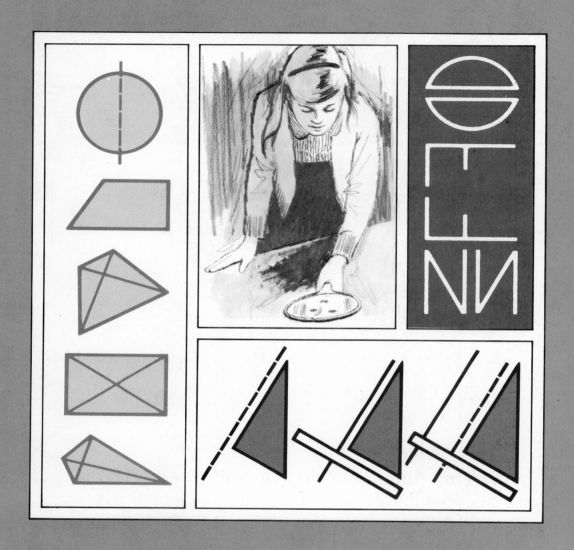

CHAPTER FOUR

Geometry

RAYS AND LINES

1. Mark two points, like this.   A   B

2. Use your ruler. Draw a straight path to connect *A* and *B*.

3. Extend the path, like this. Use your ruler.

4. If you had a very large sheet of paper, how far could you extend the path?

A straight path that goes on forever in one direction is called a **ray.**

5. Put an arrow on your drawing, like this.

This shows that the path goes on forever in one direction.

We can name this ray $\overrightarrow{AB}$. The **endpoint** is always named first.

6. What is a ray of light? How far can a ray of light from a star travel?

7. Now extend the path the other way, like this.

This path goes on forever in both ways.

A straight path that goes on forever in both directions is called a **line**.
We can name this line $\overleftrightarrow{AB}$.

EXERCISES

Which of these are rays? lines? Write names for them.

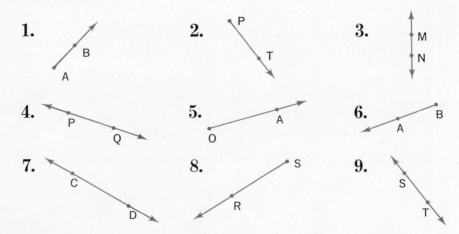

10. Mark two points P and Q. Draw the ray $\overrightarrow{PQ}$.

11. Mark two points P and Q. Draw the ray $\overrightarrow{QP}$.

12. Mark two points P and Q. Draw the line $\overleftrightarrow{PQ}$.

UNEXPLORED TERRITORY

Which one of the set is different? How is it different?

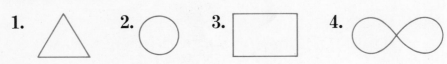

LINE SEGMENTS

1. Mark two points. A   B

2. Use your ruler.

   Draw a straight path from *A* to *B*.

3. Draw different paths from *A* to *B*. Are they straight?

4. How many straight paths are there from *A* to *B*?

> We call such a straight path a **line segment,** or **segment.**
> We can name your segment $\overline{AB}$.

5. Mark two points. A   B

6. Use your ruler. Draw the line $\overleftrightarrow{AB}$.

7. How many lines can you draw through points *A* and *B*?

EXERCISES

1. Mark two points *R* and *S*. Use your ruler. Draw the line segment $\overline{RS}$.

Which of these are segments? rays? lines? Write names for them.

2. P
   Q

3. S
   R

4. C
   D

TRIANGLES

1. Mark three points.

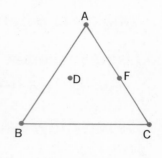

2. Use a ruler. Draw $\overline{AB}$. Draw $\overline{BC}$. Draw $\overline{CA}$. What kind of figure did you draw?

3. Points A, B, and C are on the triangle. Mark another point on the triangle. Name it F.

4. Mark a point inside the triangle. Name it D.

5. Mark a point outside the triangle. Name it E.

The segments $\overline{AB}$, $\overline{BC}$, and $\overline{CA}$ are called the **sides** of the triangle.

6. A square corner is called a *right angle*. Which of these triangles have a right angle?

   a.   b.    c.   d.

A triangle with a right angle is called a **right triangle.**

7. Can you draw a triangle which has two right angles? three right angles?

8. In the world around you, find some right angles and some right triangles.

9. Use your drawing triangle to draw a right triangle.

    a. Draw segment $\overline{AB}$.

    b. Place your drawing triangle, like this. Draw segment $\overline{AC}$. Draw segment $\overline{CB}$.

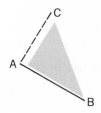

Triangle ABC has three **angles**. We can call them angle A, angle B, and angle C.

10. Which angle of triangle ABC is a right angle? Are the other angles smaller (sharper) or larger (wider) than the right angle?

EXERCISES

1. Use your drawing triangle. Draw a right triangle. Label the right angle P. Label the other angles Q and R.

2. Name the sides of the triangle you drew.

3. Draw an angle larger (wider) than a right angle. Now make it a triangle. Are the other two angles larger or smaller (sharper) than a right angle?

4. Can all three angles of a triangle be smaller than a right angle? Try to draw such a triangle.

5. How many right angles can a triangle have?

KINDS OF TRIANGLES

1. Draw two segments $\overline{AB}$, and $\overline{AC}$, like this. Each segment should be 2 inches long.

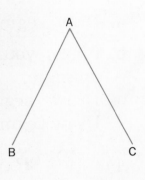

2. Draw $\overline{BC}$. Now you have a triangle. Two of its sides are the same length.

> If two sides of a triangle are the same length, it is called an **isosceles triangle.**

3. Which of these are isosceles triangles?

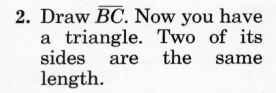

> If a triangle has three sides the same length, it is called an **equilateral triangle.**

4. Which of these are equilateral triangles? Which are isosceles triangles?

a.   b.   c.

d.   e.   f.

ANGLES AND RAYS

An angle is made of two rays. Here is a right angle. Its sides are rays $\overrightarrow{AB}$ and $\overrightarrow{AC}$. These sides go on forever.

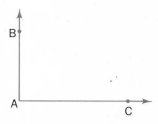

Point *A* is called the **vertex.** A name for this angle is $\angle BAC$.

1. Draw right angle $\angle PQR$. Its sides are the rays $\overrightarrow{QP}$ and $\overrightarrow{QR}$. What is its vertex?

2. Draw angle $\angle ACB$ smaller than a right angle. Draw angle $\angle RST$ larger than a right angle.

EXERCISES

Name each angle. Name the sides. Name each vertex.

1.

2.

3.

4.

5. Use your drawing triangle. Draw right angle $\angle CPT$.

6. Draw an angle smaller than a right angle. Label the vertex *R*.

7. Draw an angle larger than a right angle. Label the vertex *T*.

99

ANGLES AND TRIANGLES

Angles are made of two rays.

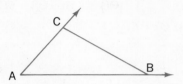

1. Draw a triangle like this.

2. Draw ray $\overrightarrow{AB}$.
   Draw ray $\overrightarrow{AC}$.
   Now you see $\angle BAC$.

3. Draw ray $\overrightarrow{BA}$. Draw ray $\overrightarrow{BC}$. Name the angle formed by these rays. Name its vertex.

4. The triangle has another angle at C. Draw rays to show this angle. Name the sides of $\angle C$. Name the vertex.

> An angle of a triangle fits on the triangle, but is not part of the triangle.

EXERCISES

1. a. Draw right triangle ABC, with the right angle at B.

   b. Draw rays to show the angle at B.

   c. Draw rays to show the angle at C.

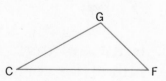

2. a. Name the angles of this triangle.

   b. What rays form an angle at C?

   c. What rays form an angle at G?

   d. What rays form an angle at F?

DO YOU REMEMBER?

Add or subtract.

1.
$$\begin{array}{r} 423 \\ +391 \end{array}$$

2.
$$\begin{array}{r} \$9.06 \\ -2.98 \end{array}$$

3.
$$\begin{array}{r} 7,036 \\ -281 \end{array}$$

4.
$$\begin{array}{r} 3,276 \\ +9,147 \end{array}$$

5.
$$\begin{array}{r} 5,090 \\ -2,381 \end{array}$$

6.
$$\begin{array}{r} \$\ .26 \\ 3.07 \\ .94 \end{array}$$

7.
$$\begin{array}{r} 8,026 \\ 753 \\ 3,565 \end{array}$$

8.
$$\begin{array}{r} \$26.31 \\ -19.83 \end{array}$$

Solve each problem.

9. The new airport at Big City covers 4,600 acres. The old airport covered 1,400 acres. How many more acres does the new airport cover?

10. One parking lot at the airport has space for 1,200 cars. Another lot has space for 568 cars. How many cars in all can park in the two lots?

11. A new parking garage has space for 2,000 cars. In the next block there are 3 older garages that have spaces for 325 cars, 624 cars, and 129 cars.

   a. How many cars can park in the 3 older garages?

   b. How many more cars can park in the new garage than in the 3 older garages?

   c. How many cars in all can park in the 4 garages?

   d. How many more cars can park in the new garage than in the garage with space for 325 cars?

PARALLEL SEGMENTS

1. When segments or lines touch or cross, we say that they *intersect*.

   a. Draw two segments that intersect.

   b. Draw two segments that do not intersect.

2. Do these segments intersect? If we make them longer, will they intersect?

3. Draw two segments that would not intersect even if you made them very long.

> Segments on a flat surface that do not intersect, no matter how long you make them, are **parallel segments**. Lines on a flat surface that do not intersect are **parallel lines.**

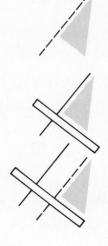

4. **a.** Use your ruler to draw a segment. Place your drawing triangle beside it.

   b. Put your ruler along the other edge of the drawing triangle, as shown.

   c. Hold the ruler. Slide the triangle along the ruler. Draw another segment.

5. Do the line segments you drew intersect? Would they intersect if you made them longer? Are they parallel?

6. Name some objects that look like parallel segments.

EXERCISES

1. Draw two segments that intersect.

2. Draw two segments that would intersect if you made them longer.

3. Draw two segments that are parallel. Use your ruler and drawing triangle.

4. Which pairs of segments look parallel?

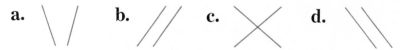

a.   b.   c.   d.

5. Which pairs of lines look parallel?

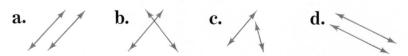

a.   b.   c.   d.

6. Which pairs of lines in Item 5 do not look parallel?

103

PERPENDICULAR SEGMENTS

1. Use your drawing tri-
   angle to draw a right
   angle.

2. Extend the rays to make
   lines, like this.

3. **a.** How many angles do
   you now have?

   b. How many of them are right angles?

When lines or segments make a right angle,
we say they are **perpendicular.** The four
angles are all right angles.

4. Find some objects that make you think of
   perpendicular segments.

EXERCISES

1. Use your triangle.
   Draw perpendicular
   segments, like this.

2. Draw perpendicular lines, like this.

3. Which pairs of segments or lines are perpendicular?

a. **b.** **c.** **d.**

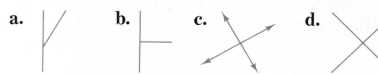

4. Which pairs of sides are perpendicular?

a. **b.** **c.**

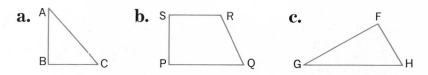

Let's Practice

Solve each problem.

1. Mr. Davis sold 1,782 pairs of shoes during July and 2,450 pairs during August.

   a. How many pairs of shoes did he sell in both months?

   b. How many more pairs of shoes did he sell in August than in July?

2. **a.** Mr. Davis sells nurse's shoes for $16.98 a pair. Mrs. Crane bought a pair on sale for $8.99. How much money did Mrs. Crane save?

   b. Mrs. Crane paid for the shoes with a twenty-dollar bill. How much change did she receive?

RECTANGLES

What can we discover about rectangles?

1. A rectangle has four right angles. Which of these are rectangles?

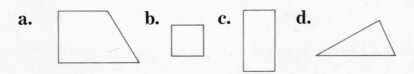

a.   b.   c.   d.

2. This is a rectangle. It has four sides $\overline{DC}$, $\overline{CB}$, $\overline{BA}$, and $\overline{AD}$. Measure the sides in centimeters.

3. Measure the sides of these rectangles in centimeters.

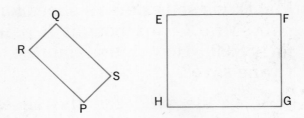

4. What did you discover?

106

In a rectangle opposite pairs of sides are the same length.

5. Which sides are parallel?

a.

b.

In a rectangle opposite pairs of sides are parallel.

6. This rectangle is a square. Measure the sides in centimeters.

In a square all sides are the same length.

EXERCISES

Use your ruler and drawing triangle.

1. Draw a rectangle, one side 5 centimeters long and one side 7 centimeters long.

2. Draw a square, one side 3 inches long.

3. How long is each side?

DIAGONALS

1. Segment $\overline{AC}$ is called a *diagonal*. This rectangle has another diagonal. Where is it? Name it.

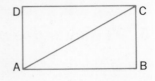

2. Measure the diagonals in centimeters.

a.    b.    c.

3. What did you discover?

> In a rectangle the diagonals are the same length.

4. These rectangles are squares. The diagonals are the same length. What else can you discover about the diagonals?

a.   b.   c.

> In a square the diagonals are **perpendicular.**

5. Any four-sided figure is a *quadrilateral*. Measure the diagonals of these quadrilaterals in centimeters.

a.   b.   c.

108

EXERCISES

1. Draw a rectangle, one side 3 inches long, the other 4 inches long. Draw its diagonals. Measure them.

2. Draw a square, each side 6 centimeters long. Draw its diagonals. Measure them.

3. Name the diagonals.

a. 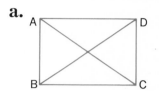 **b.** 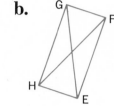 **c.**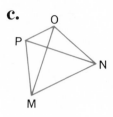

4. This is a rectangle. Are its diagonals the same length?

5. In this quadrilateral the diagonals are the same length. Is it a rectangle?

6. This is a square. Are its diagonals perpendicular? Are the diagonals the same length?

7. In this quadrilateral the diagonals are perpendicular. Is it a square?

8. In this quadrilateral the diagonals are perpendicular. Is it a square?

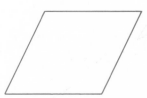

PERIMETER

Patty is making a sewing box. She wants enough ribbon to tack around the lid. She put a string around the lid. She measured the string to find how much ribbon to buy. David said she could measure the sides of the lid and then add.

Miss Burns told them they were finding the *perimeter* of the top of the box.

> The **perimeter** of a figure is the distance around it. It is also the sum of the lengths of the sides.

1. What is the perimeter of each figure?

a.

9 in.

6 in.   6 in.

9 in.

b.

8 ft   6 ft

5 ft   9 ft

2. What is the perimeter of each figure?

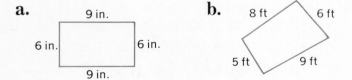

a.

6 cm

4 cm

b.

5 yd

110

Find the perimeters.

1.

2.

3.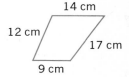

4.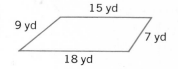

5.

6.

7. Mr. Johnson has a garden. It is in the shape of a rectangle, 16 feet long and 14 feet wide. How much fence will he need to go around it?

8. A baseball diamond is a square, 90 feet on each side. How far does a man walk if he goes around it?

Let's Practice

Think of each pair of numbers as addends. Use them to write two true addition sentences.

1. 7, 9	**2.** 6, 5	**3.** 9, 6	**4.** 9, 3
5. 9, 1	**6.** 5, 7	**7.** 8, 6	**8.** 4, 8
9. 8, 7	**10.** 9, 8	**11.** 8, 5	**12.** 9, 5
13. 7, 4	**14.** 3, 8	**15.** 9, 2	**16.** 9, 4

SYMMETRY

1. If you fold along the dotted line in each figure, would the two halves match?

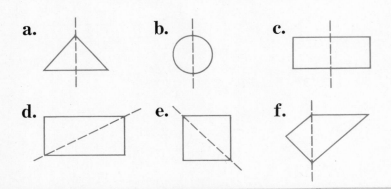

a.   b.   c.

d.   e.   f.

> If a figure can be folded so that the two halves match, it is **symmetric**. The line of folding is called a **line of symmetry.**

2. Copy these. Draw a line of symmetry in each.

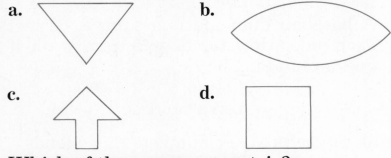

a.   b.

c.   d.

3. Which of these are symmetric?

112

4. Which of these have more than one line of symmetry?

a.   b.   c.

EXERCISES

Copy and draw lines of symmetry.

1.   **2.**    **3.**

4.   **5.**   **6.**

Let's Practice

Write three expanded numerals for each number.

Example $249 = 200 + 40 + 9$
$249 = 2 \text{ hundreds} + 4 \text{ tens}$
$+ 9 \text{ ones}$
$249 = (2 \times 100) + (4 \times 10)$
$+ (9 \times 1)$

1. 532   **2.** 98   **3.** 1,224   **4.** 756

Subtract.

5. 93
−24

6. 81
−7

7. 424
−78

8. 526
−209

9. 403
−98

10. 600
−289

11. 9,324
−2,615

12. 3,925
−386

113

REFLECTIONS

Jerry is looking at his reflection in a mirror.
Jerry and his reflection look like this.

The mirror is a line of symmetry. It is also called a **line of reflection.**

Triangle *DEF* is a reflection of triangle *ABC*. Triangle *ABC* is a reflection of triangle *DEF*.

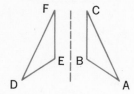

1. Copy and draw a line of reflection.

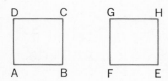

2. Point *B* is the reflection of point *F*. What is the reflection of point *G*? of point *D*? of point *A*? of point *B*?

3. Segment $\overline{BC}$ is the reflection of $\overline{FG}$. What is the reflection of $\overline{AD}$? of $\overline{GH}$? of $\overline{BC}$?

4. Copy this triangle and line of reflection on graph paper.

114

5. Point *D* is the reflection of *A*. Mark the reflection of *B* on your paper. Mark the reflection of *C* on your paper.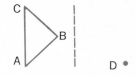
Draw the reflection of triangle *ABC*.

EXERCISES

Which pairs of figures are reflections of each other?

1.   **2.**   **3.**

4.   **5.**   **6.**

Copy and draw a line of reflection.

7.   **8.**   **9.**

10.   **11.**   **12.**

Use graph paper. Copy this figure and line of reflection.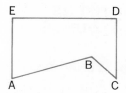

13. Mark the reflection of point *A*.

14. Mark the reflections of points *B*, *C*, *D*, and *E*.

15. Draw the reflection of the whole figure.

DO YOU REMEMBER?

Make each sentence true.

1. $8 + 7 + 6 = 9 + 2 + \triangle$

2. $(9 + 7) + \square = 9 + (7 + 2)$

3. $4 + 3 + 2 + 287 + 386 = \square$

4. $8 + 7 = \square + 9$

5. $5 + 1 + \triangle = 4 + 3 + 2$

6. $\square + 8 = 8 + 3$

7. $8 + (4 + 7) = \square + (8 + 4)$

Add.

8.	9.	10.	11.
384	$49.72	497	39,872
297	84.38	4,731	47,684
386	27.84	2,864	24,907

Solve each problem.

12. There are 286 girls and 279 boys in Hayes School. How many children attend Hayes School?

Western High School played its first five basketball games.

Western	Opponents
94	86
67	83
82	49
37	63
81	79

13. How many points has Western scored in the five games?

14. How many points have their opponents scored?

116

LOOKING FOR PATTERNS

Which one in each set is different? How is it different?

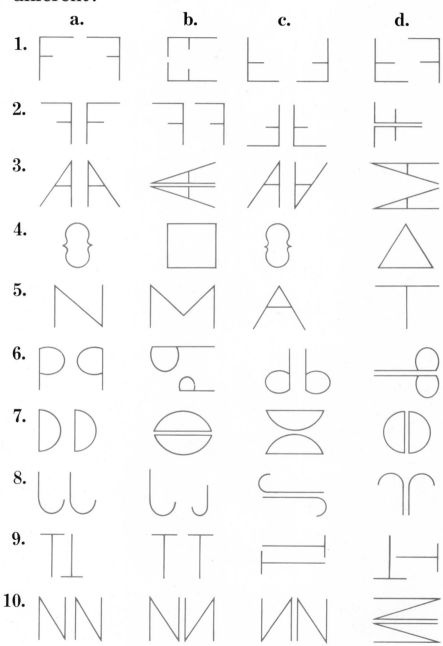

ROTATIONS

1. Are these two pictures exactly alike?
   Explain.

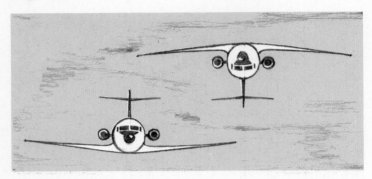

What could you do to make them exactly
alike?

2. We can *rotate* (turn) one of these figures to
   make it exactly like the other.

Can you do that with these?

a.   b.

c.   d.

Sometimes we can rotate (turn) a figure to
make it look just like another.

EXERCISES

Which one in each set is different? How is it different?

<table>
<tr><td></td><td>a.</td><td>b.</td><td>c.</td><td>d.</td></tr>
</table>

1.

2.

3.

4.

5.

6.

7.

8.

119

1. Match each picture with a term that describes that picture.

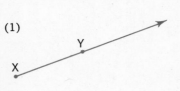
(1)

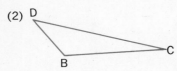
(2)

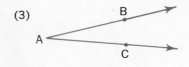
(3)

(4)

(a) Triangle with angle larger than a right angle

(b) Figure with only one line of symmetry

(c) Line $\overleftrightarrow{XY}$

(d) Ray $\overrightarrow{XY}$

(e) Angle BAC

Find the perimeters.

2. 6 ft / 4 ft

3. 27 in.

4. 15 yd / 15 yd / 18 yd / 26 yd

5. Draw an isosceles triangle with two sides $1\frac{1}{2}$ inches long.

6. Name the sides and the angles of this triangle.

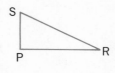

7. Draw a rectangle 3 centimeters wide and 4 centimeters long. How long are its diagonals?

Which one in each set is different? How is it different?

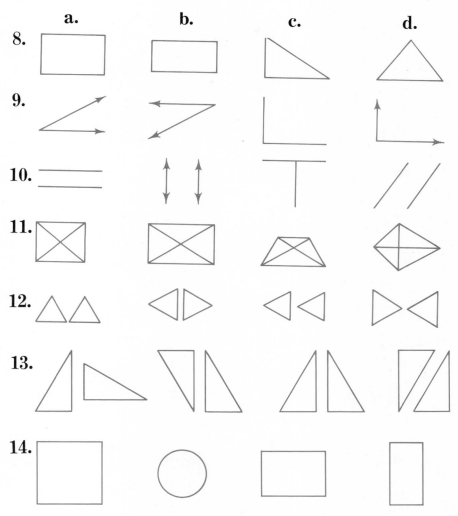

a. **b.** **c.** **d.**

8.

9.

10.

11.

12.

13.

14.

Terms You Should Know

ray	line	triangle
rectangle	isosceles	right angle
vertex	intersect	perpendicular
quadrilateral	diagonal	reflection
symmetry	segment	equilateral
perimeter	parallel	rotation

CHAPTER TEST

Find the perimeters.

1. 9 cm 7 cm

2. 137 ft 115 ft 120 ft 153 ft

3. 1,345 cm

4. Which is ray $\overrightarrow{CD}$?

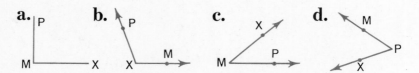

a. D C

b. D C

c. D C

5. Which is $\angle PMX$?

a. P M X

b. P M X

c. X P M

d. M P X

6. Match each picture with a term that describes that picture.

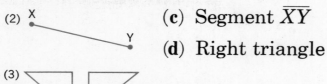

(1) B A C

(2) X Y

(3)

(**a**) Figures are reflections

(**b**) Equilateral triangle

(**c**) Segment $\overline{XY}$

(**d**) Right triangle

7. Draw an angle smaller than a right angle. Name it $\angle ACB$.

8. Draw a rectangle 2 centimeters wide and 3 centimeters long.

9. Which figures below have a pair of parallel sides?

10. Which figures have diagonals the same length?

11. Which figures have perpendicular sides?

a. b. c.

Which one in each set is different? How is it different?

a.	b.	c.	d.

12.

13.

14.

15. Which are parallel lines?

16. Which are perpendicular lines?

17. Which are intersecting lines?

CHAPTER FIVE

Multiplication
and Division

MULTIPLICATION

1. John bought 3 packs of soda pop. There were 6 cans in each pack. How many cans of pop did he buy?

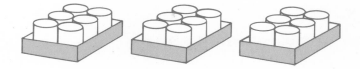

   a. We can add: $6 + 6 + 6 = \square$.

   b. We can think of $6 + 6 + 6$ as 3×6.

   $$6 + 6 + 6 = 18 \qquad 3 \times 6 = \square$$

2. We can think of $4 + 4 + 4 + 4 + 4$ as 5×4.

   a. Write a multiplication sentence for $4 + 4 + 4 + 4 + 4 + 4 + 4 + 4$.

   b. Write an addition sentence for 4×3.

3. We can use arrays to show multiplication. This array shows 3×5.

   Write a true multiplication sentence for each array.

   a.   b.   c.

4. Draw arrays for 4×6 and 3×8.

5. Numbers which are multiplied are called factors. The answer is called the product.

Factor		*Factor*		*Product*
4	×	6	=	24

Consider 8 × 3 = 24. Name the factors and the product.

6. a. Draw an array for 3 × 7.

   b. Write an addition sentence for 3 × 7.

   c. Make the sentence 3 × 7 = □ true.

7. We show multiplication on a number line.

   a. Explain how 3 × 4 or 3 fours is shown.

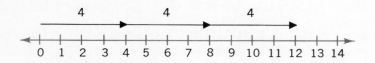

   b. Explain how 4 × 3 or 4 threes is shown.

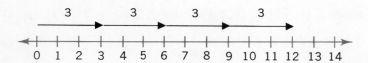

   c. What multiplications are shown?

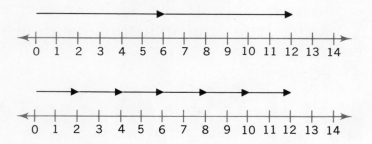

8. Solve: 2 + 2 + 2 + 2 = □.
Write an addition sentence for 4 × 3.

126

Write an addition sentence for each multiplication. Then find the sum.

1. 4×6　　**2.** 9×3　　**3.** 8×4　　**4.** 4×8

Write a multiplication sentence for each addition. Find the product.

5. $2 + 2 + 2 + 2$　　　**6.** $1 + 1 + 1 + 1 + 1 + 1$

7. $6 + 6$　　　　　　**8.** $3 + 3 + 3 + 3 + 3 + 3$

Write a multiplication sentence for each array.

Draw an array for each multiplication. Then find the products.

13. 2×4　　**14.** 3×5　　**15.** 4×6　　**16.** 6×4

Make each sentence true.

17. $3 + 3 + 3 = \triangle \times 3$　　**18.** $\square \times 5 = 5 + 5 + 5$

19. $7 + 7 = \triangle \times 7$　　　**20.** $\square \times 8 = 8 + 8 + 8$

21. $4 + 4 + 4 = \triangle \times 4$　　**22.** $\square \times 6 = 6 + 6$

Solve each problem.

23. Brenda saved 5 cents each day for 7 days. How much did she save?

24. Steve drinks 4 glasses of milk each day. How much milk does he drink in 6 days?

1. Look at this array.

   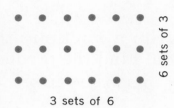

   3 sets of 6

   a. How many members are in 3 sets of 6?

   b. Turn your book. How many members are in 6 sets of 3?

2. Write a multiplication sentence for each.

   a. 3 sets of 6   b. 6 sets of 3

3. Does it look as if $3 \times 6 = 6 \times 3$? Explain.

4. Study the arrays. Make each sentence true.

   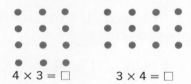

   $4 \times 3 = \square$ $3 \times 4 = \square$

   Does $4 \times 3 = 3 \times 4$? Explain.

5. a. Draw an array to show 3×2.

   b. Draw another to show 2×3.

   c. What is 3×2? What is 2×3?

   d. Does $3 \times 2 = 2 \times 3$? Why?

When we change the order of the factors, we get the same product. This is called the **commutative property of multiplication.**

6. Since $4 \times 3 = 12$, we know that $3 \times 4 = 12$.

    a. Since $4 \times 6 = 24$, we know $6 \times 4 =$ ___.

    b. Since $8 \times 7 = 56$, we know $7 \times 8 =$ ___.

    c. Since $9 \times 6 = 54$, we know $6 \times 9 =$ ___.

7. Look at $\square \times \triangle = \triangle \times \square$.

    a. Replace each $\square$ with 4 and each $\triangle$ with 2. Is the sentence true?

    b. Replace each $\square$ with 2 and each $\triangle$ with 5. Is the sentence true?

    c. Does $\square \times \triangle = \triangle \times \square$ for all numbers?

EXERCISES

Draw arrays to show these multiplications.

  1. 3×5 **2.** 5×3 **3.** 6×2 **4.** 2×6

Make each sentence true.

  5. Since $4 \times 9 = 36$, $9 \times 4 = \square$.

  6. Since $3 \times 9 = 27$, $9 \times 3 = \square$.

  7. Since $3 \times 8 = 24$, $8 \times 3 = \square$.

  8. Since $7 \times 3 = 21$, $3 \times 7 = \square$.

  9. Since $56 \times 38 = 2{,}128$, $38 \times 56 = \square$.

Make each sentence true.

  10. $4 \times 8 = \square \times 4$ **11.** $8 \times 3 = 3 \times \square$

  12. $3 \times 6 = 6 \times \square$ **13.** $\square \times 5 = 5 \times 7$

  14. $5 \times 4 = \square \times 5$ **15.** $\square \times 9 = 9 \times 2$

USING THE MULTIPLICATION TABLE

As we learn the multiplication facts, we can name the products in a table like this. Copy it.

X	0	1	2	3	4	5	6	7	8	9
0										
1										
2										
3										
4										
5										
6										
7										
8										
9										

1. Think of $3 \times 2 = 6$. Find 3 on the left. Find 2 on the top of the table. Follow the arrows to the box where they meet. We name the product, 6, in this box.

X	0	1	2	3
0				
1				
2				
3				6

2. We know $2 \times 3 = 6$. Find 2 on the left. Find 3 on the top. Trace across and down to where the row and the column meet. Write 6 in your table.

3. We know $4 \times 3 = 12$. Record it in your table.

4. Save your table to use in the next lesson.

ZERO AND ONE AS FACTORS

1. Think of zero as a factor.

   a. Study each sentence. Find a pattern.

$3 \times 1 = 3$	$3 \times 2 = 6$	$1 \times 3 = 3$
$2 \times 1 = 2$	$2 \times 2 = 4$	$1 \times 2 = 2$
$1 \times 1 = 1$	$1 \times 2 = 2$	$1 \times 1 = 1$
$0 \times 1 = \square$	$0 \times 2 = \square$	$1 \times 0 = \square$

   b. What is 0×1? Name the product 0×1 in your table.

   c. What is 0×2?

2. Look at $0 \times \square = 0$.

   a. What can replace the $\square$? Try 4. Try 3.

   b. When zero is a factor, what is the product?

   c. Name these products in your table.

0×0	0×7	4×0
0×2	0×8	5×0
0×3	0×9	6×0
0×4	1×0	7×0
0×5	2×0	8×0
0×6	3×0	9×0

3. We know that $0 \times 2 = 0$ and $2 \times 0 = 0$. Then $0 \times 2 = 2 \times 0$. Consider $0 \times \square = \square \times 0$.

   a. Replace each $\square$ with 6. Is the sentence true?

   b. Replace each $\square$ with 8. Is the sentence true?

   c. Does $0 \times \square = \square \times 0$ for all numbers?

4. Make each sentence true.

    a. $1 \times 5 = \square$ **b.** $1 \times 6 = \square$

    c. $1 \times 2 = \square$ **d.** $1 \times 8 = \square$

5. Consider $1 \times \square = \square$.

    a. What can replace each $\square$? Try 6. Try 7.

    b. When one is a factor what is the product?

    c. Name these products in your table.

2×1	6×1	8×1	5×1
1×2	1×6	1×8	1×5
3×1	7×1	9×1	4×1
1×3	1×7	1×9	1×4

EXERCISES

Multiply.

  1. 8×0 **2.** 1×6

  3. 0×1 **4.** 0×8

  5. 6×1 **6.** 0×0

  7. 2×0 **8.** 9×1

  9. 1×7 **10.** 4×0

11. 1×1 **12.** 5×0

13. 0×9 **14.** 1×8

15. 3×1 **16.** 7×0

Make each sentence true. Can you find more than one answer?

17. $\square \times 0 = 0$ **18.** $1 \times \square = \square$

TWO AS A FACTOR

1. Name each new product in your table.

X	0	1	2	3	4	5	6	7	8	9
0	0	0	0	0	0	0	0	0	0	0
1	0	1	2	3	4	5	6	7	8	9
2	0	2								
3	0	3								
4	0	4								
5	0	5								
6	0	6								
7	0	7								
8	0	8								
9	0	9								

2. a. Draw arrays to show 2×3 and 3×2.

b. We know $2 \times 3 = 3 \times 2$. Why? What is 3×2?

3. Multiply. Use an array or a number line if you need help.

a. 2×9 **b.** 2×4 **c.** 2×5

d. 2×6 **e.** 2×8 **f.** 2×7

4. Make each sentence true.

a. $2 \times 4 = 8$, so $4 \times 2 = \square$

b. $2 \times 6 = \square$, so $6 \times 2 = \square$

c. $2 \times 8 = \square$, so $8 \times 2 = \square$

d. $2 \times 9 = \square$, so $9 \times 2 = \square$

e. $2 \times 7 = \square$, so $7 \times 2 = \square$

f. $2 \times 5 = \square$, so $5 \times 2 = \square$

Make each sentence true.

1. $2 \times 0 = \square$ 2. $\square = 2 \times 7$ 3. $7 \times 2 = \square$

4. $9 \times 2 = \square$ 5. $6 \times 2 = \square$ 6. $5 \times 2 = \square$

7. $1 \times 2 = \square$ 8. $4 \times 2 = \square$ 9. $2 \times 2 = \square$

10. $2 \times 8 = \square$ 11. $6 \times 1 = \square$ 12. $\square = 4 \times 0$

13. $\square = 3 \times 2$ 14. $2 \times 9 = \square$ 15. $8 \times 2 = \square$

LET'S EXPLORE

1. We say that 2 and 5 are factors of 10 because $10 = 2 \times 5$. What are the factors in each of these sentences?

   a. $2 \times 6 = 12$ b. $2 \times 7 = 14$ c. $2 \times 4 = 8$

Any whole number that has 2 as a factor is an **even number.**
Any whole number that is not even is an **odd number.**

2. a. Show that 18 is an even number.

   b. Which of these numbers are even? Which are odd numbers?
      1, 2, 3, 4, 7, 12, 15, 19, 20

3. Think of adding two even numbers.

   a. Add 4 and 2. Is the sum an even or an odd number?

   b. Try $2 + 6$, $4 + 8$, and $2 + 10$.

   c. What is the sum of two even numbers?

4. Think of adding two odd numbers.

   a. Add 3 and 9. Is the sum an even number, or an odd number?

   b. Try $7 + 3$, $5 + 3$, and $9 + 3$.

   c. What is the sum of two odd numbers?

5. Think of adding an even and an odd number.

   a. Add 6 and 3. Is the sum an even number, or an odd number?

   b. Try $7 + 2$, $8 + 3$, and $5 + 4$.

   c. Is the sum in each addition an even number, or an odd number?

Let's Practice

Find the sum or difference.

1. 429 $+124$	**2.** 827 $+914$	**3.** 400 -196	**4.** 107 -98
5. 117 -92	**6.** 102 -91	**7.** 606 -149	**8.** 749 $+38$
9. 9,477 $+6,898$	**10.** 1,438 $+9,783$	**11.** 7,001 $-2,080$	**12.** 4,724 $+6,328$

Find a pattern. Name the missing numbers.

13. 112, 114, 116, 118, ____, ____, ____, ____

14. 150, 152, ____, ____, 158, ____, ____

15. 210, ____, ____, 240, ____, ____

16. 445, ____, ____, 460, ____, 470, ____

LET'S EXPLORE

1. Consider these arrays.

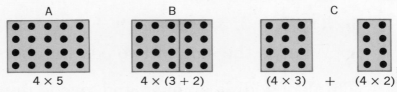

A   4 × 5

B   4 × (3 + 2)

C   (4 × 3) + (4 × 2)

a. Picture A shows 4 × □.

b. In B the array is broken apart. Each row has ▽ + △ members. We renamed 5 as ▽ + △.

c. The first array in C shows 4 × ▽. The second one shows 4 × △.

d. Do picture A and picture B have the same number of members?

2. Think of 2 × 8.

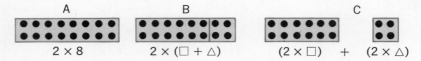

A   2 × 8

B   2 × (□ + △)

C   (2 × □) + (2 × △)

a. What replaces □ and △?

b. How was the factor 8 renamed?

c. We multiply 2 × □ and 2 × △.

d. Do pictures A and B have the same number of members?

3. Copy and complete.

$$2 \times 8 = 2 \times (6 + \underline{})$$
$$= (2 \times 6) + (2 \times \underline{})$$
$$= 12 + \underline{}$$
$$= \underline{}$$

When we multiply, we can rename one factor as two addends. The addends are then multiplied by the other factor. This is the **distributive property of multiplication over addition.**

Copy and complete.

1. $6 \times 6 = 6 \times (4 + \underline{2})$
   $= (6 \times 4) + (6 \times \underline{2})$

2. $5 \times 9 = 5 \times (\underline{} + 4)$
   $= (5 \times \underline{}) + (5 \times 4)$

3. $4 \times \underline{} = 4 \times (6 + 2)$
   $= (4 \times 6) + (4 \times 2)$

4. $4 \times 9 = 4 \times (\underline{} + 5)$
   $= (4 \times \underline{}) + (4 \times 5)$

Let's Practice

Find the sum or difference.

1.	2.	3.	4.
628	780	6,864	34,187
+279	+787	+3,894	+26,604

5.	6.	7.	8.
737	6,000	2,861	3,146
−389	−2,134	−947	+4,197

9.	10.	11.	12.
861	2,861	31,943	40,102
−861	−947	−29,943	+93,905

Make each sentence true.

13. $\square + 17 = 34$ 14. $21 - \triangle = 8$

THREE AND FOUR AS FACTORS

1. **a.** Copy this number line. Name the missing factors.

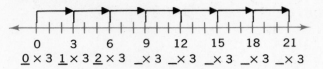

   0   3   6   9   12   15   18   21
   <u>0</u>× 3 <u>1</u>× 3 <u>2</u>× 3 _× 3 _× 3 _× 3 _× 3 _× 3

   b. Each number named is a multiple of 3. What are the multiples of 3 up to 30?

2. Multiply. Use the number line and the commutative property.

   a. 4 × 3   3 × 4

   b. 5 × 3   3 × 5

   c. 6 × 3   3 × 6

   d. 7 × 3   3 × 7

   e. 3 × 3

   f. Name the products in your table.

3. Use the distributive property and the commutative property. Copy and complete.

   a. 3 × 8 = 3 × (3 + 5)
   = (3 × 3) + (3 × ___)
   = ___ + ___
   = ___   8 × 3 = ___

   b. 3 × 9 = 3 × (5 + 4)
   = (3 × ___) + (3 × ___)
   = ___ + ___
   = ___   9 × 3 = ___

4. Count by fours to 36.

5. Make each sentence true. Use a number line and the commutative property.

    a. $4 \times 4 = \square$

    b. $5 \times 4 = \square$ so $4 \times 5 = \square$

    c. $6 \times 4 = \square$ so $4 \times 6 = \square$

    d. $7 \times 4 = \square$ so $4 \times 7 = \square$

6. Find the products. Copy and complete.

    a. $4 \times 8 = 4 \times (5 + 3)$
             $= (4 \times 5) + (\underline{\hspace{1em}} \times \underline{\hspace{1em}})$

    b. $8 \times 4 = \underline{\hspace{1em}}$

    c. $4 \times 9 = 4 \times (5 + \underline{\hspace{1em}})$
             $= (4 \times 5) + (4 \times \underline{\hspace{1em}})$

    d. $9 \times 4 = \underline{\hspace{1em}}$

7. We can show a multiplication this way.

    a. $6 \times 4 = \underline{\hspace{1em}}$ $\begin{array}{r} 4 \\ \times 6 \\ \hline \end{array}$ b. $4 \times 6 = \underline{\hspace{1em}}$ $\begin{array}{r} 6 \\ \times 4 \\ \hline \end{array}$

    c. Do this for 3×8 and 8×3.

EXERCISES

Multiply.

1. $\begin{array}{r} 8 \\ \times 3 \\ \hline \end{array}$	2. $\begin{array}{r} 3 \\ \times 6 \\ \hline \end{array}$	3. $\begin{array}{r} 4 \\ \times 3 \\ \hline \end{array}$	4. $\begin{array}{r} 3 \\ \times 2 \\ \hline \end{array}$	5. $\begin{array}{r} 1 \\ \times 3 \\ \hline \end{array}$
6. $\begin{array}{r} 3 \\ \times 3 \\ \hline \end{array}$	7. $\begin{array}{r} 5 \\ \times 3 \\ \hline \end{array}$	8. $\begin{array}{r} 0 \\ \times 3 \\ \hline \end{array}$	9. $\begin{array}{r} 9 \\ \times 4 \\ \hline \end{array}$	10. $\begin{array}{r} 8 \\ \times 4 \\ \hline \end{array}$
11. $\begin{array}{r} 4 \\ \times 6 \\ \hline \end{array}$	12. $\begin{array}{r} 4 \\ \times 4 \\ \hline \end{array}$	13. $\begin{array}{r} 7 \\ \times 3 \\ \hline \end{array}$	14. $\begin{array}{r} 1 \\ \times 4 \\ \hline \end{array}$	15. $\begin{array}{r} 9 \\ \times 3 \\ \hline \end{array}$

FIVE AND SIX AS FACTORS

1. Ellen bought 5 candy
   bars at 5 cents apiece.
   How much did she pay
   for all of them?

   $5 + 5 + 5 + 5 + 5 = \square$
   $5 \times 5 = \square$

2. Multiply. List the
   products in the table.

   a. $5 \times 6 = 5 \times (5 + 1)$
   $= (5 \times \underline{\quad}) + (5 \times \underline{\quad})$
   $= 25 + \underline{\quad}$
   $= \underline{\quad}$ $6 \times 5 = \underline{\quad}$

   b. $5 \times 7 = 5 \times (5 + 2)$
   $= (5 \times 5) + (5 \times \underline{\quad})$
   $= 25 + \underline{\quad}$
   $= \underline{\quad}$ $7 \times 5 = \underline{\quad}$

   c. $5 \times 8 = (5 \times \underline{\quad}) + (5 \times 3)$
   $= \underline{\quad} + 15$
   $= \underline{\quad}$ $8 \times 5 = \underline{\quad}$

   d. $5 \times 9 = (5 \times \underline{\quad}) + (5 \times 4)$
   $= \underline{\quad} + \underline{\quad}$
   $= \underline{\quad}$ $9 \times 5 = \underline{\quad}$

   e. $6 \times 6 = 6 \times (4 + \underline{\quad})$
   $= (6 \times 4) + (6 \times \underline{\quad})$
   $= 24 + \underline{\quad}$
   $= \underline{\quad}$

3. Find these products. Use any method.

   a. 6×7 **b.** 7×6 **c.** 6×8

   d. 8×6 **e.** 6×9 **f.** 9×6

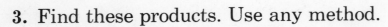

Multiply.

1. 5×3	**2.** 3×9	**3.** 5×9
4. 6×3	**5.** 8×6	**6.** 6×4
7. 4×7	**8.** 2×6	**9.** 6×5
10. 9×5	**11.** 8×5	**12.** 3×7
13. 6×7	**14.** 7×5	**15.** 5×6
16. 4×9	**17.** 3×6	**18.** 4×5
19. 5×7	**20.** 5×8	**21.** 6×6
22. 9×6	**23.** 7×6	**24.** 6×8
25. 4×8	**26.** 6×9	**27.** 4×6
28. 5×4	**29.** 3×5	**30.** 6×1
31. 6×2	**32.** 0×6	**33.** 5×5

Solve each problem.

34. Mrs. Smith's family uses 9 pounds of meat each week. How many pounds do they use in 5 weeks?

35. Mr. Jones can pack 6 baseballs in one box. How many baseballs can he put in 7 boxes?

36. A bar of soap costs 8 cents. How much will 7 bars cost?

37. Jack's mother gave each of the three boys 4 cookies. How many cookies in all did she give the boys?

SEVEN AND EIGHT AS FACTORS

1. Name the missing numbers.

   0, 7, 14, ___, ___, ___, ___, 49, ___, ___.

   These numbers are multiples of what number?

2. Use addition to find 7×7. Name the product in your table.

   $$7 + 7 + 7 + 7 + 7 + 7 + 7 = \text{\underline{\hspace{1em}}}$$
   $$7 \times 7 = \text{\underline{\hspace{1em}}}$$

3. Use the distributive and commutative properties to find these products. Name them in your table.

   a. $7 \times 8 = 7 \times (7 + 1)$
   $ = (7 \times \text{\underline{\hspace{1em}}}) + (7 \times \text{\underline{\hspace{1em}}})$
   $ = \text{\underline{\hspace{1em}}} + 7$
   $ = \text{\underline{\hspace{1em}}} \qquad 8 \times 7 = \text{\underline{\hspace{1em}}}$

   b. $7 \times 9 = 7 \times (\text{\underline{\hspace{1em}}} + 3)$
   $ = (7 \times \text{\underline{\hspace{1em}}}) + (7 \times \text{\underline{\hspace{1em}}})$
   $ = \text{\underline{\hspace{1em}}} + \text{\underline{\hspace{1em}}}$
   $ = \text{\underline{\hspace{1em}}} \qquad 9 \times 7 = \text{\underline{\hspace{1em}}}$

4. Make an array for 8×8. Name the product 8×8 in your table.

5. Find the products. Name them in the table.

   a. $8 \times 9 = 8 \times (\text{\underline{\hspace{1em}}} + 1)$
   $ = (\text{\underline{\hspace{1em}}} \times 8) + (\text{\underline{\hspace{1em}}} \times 1)$
   $ = 64 + \text{\underline{\hspace{1em}}}$
   $ = \text{\underline{\hspace{1em}}} \qquad 9 \times 8 = \text{\underline{\hspace{1em}}}$

Multiply.

1. 8 2. 7 3. 9 4. 7 5. 8 6. 5
   ×5   ×7   ×8   ×6   ×8   ×7

7. 7 8. 6 9. 3 10. 1 11. 7 12. 0
   ×8   ×8   ×7   ×8   ×4   ×8

13. 7 14. 8 15. 7 16. 3 17. 7 18. 5
   ×0   ×4   ×1   ×8   ×3   ×8

19. 4 20. 8 21. 6 22. 7 23. 8 24. 8
   ×7   ×7   ×7   ×9   ×6   ×9

Solve each problem.

25. Bill and his father went fishing for 5 days. Each day Bill caught 3 fish and his father caught 4 fish.

   a. How many fish did Bill catch in all?

   b. How many fish did his father catch?

   c. How many fish did they catch in all?

26. Mrs. Davis buys 5 pounds of beef and 2 pounds of veal each week.

   a. How much beef does she buy in 3 weeks?

   b. How much veal does she buy in 3 weeks?

   c. How much meat does she buy in 3 weeks?

NINE AS A FACTOR

1. Find the product 9×9 and then name it in your table.

$$9 \times 9 = 9 \times (\_\_ + 5)$$
$$= (9 \times \_\_) + (9 \times 5)$$
$$= \_\_ + \_\_$$
$$= \_\_$$

2. Nine is an interesting factor. Let's look for patterns. Name the products.

$9 \times 1 = 9$	9×6
$9 \times 2 = 18$	9×7
$9 \times 3 = 27$	9×8
9×4	9×9
9×5	9×10

a. Study the numerals for the products. Find the digit symbols in the tens place. What do you find?

b. Study the numerals for the products.

$9 \times 3 = 27$	$2 + 7 = 9$
$9 \times 4 = 36$	$3 + 6 = 9$
$9 \times 5 = 45$	$4 + 5 = 9$

What pattern do you find?

3. How can you check when 9 is a factor?

4. What pattern do you find in these sentences?

$$9 \times 2 = 18$$
$$9 \times 3 = 27$$
$$9 \times 4 = 36$$
$$9 \times 5 = 45$$
$$9 \times 6 = 54$$

144

EXERCISES

Multiply.

1. 3×9 2. 8×8 3. 0×1

4. 9×2 5. 7×7 6. 1×2

7. 1×9 8. 6×6 9. 2×3

10. 5×5 11. 9×4 12. 3×4

13. 6×7 14. 4×4 15. 5×4

16. 9×7 17. 3×3 18. 9×6

19. 9×5 20. 2×2 21. 5×6

22. 6×8 23. 1×1 24. 9×8

25. 9×9 26. 8×9 27. 0×0

28. 9×3 29. 9×0 30. 9×1

Name the first nine multiples of each.

31. 8   32. 6   33. 4   34. 5

Solve each problem.

35. Mr. McCarthy planted 8 apple trees in each of 4 rows. How many trees did he plant?

36. Mr. Martinez set 9 tomato plants in each row of his garden. How many plants did he set in the following?

   a. 3 rows   b. 9 rows

   c. 4 rows   d. 8 rows

PROBLEM SOLVING

Write a number sentence for each problem. Make each sentence true.

1. Betty had 17 cookies. She gave 8 of them to Louis. How many cookies did she keep for herself?

2. Jack's bookcase has 5 shelves. Each shelf holds 9 books. How many books can he put in the bookcase?

3. Harriet needs 16 cents for candy. She has 9 cents. How much more does she need?

4. For 9 days, 8 children came to the nurse's office each day. How many children were at the nurse's office in all?

5. David read 8 books one week. He read 6 books the next week. How many books did he read in all?

6. A rancher had 8 horses. He bought 7 more. Now how many horses does he have?

7. Mike practices on his guitar 2 hours each day. How many hours does he practice in 6 days?

8. Candy bars cost 6 cents each. Find the cost of 9 bars.

9. Find the cost of 8 pounds of potatoes at 7 cents a pound.

OPERATIONS

An operation is a way to combine a pair of numbers to give one number for an answer.

1. **a.** Consider $8 + 2 = \square$. What is the operation? If 8 and 2 are combined by addition, what number is the answer?

   b. If 8 and 2 are combined by another operation, the answer is 6. What is the opertion?

   c. Replace the ≣ in 8 ≣ 2 = 16 to make it true.

2. Make true sentences. Write +, −, or × in place of the ≣.

   a. 3 ≣ 3 = 9   **b.** 3 ≣ 3 = 6   **c.** 3 ≣ 3 = 0

   d. 4 ≣ 5 = 9   **e.** 5 ≣ 4 = 20   **f.** 5 ≣ 4 = 1

3. Let us use these operations in our machine.

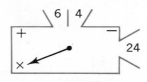

   a. We put the numbers 6 and 4 in and set the dial at ×. What is the result?

   b. What number do we get if we set the dial at +? at −?

4. Think of putting 8 and 6 in the machine. Make each sentence true.

   a. $8 + 6 = \square$ **b.** $8 \times 6 = \square$ **c.** $8 - 6 = \square$

EXERCISES

Make each sentence true. Use $+$, $-$, or $\times$.

1. $7 \equiv 7 = 49$

2. $15 \equiv 3 = 12$

3. $4 \equiv 9 = 36$

4. $7 \equiv 7 = 0$

5. $15 \equiv 3 = 18$

6. $3 \equiv 1 = 3$

7. $7 \equiv 7 = 14$

8. $7 \equiv 8 = 56$

9. $0 \equiv 0 = 0$

10. $5 \equiv 4 = 9$

11. $13 \equiv 13 = 26$

12. $13 \equiv 13 = 0$

13. $8 \equiv 7 = 56$

14. $8 \equiv 7 = 1$

15. $8 \equiv 7 = 15$

16. $9 \equiv 5 = 14$

Set the dial of each operation machine at each of the 3 operations. Write a true number sentence for each setting.

17.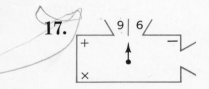

18.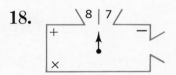

19.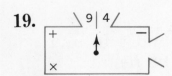

20.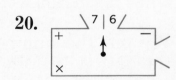

Let's Practice

Write standard numerals.

1. Fourteen thousand, two hundred seventy.

2. Three million, three thousand, three.

148

MULTIPLICATION AND DIVISION

1. Jack is pasting 24 stamps in his stamp book. If he puts 6 stamps in a row, how many rows of stamps can he make?

   a. Jack thought of the sentence $\triangle \times 6 = 24$. Is a factor or product missing?

   b. The sentence $24 \div 6 = \triangle$ is a related division sentence.

Missing Factor	Quotient
$\triangle \times 6 = 24$	$24 \div 6 = \triangle$

   c. The missing factor in $\triangle \times 6 = 24$ is the same as what number in $24 \div 6 = \triangle$?

2. a. Multiply 7 by 2. Then divide 14 by 2. What is the answer?

   $2 \times 7 = $ ___ $14 \div 2 = $ ___

   b. Multiply 8 by 3. Divide the product by 3. What is the result?

3. a. Consider $10 \div 2 = 5$. Multiply 5 by 2. What is the result?

   b. Consider $15 \div 3 = 5$ and $5 \times 3 = 15$. Compare the product and the number we started with in the related division.

Division undoes multiplication.
Multiplication undoes division.
Multiplication and division are opposite operations.

4. Complete the sentences for each array.

a.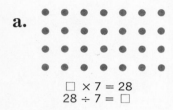

$\Box \times 7 = 28$
$28 \div 7 = \Box$

b.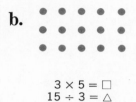

$3 \times 5 = \Box$
$15 \div 3 = \triangle$

5. Draw an array for each. Write a multiplication and a related division sentence.

   a. 18 members in all, 6 members in a row

   b. 24 members in all, 3 rows

   c. 36 members in all, 6 members in a row

EXERCISES

Replace each $\Box$ to make a true number sentence.

1. Since $7 \times 7 = 49$, then $49 \div 7 = \Box$.

2. Since $8 \times 9 = 72$, then $72 \div 9 = \Box$.

3. Since $6 \times 4 = 24$, then $24 \div 4 = \Box$.

4. Since $8 \times 7 = 56$, then $56 \div 7 = \Box$.

5. $3 \times \triangle = 21$ **6.** $7 \times \triangle = 28$ **7.** $9 \times \triangle = 72$
$21 \div 3 = \triangle$ $28 \div 7 = \triangle$ $72 \div 9 = \triangle$

8. Draw a set with 24 dots. Circle sets of 6.

$\triangle \times 6 = 24$ $24 \div 6 = \triangle$

RELATING SUBTRACTION AND DIVISION

1. We can think of division in another way.

   a. Think of a set of 24. How many groups of 6 can we make from the 24 members?

   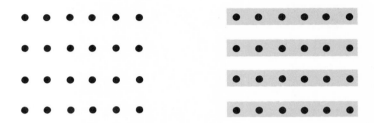

   b. We can think: $24 \div 6 = \square$. Make the sentence true.

2. We can relate division to subtraction. Study each array and the subtraction.

   $$
   \begin{array}{r}
   20 \\
   -5 \\
   \hline
   15 \\
   -5 \\
   \hline
   10 \\
   -5 \\
   \hline
   5 \\
   -5 \\
   \hline
   0
   \end{array}
   $$

   a. How many groups of 5 can we make from a set of 20?

   b. How many times did we subtract 5?

   c. We can relate this repeated subtraction to $20 \div 5 = \square$. Make the sentence true.

3. a. Draw a set with 28 members.

   b. Circle members to show $28 \div 7$.

   c. Check by using subtraction.

4. Copy this set. Circle as many sets of 4 as you can. Write a division sentence. Check by using subtraction.

5. Write a repeated subtraction for each of these divisions.

   a. $18 \div 6$ **b.** $24 \div 3$ **c.** $24 \div 8$

EXERCISES

Write a repeated subtraction for each of these divisions.

1. $20 \div 4$ **2.** $12 \div 2$ **3.** $9 \div 3$

Draw an array to show each sentence. Make each sentence true.

4. $16 \div 4 = \triangle$ **5.** $45 \div 5 = \triangle$ **6.** $36 \div 6 = \triangle$

7.-9. Write a repeated subtraction for each division in Exercises 4-6.

Write a repeated subtraction for each problem.

10. In Mrs. Moore's room 12 students needed eye tests. They went to the nurse's office two at a time. How many pairs of students went?

11. In Mrs. Nelson's class, 28 students had eye tests. They went in groups of four. How many groups of students went to the nurse's office?

152

USING RELATED SENTENCES

1. Write a related division sentence for each of these sentences.

   a. $5 \times \triangle = 15$ **b.** $2 \times \triangledown = 4$ **c.** $\square \times 7 = 14$

2. We can use an array and a multiplication sentence to find two related division sentences.

   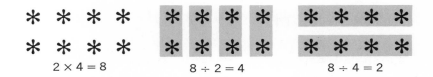

   $2 \times 4 = 8$ $8 \div 2 = 4$ $8 \div 4 = 2$

   a. Draw an array to show $2 \times 6 = 12$.

   b. Ring members to show $12 \div 2 = \triangle$.

   c. Ring members to show $12 \div 6 = \square$.

3. Write two true related division sentences for each multiplication.

   a. $7 \times 8 = 56$ **b.** $1 \times 2 = 2$

4. To find a quotient, we can think of finding a missing factor in a related multiplication.

   a. For $18 \div 2 = \triangle$, we think $2 \times \triangle = 18$

   For $14 \div 7 = \triangle$, we think $7 \times \triangle = 14$

   For $2 \div 1 = \triangle$, we think $1 \times \triangle = 2$

   b. Make each sentence in item a true.

5. Write a related multiplication sentence for each division. Make each sentence true.

   a. $16 \div 8 = \triangle$ **b.** $48 \div 6 = \square$ **c.** $18 \div 9 = \bigcirc$

153

6. We can also show $16 \div 2 = 8$ as $2\overline{)16}^{\,8}$.
Rewrite each of these divisions.

    a. $16 \div 4 = 4$ **b.** $27 \div 9 = 3$ **c.** $48 \div 6 = 8$

EXERCISES

Copy and complete. Make each sentence true.

  1. $2 \times \triangle = 16$ $16 \div 2 = \triangle$ $16 \div 8 = \triangledown$

  2. $7 \times \triangle = 14$ $14 \div 7 = \triangle$ $14 \div 2 = \triangledown$

  3. $2 \times 4 = \square$ $8 \div 2 = \triangle$ $8 \div 4 = \triangledown$

  4. $9 \times \triangle = 18$ $18 \div 9 = \triangle$ _____

  5. $\triangle \times 6 = 12$ _____ $12 \div 6 = \triangledown$

  6. _____ $6 \div 2 = \triangle$ $6 \div \triangledown = 3$

  7. _____ $10 \div 2 = \triangle$ $10 \div \triangle = 2$

Divide.

  8. $2\overline{)14}$ **9.** $2\overline{)12}$ **10.** $5\overline{)10}$ **11.** $2\overline{)6}$

12. $2\overline{)8}$ **13.** $3\overline{)6}$ **14.** $6\overline{)12}$ **15.** $1\overline{)2}$

16. $2\overline{)18}$ **17.** $8\overline{)16}$ **18.** $2\overline{)10}$ **19.** $4\overline{)8}$

20. $7\overline{)14}$ **21.** $2\overline{)4}$ **22.** $9\overline{)18}$ **23.** $2\overline{)2}$

Solve the problem.

24. Joseph borrowed $6.00 from his brother, Fred, and paid him back in 3 equal payments. How much was each payment?

THREE AND FOUR IN DIVISION

1. Study each array. Make the sentences true.

a.

3 × △ = 27
27 ÷ 3 = △
27 ÷ 9 = ▽

b.

3 × △ = 12
12 ÷ 3 = △
12 ÷ 4 = ▽

2. Make each sentence true. Draw an array if you need help.

   a. $6 \times 3 = 18$ $18 \div 3 = \triangle$ $18 \div 6 = \triangledown$

   b. $3 \times 5 = \square$ $15 \div 3 = \triangle$ $15 \div 5 = \triangledown$

   c. $3 \times 4 = \square$ $12 \div 4 = \triangle$ $12 \div 3 = \triangledown$

   d. $9 \times 4 = \square$ $36 \div 4 = \triangle$ $36 \div 9 = \triangledown$

   e. $4 \times 8 = \square$ $32 \div 8 = \triangle$ $32 \div 4 = \triangledown$

   f. $7 \times 4 = \square$ $28 \div 7 = \triangle$ $28 \div 4 = \triangledown$

   g. $9 \times 3 = \square$ $27 \div 3 = \triangle$ $27 \div 9 = \triangledown$

3. We know $4 \times 4 = 16$, so $16 \div 4 = \triangledown$.

4. Make these sentences true.

   a. $6 \times \triangledown = 24$ $24 \div 4 = \triangle$ $24 \div 6 = \triangledown$

   b. $4 \times \triangle = 20$ $20 \div 4 = \triangle$ $20 \div 5 = \triangledown$

   c. $4 \times \triangle = 4$ $4 \div 4 = \triangle$ $4 \div \triangle = 4$

   d. $2 \times \triangle = 8$ $8 \div 2 = \triangle$ $8 \div \triangle = 2$

   e. $8 \times \triangle = 24$ $24 \div 8 = \triangledown$ $24 \div 3 = \triangle$

   f. $3 \times \triangle = 21$ $21 \div 7 = \triangledown$ $21 \div 3 = \triangle$

5. We can write a related multiplication sentence for a division sentence. Make each sentence true.

a. $9 \div 3 = \triangle$ $3 \times \triangle = 9$

b. $6 \div 3 = \triangle$ $3 \times \triangle = 6$

c. $6 \div 2 = \triangle$ $2 \times \triangle = 6$

d. $8 \div 2 = \triangle$ $2 \times \triangle = 8$

e. $3 \div 3 = \triangle$ $3 \times \triangle = 3$

f. $24 \div 3 = \triangle$ $3 \times \triangle = 24$

EXERCISES

1. $3\overline{)27}$	2. $4\overline{)16}$	3. $3\overline{)3}$	4. $5\overline{)15}$
5. $8\overline{)24}$	6. $6\overline{)24}$	7. $2\overline{)8}$	8. $3\overline{)12}$
9. $7\overline{)21}$	10. $2\overline{)6}$	11. $7\overline{)28}$	12. $4\overline{)8}$
13. $4\overline{)12}$	14. $3\overline{)18}$	15. $1\overline{)3}$	16. $9\overline{)36}$
17. $6\overline{)18}$	18. $9\overline{)27}$	19. $5\overline{)20}$	20. $4\overline{)24}$
21. $4\overline{)36}$	22. $8\overline{)32}$	23. $4\overline{)4}$	24. $3\overline{)9}$
25. $3\overline{)24}$	26. $4\overline{)28}$	27. $7\overline{)14}$	28. $4\overline{)20}$
29. $8\overline{)16}$	30. $3\overline{)6}$	31. $1\overline{)4}$	32. $3\overline{)21}$
33. $3\overline{)15}$	34. $4\overline{)32}$	35. $1\overline{)9}$	36. $9\overline{)9}$
37. $8\overline{)64}$	38. $2\overline{)18}$	39. $9\overline{)18}$	40. $2\overline{)16}$

Solve the problem.

41. Susan wanted to read 18 books in 3 weeks. How many books a week should she read?

FIVE AND SIX IN DIVISION

1. The boys at Lincoln School are playing basketball. Each team has 5 players.

   a. There are 45 boys in Mr. Allen's gym class. How many teams will he have?
   Think: $45 \div 5 = \triangle$ or $5 \times \triangle = 45$

   b. There are 35 boys in Mr. Lee's first gym class. How many teams can he form?
   Draw an array to check your answer.

   c. There are 40 boys in Mr. Lee's second class. How many teams can he form?

2. Make these related sentences true.

   a. $8 \times \triangle = 40$ $40 \div 8 = \triangle$

   b. $9 \times \triangle = 45$ $45 \div 9 = \triangle$

   c. $7 \times \triangle = 35$ $35 \div 7 = \triangle$

   d. $5 \times \triangle = 30$ $30 \div 5 = \triangle$

   e. $5 \times \triangle = 20$ $20 \div 5 = \triangle$

3. Rudy is packing 6 golf balls in a box. He has 54 balls in all. How many boxes does he need?

   $$6 \times \triangle = 54$$
   $$54 \div 6 = \triangle$$

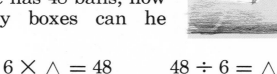

4. If he has 48 balls, how many boxes can he fill?

   $$6 \times \triangle = 48 \qquad 48 \div 6 = \triangle$$

5. Make these related sentences true.

a. $9 \times \triangle = 54$ $54 \div 9 = \triangle$ $54 \div 6 = \triangledown$

b. $8 \times \triangle = 48$ $48 \div 8 = \triangle$ $48 \div 6 = \triangledown$

c. $7 \times \triangle = 42$ $42 \div 6 = \triangledown$ $42 \div 7 = \triangle$

d. $6 \times 6 = \triangledown$ $36 \div 6 = \triangle$ $36 \div \triangle = 6$

e. $6 \times \triangle = 6$ $6 \div 6 = \triangle$ $6 \div \triangle = 6$

f. $5 \times \triangle = 5$ $5 \div 5 = \triangle$ $5 \div \triangle = 5$

6. Write a related sentence for each division sentence. Make each sentence true.

Example $30 \div 6 = \triangle$ $6 \times \triangle = 30$

a. $20 \div 5 = \triangle$ **b.** $25 \div 5 = \triangle$

c. $15 \div 5 = \triangle$ **d.** $18 \div 6 = \triangle$

e. $24 \div 6 = \triangle$ **f.** $12 \div 6 = \triangle$

EXERCISES

Divide.

1. $5\overline{)45}$ **2.** $5\overline{)25}$ **3.** $5\overline{)30}$ **4.** $6\overline{)36}$

5. $7\overline{)42}$ **6.** $4\overline{)20}$ **7.** $6\overline{)24}$ **8.** $5\overline{)35}$

9. $6\overline{)48}$ **10.** $4\overline{)24}$ **11.** $5\overline{)20}$ **12.** $3\overline{)15}$

13. $2\overline{)12}$ **14.** $6\overline{)18}$ **15.** $8\overline{)40}$ **16.** $2\overline{)10}$

17. $1\overline{)6}$ **18.** $9\overline{)54}$ **19.** $5\overline{)15}$ **20.** $6\overline{)12}$

21. $9\overline{)45}$ **22.** $6\overline{)42}$ **23.** $7\overline{)35}$ **24.** $5\overline{)40}$

25. $6\overline{)6}$ **26.** $1\overline{)5}$ **27.** $8\overline{)48}$ **28.** $5\overline{)5}$

USING THE TABLE

1. Think of the sentence $4 \times \triangle = 12$. In the table find the 4 on the left. Trace to the right until you find 12. Follow the arrow up the column. What is the missing factor in $4 \times \triangle = 12$?

X	1	2	3	4
1	1	2	3	4
2	2	4	6	8
3	3	6	9	12
4	4	8	12	16

2. Consider $\triangle \times 4 = 8$. We can find 4 at the top of the table, and trace down to 8. Trace to the far left. What is the missing factor?

EXERCISES

Use the table below to find the missing factor. Make each sentence true.

1. $6 \times \triangle = 54$

2. $\triangle \times 8 = 48$

3. $5 \times \triangle = 25$

4. $\triangle \times 5 = 35$

5. $6 \times \triangle = 48$

6. $8 \times \triangle = 40$

7. $\triangle \times 7 = 42$

X	1	2	3	4	5	6	7	8	9
1	1	2	3	4	5	6	7	8	9
2	2	4	6	8	10	12	14	16	18
3	3	6	9	12	15	18	21	24	27
4	4	8	12	16	20	24	28	32	36
5	5	10	15	20	25	30	35	40	45
6	6	12	18	24	30	36	42	48	54
7	7	14	21	28	35	42	49	56	63
8	8	16	24	32	40	48	56	64	72
9	9	18	27	36	45	54	63	72	81

8. $7 \times \triangle = 49$

9. $8 \times \triangle = 32$

10. $\triangle \times 7 = 63$

11. $\triangle \times 8 = 40$

DO YOU REMEMBER?

Divide.

1. $3\overline{)15}$ 2. $7\overline{)35}$ 3. $2\overline{)12}$ 4. $5\overline{)20}$

5. $6\overline{)24}$ 6. $5\overline{)30}$ 7. $5\overline{)40}$ 8. $8\overline{)48}$

9. $2\overline{)10}$ 10. $4\overline{)20}$ 11. $6\overline{)30}$ 12. $6\overline{)42}$

13. $6\overline{)6}$ 14. $9\overline{)54}$ 15. $6\overline{)12}$ 16. $6\overline{)54}$

17. $3\overline{)18}$ 18. $5\overline{)25}$ 19. $4\overline{)24}$ 20. $5\overline{)10}$

21. $6\overline{)36}$ 22. $7\overline{)42}$ 23. $8\overline{)40}$ 24. $5\overline{)35}$

25. $5\overline{)15}$ 26. $5\overline{)45}$ 27. $6\overline{)18}$ 28. $9\overline{)45}$

29. $6\overline{)48}$ 30. $5\overline{)5}$ 31. $2\overline{)8}$ 32. $9\overline{)18}$

Let's Practice

Solve each problem.

1. Bob's father gave him 24 pencils to share equally with Mary and Joe. How many pencils should each of the 3 children receive?

2. Ann put 6 hangers in each of the closets. She had 42 hangers. How many closets are in Ann's house?

3. Mrs. Gray folded 32 towels. She put 8 towels in each stack. How many stacks did she make?

4. Jim read 5 books each week for 4 weeks. How many books did he read in all?

USING 7, 8, AND 9 IN DIVISION

1. Mary has 49 pictures to paste in her album. If she puts 7 pictures on each page, how many pages does she use?

   a. Think: $49 \div 7 = \triangle$ or $7 \times \triangle = 49$.

   b. Write a repeated subtraction for $49 \div 7 = \triangle$.

2. Copy and complete. Make each sentence true.

   a. $9 \times \triangle = 63$ $63 \div 9 = \triangle$ $63 \div 7 = \triangledown$

   b. $8 \times \triangle = 64$ $64 \div 8 = \triangle$

   c. $8 \times \triangle = 56$ $56 \div 8 = \triangle$ $56 \div 7 = \triangledown$

   d. $9 \times \triangle = 72$ $72 \div 9 = \triangle$ $72 \div 8 = \triangledown$

   e. $9 \times \triangle = 9$ _____   _____

   f. $9 \times \triangle = 81$ _____

3. Write a related multiplication sentence for each division. Make the sentences true.

   a. $8 \div 1 = \triangle$ b. $42 \div 7 = \triangle$

   c. $48 \div 8 = \triangle$ d. $54 \div 9 = \triangle$

   e. $36 \div 9 = \triangle$ f. $45 \div 9 = \triangle$

4. Jane was returning 56 soda bottles to the store in cartons. Each carton held 8 bottles. How many cartons did she need?

EXERCISES

Divide.

1. 4)32 2. 2)18 3. 6)42 4. 8)24

5. 9)81 6. 5)35 7. 2)16 8. 9)9

9. 7)28 10. 8)40 11. 7)49 12. 8)72

13. 8)8 14. 2)14 15. 7)35 16. 9)54

17. 8)56 18. 9)63 19. 8)64 20. 6)48

21. 7)42 22. 8)32 23. 4)28 24. 9)36

25. 1)7 26. 3)24 27. 9)72 28. 5)45

29. 7)21 30. 5)40 31. 8)16 32. 3)27

33. 9)18 34. 6)54 35. 1)9 36. 7)14

37. 7)56 38. 7)7 39. 7)63 40. 3)21

41. 9)45 42. 8)48 43. 9)27 44. 4)36

45. 1)8 46. 3)18 47. 6)30 48. 5)10

UNEXPLORED TERRITORY

Copy the table below. Compare each number in row A with the number named below it in row B. How is each pair of numbers related? Name the missing numbers in row B.

Row A	1	2	3	4	5	6	7	8	9
Row B	2	4	6	8					

DO YOU REMEMBER?

Add.

1. $266 + 36 + 365 + 1,000$

2. $4,973 + 3,892 + 3,899 + 902$

3. $6,439 + 439 + 39 + 9$

4. $1,428 + 224 + 829$

Subtract.

5. $1,986 - 539$ 6. $28,712 - 19,438$

7. $70,000 - 4,123$ 8. $70,005 - 38,199$

In Exercises 9–12 write the standard numerals.

9. Fifty-five thousand, two hundred thirty-seven

10. One hundred six thousand, thirty-nine

11. One hundred six million, thirty-nine thousand

12. Three hundred twenty-seven million, forty-two thousand, one hundred twenty

13. Draw line segment $\overline{EF}$.

14. Draw triangle CDE.

15. Draw ray $\overrightarrow{DE}$.

16. Draw a right triangle.

17. Draw the angle BCD.

Multiply.

18. 8×8 **19.** 9×7 **20.** 8×4

21. 9×3 **22.** 5×7 **23.** 7×7

24. 8×6 **25.** 9×5 **26.** 6×9

27. 4×9 **28.** 9×9 **29.** 9×7

Solve each problem.

30. Bill had $435 in his bank account. His father gave him $28 more. How much money does Bill have now?

31. Mrs. Hansen spent $20 for 5 tickets to the circus. How much did each ticket cost?

32. Ruth had 24 cupcakes. She divided them equally among 8 girls. How many cupcakes did each girl receive?

UNEXPLORED TERRITORY

1. Consider $\square \div 1 = \square$.

  a. Replace each $\square$ with 8. Is the sentence true?

  b. Try 6; then try 9. Is each sentence true?

  c. What do you find when you divide by 1?

2. Name each quotient.

  a. $9 \div 9$ **b.** $3 \div 3$ **c.** $12 \div 12$

  d. $226 \div 226$ **e.** $10 \div 10$ **f.** $325 \div 325$

  g. If you divide any number greater than 0 by itself, what is the quotient?

ZERO IN DIVISION

1. **a.** Make the sentence $9 \times 0 = \square$ true.

   b. When zero is a factor, what is the product?

2. Study these sentences. Make them true.

   a. $15 \div 5 = \triangle$ because $5 \times \triangle = 15$

   b. $0 \div 4 = 0$ because $4 \times \triangle = 0$

   c. $0 \div 8 = 0$ because $8 \times \triangle = 0$

   d. $0 \div 1 = \triangle$ because $1 \times \triangle = 0$

3. Think of $1 \div 0 = \square$. A related multiplication is $\square \times 0 = 1$. We know $\square \times 0 = 0$. Can we make the related sentences $\square \times 0 = 1$ and $1 \div 0 = \square$ true?

4. **a.** Write a related multiplication sentence for $5 \div 0 = \square$.

   b. Can you make the sentence true?

   c. What can you say about $5 \div 0 = \square$?

5. **a.** Consider $0 \div 0 = \square$. A related multiplication is $\square \times 0 = 0$. Replace the $\square$ in each sentence. Try 2. Try 6. Try 8.

   b. Can any number replace the $\square$ in $\square \times 0 = 0$?

   c. Can any number replace the $\square$ in $0 \div 0 = \square$?

   d. When we try to divide 0 by 0, do we get only one number for an answer?

There is no division by zero.

MORE ABOUT DIVISION

In the division operation we combine two numbers. The result is one number that we call the *quotient*.

1. Consider 12 ÷ 3 = 4. What numbers were combined? What is the quotient?

2. Find the quotient.

   a. 81 ÷ 9   **b.** 72 ÷ 8   **c.** 49 ÷ 7

   d. 56 ÷ 7   **e.** 48 ÷ 6   **f.** 18 ÷ 2

3. Make each sentence true. Use +, −, ×, or ÷.

   a. 8 ▤ 8 = 64   **b.** 6 ▤ 6 = 0
      8 ▤ 8 = 1   6 ▤ 6 = 1
      8 ▤ 8 = 0   6 ▤ 6 = 12
      8 ▤ 8 = 16   6 ▤ 6 = 36

4. Set the dial on the machine for each of the 4 operations. Write a true number sentence for each operation.

   a.    **b.**

   c. 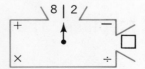   **d.**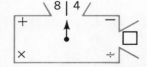

   e. 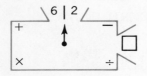   **f.**

166

PROBLEM SOLVING

1. Jerry is mounting 24 pictures. How many pictures are in each row if he places them in 8 rows? in 6 rows? in 4 rows?

2. Bill has 18 pictures. How many can he put in each row if he makes 3 rows? 9 rows? 6 rows?

3. Jill needs 27 cents to buy bananas. They sell for 15 cents a pound. She has only 10 cents. How much more money does she need?

4. Bill has 29 cents. He wants to buy a ball. How much more money does he need?

Let's Practice

Divide.

1. 8)24   2. 9)81   3. 4)36   4. 8)64

5. 8)56   6. 9)63   7. 9)27   8. 9)72

9. 8)72   10. 3)24   11. 9)36   12. 7)63

13. 9)45   14. 9)54   15. 8)48   16. 6)54

17. 8)40   18. 3)27   19. 8)32   20. 9)18

21. 8)16   22. 8)24   23. 7)49   24. 7)42

25. 3)21   26. 6)24   27. 5)25   28. 4)20

ANOTHER PROPERTY OF MULTIPLICATION

1. In addition we found that addends may be regrouped without changing the sum. Copy and complete.

   a. $(9 + 4) + 8 = $ ___ $+ 8$
   $= $ ___

   b. $9 + (4 + 8) = 9 + $ ___
   $= $ ___

   c. What property of addition did you use?

2. Consider $3 \times 2 \times 4$.

   a. $(3 \times 2) \times 4 = 6 \times $ ___
   $= $ ___

   b. $3 \times (2 \times 4) = 3 \times $ ___
   $= $ ___

   c. What factors did we group in item a? item b?

   d. Is $(3 \times 2) \times 4 = 3 \times (2 \times 4)$ a true sentence? Why?

3. Make each sentence true.

   a. $(2 \times 4) \times 3 = 2 \times (\square \times 3)$

   b. $(4 \times 5) \times 3 = \triangle \times (5 \times 3)$

4. Rewrite the sentence $(4 \times 4) \times 5 = \square$ to show another grouping of the factors.

Factors may be grouped in different ways when we multiply. The product is unchanged. This is the **associative property of multiplication.**

Write a true multiplication sentence for each picture.

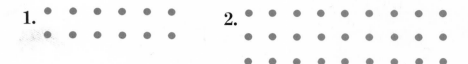

1.

2.

3. Think of $4 \times 2 = 8$. Name the factors and product.

4. Write a true multiplication sentence for $6 + 6 + 6 + 6 = \square$.

5. Make the sentence $\square \times \triangle = \triangle \times \square$ true. What property is shown?

Make each sentence true.

6. Since $4 \times 8 = 32$, then $32 \div 8 = \square$, and $32 \div 4 = \triangle$.

7. Since $7 \times 6 = \square$, then $\square \div 6 = 7$, and $\square \div 7 = 6$.

Write two division sentences for each.

8. $9 \times 8 = 72$ 9. $4 \times 6 = \square$ 10. $5 \times 8 = \square$

11. Copy and complete.

$$7 \times 9 = 7 \times (6 + \underline{\quad})$$
$$= (7 \times 6) + (7 \times \underline{\quad})$$
$$= 42 + \underline{\quad}$$
$$= \underline{\quad}$$

12. What property is shown?
$$4 \times (5 + 6) = (4 \times 5) + (4 \times 6)$$

169

Make each sentence true.

13. $(3 \times 4) \times 2 = 3 \times (4 \times \triangle)$

14. $(5 \times \square) \times 6 = \triangle \times (7 \times 6)$

15. $7 \times 1 = \square$ **16.** $1 \times 28 = \triangle$

17. $\square \times 1 = \square$ **18.** $9 \times 0 = \square$

19. $0 \times 4 = \square$ **20.** $8 \times \square = \square$

Make each sentence true. Use $+$, $-$, $\times$, or $\div$.

21. $27 \equiv 3 = 9$ **22.** $27 \equiv 3 = 24$ **23.** $9 \equiv 3 = 27$

24. $7 \equiv 2 = 9$ **25.** $7 \equiv 2 = 5$ **26.** $7 \equiv 2 = 14$

27. Name the even numbers greater than 1 but less than 15.

28. Name the odd numbers less than 10.

29. There are 8 chairs at each table in the library. How many chairs are at 3 tables?

30. Erasers cost 6 cents each. Find the cost of 8 erasers.

Terms You Should Know

array   product
factor   quotient
multiple   even numbers
multiplication   odd numbers
commutative property of multiplication
associative property of multiplication
distributive property of multiplication
                over addition

CHAPTER TEST

1. Draw an array to show 4 × 6. Write an addition sentence for 4 × 6.

2. Make the sentence 4 × 6 = □ true. Name the factors. Name the product.

3. Write a related multiplication sentence for each division. Make both sentences true.

   a. 8 ÷ 4 = □ **b.** 24 ÷ 6 = □ **c.** 10 ÷ △ = 2

4. Write a related division sentence for each multiplication. Make both sentences true.

   a. □ × 8 = 48   **b.** 9 × □ = 36

   c. 72 = 9 × □   **d.** 81 = 9 × △

Make each sentence true.
What property is shown in each sentence?

5. (4 × 2) × 3 = 4 × (2 × ___)

6. 6 × (5 + 3) = (6 × ___) + (6 × ___)

7. 6 × 8 = 8 × ___

Multiply.

8. 8 × 9   9. 4 × 6   10. 7 × 9

11. 9 × 7   12. 6 × 7   13. 8 × 8

Divide.

14. 4)‾12‾   15. 6)‾12‾   16. 8)‾48‾   17. 7)‾63‾

18. 9)‾81‾   19. 8)‾72‾   20. 6)‾18‾   21. 3)‾27‾

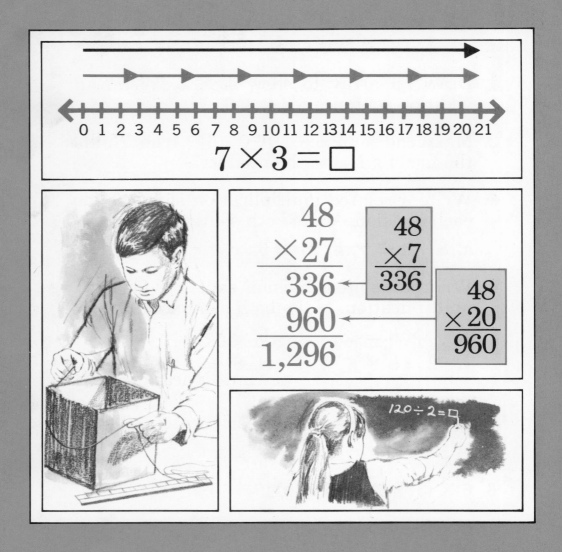

$7 \times 3 = \square$

$$
\begin{array}{r}
48 \\
\times 27 \\
\hline
336 \\
960 \\
\hline
1{,}296
\end{array}
$$

$$
\begin{array}{r}
48 \\
\times 7 \\
\hline
336
\end{array}
$$

$$
\begin{array}{r}
48 \\
\times 20 \\
\hline
960
\end{array}
$$

$120 \div 2 = \square$

CHAPTER SIX

Multiplication of Whole Numbers

REVIEWING MULTIPLICATION

1. a. What do we call two numbers that are multiplied?

   b. What do we call the result of a multiplication?

2. What multiplication is shown on this number line?

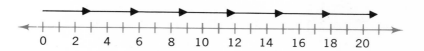

3. a. Write a true addition sentence for 6×9.

   b. What is the product 6×9?

4. What properties of multiplication are shown?

   a. $9 \times 7 = 7 \times 9$

   b. $4 \times (3 \times 2) = (4 \times 3) \times 2$

   c. $6 \times (5 + 4) = (6 \times 5) + (6 \times 4)$

EXERCISES

Name the products.

1. $\begin{array}{r} 9 \\ \times 9 \\ \hline \end{array}$	**2.** $\begin{array}{r} 8 \\ \times 8 \\ \hline \end{array}$	**3.** $\begin{array}{r} 9 \\ \times 8 \\ \hline \end{array}$	**4.** $\begin{array}{r} 7 \\ \times 7 \\ \hline \end{array}$	**5.** $\begin{array}{r} 7 \\ \times 8 \\ \hline \end{array}$	**6.** $\begin{array}{r} 9 \\ \times 3 \\ \hline \end{array}$
7. $\begin{array}{r} 9 \\ \times 4 \\ \hline \end{array}$	**8.** $\begin{array}{r} 7 \\ \times 4 \\ \hline \end{array}$	**9.** $\begin{array}{r} 5 \\ \times 8 \\ \hline \end{array}$	**10.** $\begin{array}{r} 7 \\ \times 6 \\ \hline \end{array}$	**11.** $\begin{array}{r} 8 \\ \times 6 \\ \hline \end{array}$	**12.** $\begin{array}{r} 4 \\ \times 4 \\ \hline \end{array}$
13. $\begin{array}{r} 4 \\ \times 7 \\ \hline \end{array}$	**14.** $\begin{array}{r} 9 \\ \times 6 \\ \hline \end{array}$	**15.** $\begin{array}{r} 7 \\ \times 9 \\ \hline \end{array}$	**16.** $\begin{array}{r} 9 \\ \times 2 \\ \hline \end{array}$	**17.** $\begin{array}{r} 8 \\ \times 4 \\ \hline \end{array}$	**18.** $\begin{array}{r} 3 \\ \times 7 \\ \hline \end{array}$

MORE PRODUCTS

1. Do you remember 0 and 1 in multiplication?
   a. $0 \times 10 = 0$. Why?
   b. Make the sentence $0 \times 300 = \square$ true.
   c. $1 \times 10 = 10$. Why?
   d. Make the sentence $1 \times 400 = \square$ true.

2. Make each sentence true.

   a. $1 \times 10 = \square$
   $3 \times \square = 30$
   $\square \times 10 = 50$
   $6 \times \square = 60$
   $8 \times 10 = \square$

   b. $10 \times 10 = \square$
   $11 \times 10 = \square$
   $25 \times 10 = \square$
   $30 \times 10 = \square$
   $49 \times 10 = \square$

   c. What pattern do you see for multiplying by 10?

3. Make each sentence true.

   a. $1 \times \square = 100$
   $2 \times 100 = \square$
   $4 \times 100 = \square$
   $\square \times 100 = 800$
   $9 \times 100 = \square$

   b. $10 \times 100 = \square$
   $11 \times 100 = \square$
   $13 \times 100 = \square$
   $20 \times 100 = \square$
   $23 \times 100 = \square$

   c. What pattern do you see for multiplying by 100?

4. Make each sentence true.

   a. $1 \times 1{,}000 = \square$
   $9 \times \square = 9{,}000$
   $\square \times 1{,}000 = 10{,}000$

   b. $15 \times 1{,}000 = \square$
   $\square \times 1{,}000 = 35{,}000$
   $39 \times \square = 39{,}000$

   c. What pattern do you see for multiplying by 1,000?

Multiply.

1. 8 × 10   2. 82 × 10   3. 10 × 10

4. 7 × 100   5. 82 × 100   6. 10 × 100

7. 9 × 1,000   8. 82 × 1,000   9. 421 × 100

10. 0 × 200   11. 10 × 54   12. 10 × 1,000

13. 1 × 3,000   14. 10 × 89   15. 100 × 89

Let's Practice

Study these triangles.

1. Which triangles shown above are isosceles?

2. Which triangle is a right triangle?

3. Find the perimeter of the triangle in picture C.

4. Can a triangle have two right angles? three right angles?

5. Find the perimeter of the triangles in pictures A, B, and D.

6. Label each vertex in triangle A.

175

MULTIPLES OF TEN

1. Rename these multiples of ten.

   a. $30 = 3 \times \triangle$ **b.** $50 = \triangle \times 10$ **c.** $60 = \triangle \times 10$

2. Think of 2×30.

   number
   5 like this

$2 \times 30 = 2 \times (3 \times 10)$	How is 30 renamed?
$= (2 \times 3) \times 10$	What property is used?
$= 6 \times 10$	What is 2×3?
$= 60$	What is 6×10?

3. Find the product 6×30. Copy and complete.

   $$6 \times 30 = 6 \times (\underline{\quad} \times 10)$$
   $$= (6 \times \underline{\quad}) \times 10$$
   $$= \underline{\quad} \times 10$$
   $$= \underline{\quad}$$

4. Multiply. Look for a pattern.

   a. $2 \times 90 = (2 \times 9) \times 10$ $\begin{array}{r} 90 \\ \times 2 \\ \hline \end{array}$
   $= \underline{\quad}$

   b. $7 \times 40 = (7 \times 4) \times 10$ $\begin{array}{r} 40 \\ \times 7 \\ \hline \end{array}$
   $= \underline{\quad}$

   c. $8 \times 70 = (8 \times 7) \times 10$ $\begin{array}{r} 70 \\ \times 8 \\ \hline \end{array}$
   $= \underline{\quad}$

   d. $5 \times 50 = (5 \times 5) \times 10$ $\begin{array}{r} 50 \\ \times 5 \\ \hline \end{array}$
   $= \underline{\quad}$

5. Multiply.

   a. 2×50 **b.** 3×40 **c.** 8×70

   d. 9×30 **e.** 7×20 **f.** 9×90

   g. 7×60 **h.** 3×20 **i.** 6×80

USING THE ASSOCIATIVE PROPERTY

1. Rename these multiples of 100 and 1,000.

    a. $500 = 5 \times \triangledown$

    b. $5,000 = 5 \times \triangledown$

    c. $600 = \triangledown \times 100$

    d. $6,000 = \triangledown \times 1,000$

2. Consider 7×400.

$$7 \times 400 = 7 \times (4 \times 100)$$
$$= (7 \times 4) \times 100$$
$$= 28 \times 100$$
$$= \underline{\quad}$$

   How is 400 renamed? What property is used?

3. Copy and complete.

    a. $8 \times 600 = 8 \times (\underline{\quad} \times 100)$
    $= (8 \times \underline{\quad}) \times 100$
    $= \underline{\quad} \times 100$
    $= \underline{\quad}$

    b. $9 \times 2,000 = 9 \times (2 \times \underline{\quad})$
    $= (9 \times 2) \times \underline{\quad}$
    $= 18 \times \underline{\quad}$
    $= \underline{\quad}$

4. Multiply. Look for a pattern.

    a. $5 \times 500 = (5 \times 5) \times 100$
    $= \underline{\quad}$

    $\begin{array}{r} 500 \\ \times 5 \\ \hline \end{array}$

    b. $5 \times 5,000 = (5 \times 5) \times 1,000$
    $= \underline{\quad}$

    $\begin{array}{r} 5,000 \\ \times 5 \\ \hline \end{array}$

    c. $7 \times 600 = (7 \times 6) \times 100$
    $= \underline{\quad}$

    $\begin{array}{r} 600 \\ \times 7 \\ \hline \end{array}$

    d. $7 \times 6,000 = (7 \times 6) \times 1,000$
    $= \underline{\quad}$

    $\begin{array}{r} 6,000 \\ \times 7 \\ \hline \end{array}$

5. Study items a and b. Copy and complete items c and d.

a. $\begin{array}{r} 500 \\ \times 6 \\ \hline 3,000 \end{array}$ b. $\begin{array}{r} 5,000 \\ \times 6 \\ \hline 30,000 \end{array}$ c. $\begin{array}{r} 900 \\ \times 9 \\ \hline \end{array}$ d. $\begin{array}{r} 9,000 \\ \times 9 \\ \hline \end{array}$

EXERCISES

Copy and complete.

1. $5 \times 300 = (5 \times \underline{\hspace{1cm}}) \times 100$
   $= \underline{\hspace{1cm}}$

2. $7 \times 4,000 = (7 \times \underline{\hspace{1cm}}) \times 1,000$
   $= \underline{\hspace{1cm}}$

3. $6 \times 600 = (6 \times 6) \times \underline{\hspace{1cm}}$
   $= \underline{\hspace{1cm}}$

Multiply.

4. 4×3
   4×30
   4×300
   $4 \times 3,000$

5. 8×7
   8×70
   8×700
   $8 \times 7,000$

Multiply.

6. 9×20

7. 20×9

8. $9 \times 3,000$

9. 8×400

10. $3 \times 7,000$

11. 600×2

12. 70×4

13. $8 \times 8,000$

14. 30×9

15. 9×900

16. $5 \times 7,000$

17. $4 \times 6,000$

MULTIPLES OF TEN AND HUNDRED

1. Make each sentence true.

    a. $10 \times 10 = \square$ **b.** $10 \times 100 = \square$

2. There are 10 hot dogs in a package. How many are in 20 packages?

$$20 \times 10 = (2 \times 10) \times 10$$
$$= 2 \times (10 \times 10)$$
$$= 2 \times 100$$
$$= \underline{}$$

3. Copy and complete.

$$50 \times 100 = (5 \times 10) \times 100$$
$$= 5 \times (10 \times 100)$$
$$= 5 \times \underline{}$$
$$= \underline{}$$

4. Find the products.

    a. $60 \times 10 = 6 \times 10 \times 10$
$$= \underline{}$$

    b. $80 \times 100 = 8 \times 10 \times 100$
$$= \underline{}$$

5. a. $2 \times 20 = 40$, so $20 \times 2 = \square$. Why?

    b. $2 \times (2 \times 10) = (2 \times 2) \times 10$. Why?

6. Multiply. Compare the factors and products. What do you find?

    a. $(3 \times 2) \times (1 \times 4)$ **b.** $(3 \times 2) \times (4 \times 1)$

    c. $(4 \times 1) \times (3 \times 2)$ **d.** $(4 \times 3) \times (1 \times 2)$

179

7. Think of 30 × 20. Name the product. Study the vertical form.

$$30 \times 20 = (3 \times 10) \times (2 \times 10)$$
$$= (3 \times 2) \times (10 \times 10)$$
$$= 6 \times 100$$
$$= \underline{}$$

$$\begin{array}{r} 20 \\ \times 30 \\ \hline 600 \end{array}$$

8. Multiply. Copy and complete.

a.
$$30 \times 40 = (\underline{} \times 10) \times (\underline{} \times 10)$$
$$= (\underline{} \times 4) \times (10 \times 10)$$
$$= \underline{} \times 100$$
$$= \underline{}$$

$$\begin{array}{r} 40 \\ \times 30 \\ \hline 1{,}200 \end{array}$$

b.
$$30 \times 400 = (3 \times \underline{}) \times (4 \times 100)$$
$$= (3 \times 4) \times (\underline{} \times 100)$$
$$= 12 \times \underline{}$$
$$= \underline{}$$

$$\begin{array}{r} 400 \\ \times 30 \\ \hline 12{,}000 \end{array}$$

9. Find the products.

a.
$$50 \times 30 = (5 \times 3) \times (10 \times 10)$$
$$= \underline{}$$

b.
$$50 \times 300 = (5 \times 3) \times (10 \times 100)$$
$$= \underline{}$$

c.
$$900 \times 50 = (9 \times 5) \times (100 \times 10)$$
$$= \underline{}$$

d.
$$70 \times 700 = (7 \times 7) \times (\underline{} \times 100)$$
$$= \underline{}$$

10. Multiply.

a.
$$\begin{array}{r} 50 \\ \times 60 \end{array}$$

b.
$$\begin{array}{r} 80 \\ \times 60 \end{array}$$

c.
$$\begin{array}{r} 700 \\ \times 40 \end{array}$$

d.
$$\begin{array}{r} 900 \\ \times 30 \end{array}$$

e. 40 × 50   f. 60 × 70   g. 40 × 80

Multiply.

1. 40 × 70   2. 40 × 30   3. 80 × 20

4. 60 × 400   5. 40 × 300   6. 50 × 500

7. 40 × 4   8. 50 × 30   9. 70 × 70

10. 60 × 300   11. 20 × 900   12. 80 × 700

13.   70
   ×60   14.   90
   ×40   15.   80
   ×30   16.   70
   ×80

17.   700
   ×90   18.   60
   ×80   19.   40
   ×90   20.   700
   ×80

21.   600
   ×80   22.   500
   ×70   23.   900
   ×50   24.   60
   ×60

Solve each problem.

25. There are 60 minutes in one hour. How many minutes are there in 20 hours?

26. How many minutes are there in 40 hours?

27. How many minutes are there in 100 hours?

28. How many minutes are there in 500 hours?

UNEXPLORED TERRITORY

We can rename a number by naming two or more factors. For example, $30 = 3 \times 2 \times 5$, $9 = 3 \times 3$, and $7 = 7 \times 1$. Use only 1, 2, 3, 5, and 7 as factors and rename these numbers.

1. 15   2. 24   3. 27   4. 32   5. 42

DO YOU REMEMBER?

Add.

| 1. | 479
+384 | 2. | 87,241
+98,794 | 3. | $ .64
1.98
+2.37 | 4. | 87
63
149
+238 |

Subtract.

| 5. | 784
−193 | 6. | 6,004
−3,129 | 7. | 8,994
−3,899 | 8. | $34.86
−17.49 |

Multiply.

9. 7×10 **10.** 7×100 **11.** $7 \times 1,000$

12. 238×10 **13.** 10×100 **14.** 4×30

15. 90×7 **16.** 60×40 **17.** 70×60

18. 40×200 **19.** 3×200 **20.** 8×60

| 21. | 30
×3 | 22. | 60
×4 | 23. | 20
×5 | 24. | 300
×3 |

| 25. | 400
×3 | 26. | 3,000
×3 | 27. | 7,000
×6 | 28. | 2,000
×9 |

| 29. | 200
×40 | 30. | 40
×20 | 31. | 300
×40 | 32. | 700
×40 |

Make each sentence true.

33. $60 \times \square = 180$ **34.** $\square \times 4 = 240$

35. $\square \times 30 = 120$ **36.** $\square \times 200 = 1,000$

37. $\square \times 600 = 3,600$ **38.** $\square \times 7 = 490$

USING A PATTERN

Let us use what we know about related sentences.

    Missing factor   *Quotient*

$$8 \times \square = 80 \qquad\qquad 80 \div 8 = \square$$

1. Name the missing factors and quotients.

    a. $7 \times \square = 630$ **b.** $7 \times \square = 6{,}300$
        $630 \div 7 = \square$ $6{,}300 \div 7 = \square$

2. Write a related multiplication for each division. Then make each sentence true. For $1{,}200 \div 3 = \triangle$, we write $3 \times \triangle = 1{,}200$.

    a. $80 \div 8 \ = \square$ **b.** $800 \div 8 \ = \square$

    c. $800 \div 80 = \square$ **d.** $800 \div 2 \ = \square$

    e. $800 \div 40 = \square$ **f.** $800 \div 400 = \square$

EXERCISES

Divide.

  1. $120 \div 3$ **2.** $1{,}200 \div 3$

  3. $1{,}200 \div 4$ **4.** $180 \div 3$

  5. $1{,}800 \div 6$ **6.** $100 \div 5$

  7. $240 \div 6$ **8.** $2{,}400 \div 6$

  9. $2{,}400 \div 60$ **10.** $270 \div 9$

11. $1{,}000 \div 2$ **12.** $1{,}000 \div 5$

13. $1{,}000 \div 20$ **14.** $600 \div 30$

USING THE DISTRIBUTIVE PROPERTY

We can use the distributive property to help us multiply.

1. John bought 4 boxes of candy. Each box had 12 candy bars. How many candy bars did he buy? Explain each step.

$$4 \times 12 = 4 \times (10 + 2)$$
$$= (4 \times 10) + (4 \times 2)$$
$$= 40 + 8$$
$$= \underline{\quad}$$

2. Gerald has three bags of marbles. There are 23 marbles in each bag. How many marbles does he have? Copy and complete.

$$3 \times 23 = 3 \times (20 + 3)$$
$$= (3 \times \underline{\quad}) + (3 \times \underline{\quad})$$
$$= 60 + 9$$
$$= \underline{\quad}$$

3. Copy and complete.

$$5 \times 34 = 5 \times (30 + \underline{\quad})$$
$$= (5 \times \underline{\quad}) + (5 \times \underline{\quad})$$

4. We can distribute multiplication over three or more addends.

a. $2 \times 342 = 2 \times (300 + 40 + 2)$
$= (2 \times 300) + (2 \times \underline{\hspace{1em}})$
$\qquad\qquad\qquad\qquad + (2 \times \underline{\hspace{1em}})$
$= 600 + \underline{\hspace{1em}} + 4$
$= \underline{\hspace{1em}}$

b. $3 \times 351 = 3 \times (300 + 50 + 1)$
$= (3 \times 300) + (3 \times 50) + (3 \times 1)$
$= 900 + \underline{\hspace{1em}} + \underline{\hspace{1em}}$
$= \underline{\hspace{1em}}$

5. Multiply 20 and 21.

$20 \times 21 = 20 \times (20 + 1)$
$= (20 \times \underline{\hspace{1em}}) + (20 \times \underline{\hspace{1em}})$
$= \underline{\hspace{1em}} + \underline{\hspace{1em}}$
$= \underline{\hspace{1em}}$

6. Multiply 40 and 212.

$40 \times 212 = 40 \times (200 + \underline{\hspace{1em}} + 2)$
$= (40 \times 200) + (40 \times \underline{\hspace{1em}})$
$\qquad\qquad\qquad\qquad + (\underline{\hspace{1em}} \times 2)$
$= 8,000 + \underline{\hspace{1em}} + \underline{\hspace{1em}}$
$= \underline{\hspace{1em}}$

EXERCISES

Multiply. Use the distributive property.

1. 5×11 **2.** 3×13 **3.** 4×15

4. 9×27 **5.** 2×246 **6.** 30×46

7. 20×49 **8.** 20×222 **9.** 60×532

PROBLEM SOLVING

1. Mr. Allan sold 20 bags of peanuts and 30 bags of popcorn. How many bags of food did he sell?

2. A train can travel 70 miles in one hour. How many miles can it travel in 2 hours?

3. The 30 children in Mrs. Smith's class are making scrapbooks. Each child will need 20 sheets of paper. How many sheets of paper in all are needed?

4. Mr. Wells has 120 pennies. He wants to divide them equally between Jerry and Dan. How many pennies will each boy get?
   Think: $120 \div 2 = \square$.

5. Mr. Jones is packing 30 books in a box. How many books will there be in 4 boxes? in 10 boxes? in 40 boxes? in 400 boxes?

6. Mrs. Lyon makes 400 school lunches each day. How many lunches does she make in 20 days?

7. Jack, Mary, and Bill buy 2 sandwiches each, every school day.

   a. How many sandwiches do the children buy each day?

   b. How many sandwiches do they buy altogether in 5 days?

USING PARTIAL PRODUCTS

1. We have used the distributive property to help us find products. Explain each step.

$$4 \times 238 = 4 \times (200 + 30 + 8)$$
$$= (4 \times 200) + (4 \times 30) + (4 \times 8)$$
$$= 800 + 120 + 32$$
$$= 952$$

2. a. How is the distributive property used here?

$$\begin{array}{r} 200 + 30 + 8 \\ 4 \\ \hline 800 + 120 + 32 = 952 \end{array}$$

b. The numbers 800, 120, and 32 are partial products. What is their sum?

3. Harold wrote this on the board.

$$\begin{array}{r} 200 + 30 + 8 \\ 4 \\ \hline 32 \\ 120 \\ 800 \\ \hline 952 \end{array}$$

a. How did he show the partial products?

b. Are they easier to add?

4. Name the factors for each partial product.

a.
$$\begin{array}{r} 238 \\ \times 4 \\ \hline 32 \\ 120 \\ 800 \\ \hline 952 \end{array}$$
  (4×8)
  (4×30)
  $(4 \times \underline{\quad})$

b.
$$\begin{array}{r} 463 \\ \times 7 \\ \hline 21 \\ 420 \\ 2{,}800 \\ \hline 3{,}241 \end{array}$$
  $(\underline{\quad} \times \underline{\quad})$
  $(\underline{\quad} \times \underline{\quad})$
  $(\underline{\quad} \times \underline{\quad})$

5. Use the form in Item 4. Multiply 7 by 384.

Multiply. Use this form.

$$5 \times 624 = (5 \times 600) + (5 \times 20) + (5 \times 4)$$
$$= 3,000 + 100 + 20$$
$$= 3,120$$

1. 6×735 **2.** 7×846

Multiply. Use the form in Item 4, page 187.

3. 6×246 **4.** 7×357 **5.** 8×68

Multiply. Use the form shown in Item 4.
Do not show the meaning of the partial products.

6. 7×273 **7.** 8×384 **8.** 6×162

9. $\begin{array}{r} 276 \\ \times 5 \\ \hline \end{array}$ **10.** $\begin{array}{r} 392 \\ \times 8 \\ \hline \end{array}$ **11.** $\begin{array}{r} 73 \\ \times 9 \\ \hline \end{array}$ **12.** $\begin{array}{r} 71 \\ \times 4 \\ \hline \end{array}$

13. $\begin{array}{r} 799 \\ \times 3 \\ \hline \end{array}$ **14.** $\begin{array}{r} 888 \\ \times 4 \\ \hline \end{array}$ **15.** $\begin{array}{r} 43 \\ \times 7 \\ \hline \end{array}$ **16.** $\begin{array}{r} 86 \\ \times 6 \\ \hline \end{array}$

17. $\begin{array}{r} 438 \\ \times 5 \\ \hline \end{array}$ **18.** $\begin{array}{r} 981 \\ \times 2 \\ \hline \end{array}$ **19.** $\begin{array}{r} 452 \\ \times 4 \\ \hline \end{array}$ **20.** $\begin{array}{r} 756 \\ \times 3 \\ \hline \end{array}$

Solve each problem.

21. One truck holds 468 crates of tomatoes. How many crates will 8 trucks hold?

22. A jet plane flies about 570 miles in one hour.

    a. How far will it fly in 3 hours?

    b. How far will it fly in 4 hours?

MULTIPLYING—SHORT FORM

1. We can use a short form. Multiply 23 by 3.

   Step 1
   $$\begin{array}{r} 2\,3 \\ \times 3 \\ \hline 9 \end{array}$$
   $3 \times 3 = 9$

   Step 2
   $$\begin{array}{r} 2\,3 \\ \times 3 \\ \hline 6\,9 \end{array}$$
   $3 \times (2 \text{ tens}) = 60$
   $9 + 60 = 69$

   a. Study Step 1. In what place is the 9?

   b. Study Step 2. In what place is the 6?

2. Multiply. Use the short form.

   a. $\begin{array}{r} 12 \\ \times 3 \\ \hline \end{array}$
   b. $\begin{array}{r} 43 \\ \times 2 \\ \hline \end{array}$
   c. $\begin{array}{r} 53 \\ \times 3 \\ \hline \end{array}$
   d. $\begin{array}{r} 61 \\ \times 7 \\ \hline \end{array}$

3. Find the product 4×321. Explain each step.

   a. $\begin{array}{r} 3\,2\,1 \\ \times 4 \\ \hline 4 \end{array}$
      Multiply ones.
   $4 \times 1 = \underline{\hphantom{00}}$

   b. $\begin{array}{r} 3\,2\,1 \\ \times 4 \\ \hline 8\,4 \end{array}$
      Multiply tens.
   $4 \times (2 \text{ tens}) = \underline{\hphantom{00}} \text{ tens}$

   c. $\begin{array}{r} 3\,2\,1 \\ \times 4 \\ \hline 1{,}2\,8\,4 \end{array}$
      Multiply hundreds.
   $4 \times (3 \text{ hundreds}) = \underline{\hphantom{00}}$
                          hundreds

4. Multiply. Use the short form.

   a. $\begin{array}{r} 511 \\ \times 7 \\ \hline \end{array}$
   b. $\begin{array}{r} 2{,}234 \\ \times 2 \\ \hline \end{array}$
   c. $\begin{array}{r} 323 \\ \times 3 \\ \hline \end{array}$
   d. $\begin{array}{r} 402 \\ \times 2 \\ \hline \end{array}$

EXERCISES

Multiply. Use the short form.

1.	33 ×3	2.	21 ×2	3.	11 ×3	4.	2,001 ×5
5.	123 ×3	6.	412 ×4	7.	601 ×3	8.	7,424 ×2
9.	4,323 ×3	10.	3,122 ×4	11.	4,343 ×2	12.	4,101 ×2

Solve each problem.

13. Elva bought 4 dozen eggs. How many eggs did she buy?

14. Mike traveled 2,434 miles when he flew from New York to Oregon. How many miles would he fly on a round trip?

Let's Practice

Write word names.

1. 3,489   2. 207,342   3. $28.47

Use =, >, or <. Make each sentence true.

4. $48+76+97 \equiv 500$ 5. $97-38 \equiv 27+28$

6. $8+8+8+8 \equiv 16+2$ 7. $100-64 \equiv 9 \times 4$

Add.

8.	394 296 847	9.	12,874 38,706 94,706 90,876	10.	$.19 .18 .27 .98	11.	$48.62 39.43 87.04

1. There are 28 class-rooms. If Maria is to put 3 pieces of chalk in each room, how many pieces will she need?

a. Study the long form. What are the partial products?

b. Name the product.

2. Let's try a short form. Explain each step. The small numerals are reminders. They help us remember to regroup.

a.
$$\begin{array}{r} {}^{2}\;2\,8 \\ \times\,3 \\ \hline 4 \end{array}$$
3×8 ones = ___
$24 =$ ___ tens $+ 4$
Write 4. Remember 2 tens.

b.
$$\begin{array}{r} {}^{2}\;2\,8 \\ \times\,3 \\ \hline 8\,4 \end{array}$$
$(3 \times 2$ tens$) + 2$ tens
6 tens $+ 2$ tens = ___ tens
Write 8.

3. Multiply.

a.
$$\begin{array}{r} 17 \\ \times 5 \\ \hline \end{array}$$

b.
$$\begin{array}{r} 25 \\ \times 3 \\ \hline \end{array}$$

c.
$$\begin{array}{r} 18 \\ \times 4 \\ \hline \end{array}$$

d.
$$\begin{array}{r} 26 \\ \times 6 \\ \hline \end{array}$$

4. Explain each step in this short form.

$$\begin{array}{r} {}^{1}\;2\,2\,4 \\ \times\,3 \\ \hline 2 \end{array}$$
$$\begin{array}{r} {}^{1}\;2\,2\,4 \\ \times\,3 \\ \hline 7\,2 \end{array}$$
$$\begin{array}{r} {}^{1}\;2\,2\,4 \\ \times\,3 \\ \hline 6\,7\,2 \end{array}$$

191

5. Study each step. Where do we need to regroup?

$$
\begin{array}{r}
43\boxed{2} \\
\times\boxed{4} \\
\hline
\boxed{8}
\end{array}
\qquad
\begin{array}{r}
\!^{1} \\
4\boxed{3}2 \\
\times\boxed{4} \\
\hline
\boxed{2}8
\end{array}
\qquad
\begin{array}{r}
\!^{1} \\
\boxed{4}32 \\
\times\boxed{4} \\
\hline
\boxed{1,7}28
\end{array}
$$

a. 4 × 2 ones = ____ ones

b. 4 × 3 tens = ____ tens
   12 tens = ____ hundred + 2 tens
   Name 2 tens.

c. (4 × 4 hundreds) + 1 hundred
   = ____ hundreds.

6. Multiply. Explain each step.

   a. 2 × 1,741   b. 3 × 1,803   c. 4,900 × 6

EXERCISES

Multiply.

1. $\begin{array}{r}19\\ \times5\end{array}$	2. $\begin{array}{r}26\\ \times3\end{array}$	3. $\begin{array}{r}19\\ \times4\end{array}$	4. $\begin{array}{r}27\\ \times6\end{array}$
5. $\begin{array}{r}117\\ \times3\end{array}$	6. $\begin{array}{r}328\\ \times2\end{array}$	7. $\begin{array}{r}119\\ \times5\end{array}$	8. $\begin{array}{r}2,136\\ \times2\end{array}$
9. $\begin{array}{r}416\\ \times5\end{array}$	10. $\begin{array}{r}712\\ \times7\end{array}$	11. $\begin{array}{r}502\\ \times8\end{array}$	12. $\begin{array}{r}6,224\\ \times4\end{array}$
13. $\begin{array}{r}231\\ \times4\end{array}$	14. $\begin{array}{r}161\\ \times5\end{array}$	15. $\begin{array}{r}293\\ \times3\end{array}$	16. $\begin{array}{r}831\\ \times4\end{array}$
17. $\begin{array}{r}58\\ \times7\end{array}$	18. $\begin{array}{r}86\\ \times4\end{array}$	19. $\begin{array}{r}561\\ \times5\end{array}$	20. $\begin{array}{r}993\\ \times3\end{array}$

REGROUPING MORE THAN ONCE

1. Study these ways of multiplying 347 by 4.

Partial Products

$$347$$
$$\times 4$$
$$\overline{28}$$
$$160$$
$$\underline{1,200}$$
$$1,388$$

Short Form

$$\overset{1\ 2}{347}$$
$$\underline{\times 4}$$
$$1,388$$

a. Explain the partial-products form.

b. Study the short form.

4×7 ones = ____ ones
$(4 \times 4$ tens$) + 2$ tens = ____ tens
$(4 \times 3$ hundreds$) + 1$ hundred
$$= \underline{} \text{ hundreds}$$

2. Explain each step in the two forms.

Partial Products

$$9,876$$
$$\underline{\times 5}$$
$$30$$
$$350$$
$$4,000$$
$$\underline{45,000}$$
$$49,380$$

Short Form

$$\overset{4\ 3\ 3}{9,876}$$
$$\underline{\times 5}$$
$$49,380$$

3. The small numerals in the short form are reminders. Use them when you find these products.

a. 776
$\times 3$

b. 478
$\times 4$

c. 1,591
$\times 6$

4. John bought 3 football tickets at $.75 each. Find the total cost. Explain each step.

$$\begin{array}{r} {}^{1}\ \\ \$.7\,5 \\ \times\ 3 \\ \hline 5 \end{array} \qquad \begin{array}{r} {}^{1}\ \\ \$.7\,5 \\ \times\ 3 \\ \hline \$2.2\,5 \end{array}$$

5. Multiply. Express your answer in dollars and cents.

a. $.63
   ×4

b. $1.79
   ×2

c. $22.35
   ×2

EXERCISES

Multiply.

1. 149
   ×6

2. 295
   ×3

3. 239
   ×4

4. 1,136
   ×6

5. 1,618
   ×3

6. 1,729
   ×2

7. 1,314
   ×7

8. 1,231
   ×9

9. 1,591
   ×6

10. 654
   ×8

11. 738
   ×6

12. 978
   ×2

13. 2,967
   ×3

14. 1,467
   ×6

15. 5,769
   ×9

16. 5,673
   ×7

17. 8,429
   ×9

18. 6,566
   ×6

19. 8,035
   ×9

20. 7,603
   ×8

21. $3.49
   ×6

22. $37.42
   ×8

23. $61.29
   ×7

24. $435.67
   ×2

ESTIMATING PRODUCTS

We do not always need an exact answer. Sometimes we estimate.

1. There are 32 children in each of 5 fourth-grade classes. What is the total number of children in the 5 classes?

   a. Round the greater factor to a multiple of ten. Is 32 nearer to 30 or 40?

   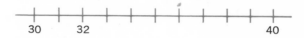

   b. Estimate: 5 × 30 = □. About how many fourth-graders are there?

   c. Multiply: 5 × 32. What is the exact number of fourth-graders?

2. Estimate the products. Round the greater factor to the nearest multiple of ten.

   a. Consider 2 × 68. What multiple of 10 is nearest to 68?
   Estimate: 2 × 70 = □. Find the exact product.

   b. Think of 2 × 35. We round 35 to what multiple of 10?
   Estimate: 2 × 40 = □. Find the exact product.

3. a. To estimate 6 × 33, think 6 × ___

   b. To estimate 3 × 36, think 3 × ___

   c. To estimate 7 × 22, think 7 × ___

   d. To estimate 5 × 55, think 5 × ___

4. The speed of a jet plane is 570 miles per hour. About how far will the plane travel in 3 hours?

    a. Round the greater factor to the nearest multiple of 100.

    b. Estimate: $3 \times 600 = \square$. About how far will the plane travel? Find the product 3×570.

5. Estimate the products.

    a. 4×328. Is 328 nearer to 300 or 400? What is the exact product?

    b. What is the exact product of 5×550?

6. a. To estimate 6×621, think $6 \times \underline{\hspace{1cm}} = \underline{\hspace{1cm}}$.

    b. To estimate 8×987, think $8 \times \underline{\hspace{1cm}} = \underline{\hspace{1cm}}$.

    c. To estimate 2×949, think $2 \times \underline{\hspace{1cm}} = \underline{\hspace{1cm}}$.

    d. To estimate 5×750, think $5 \times \underline{\hspace{1cm}} = \underline{\hspace{1cm}}$.

EXERCISES

Estimate.

1. 7×33	**2.** 6×59	**3.** 4×75
4. 2×87	**5.** 3×65	**6.** 3×64
7. 7×330	**8.** 6×751	**9.** 4×592
10. 2×875	**11.** 3×656	**12.** 3×647

13.–24. Find exact products for Exercises 1.–12.

MULTIPLES OF TEN AS A FACTOR

1. Copy and complete.

$$41 \times 20 = 41 \times (2 \times 10)$$
$$= (41 \times 2) \times 10$$
$$= \underline{\quad} \times 10$$
$$= \underline{\quad}$$

a. How was 20 renamed?

b. What property was used?

c. $41 \times 2 = \underline{\quad}$; $82 \times 10 = \underline{\quad}$

d. $41 \times 20 = \underline{\quad}$

2. Copy and complete.

a. $52 \times 40 = 52 \times (\underline{\quad} \times 10)$.
$$= (52 \times \underline{\quad}) \times 10$$
$$= \underline{\quad} \times 10$$
$$= \underline{\quad}$$

b. $52 \times 4 = \underline{\quad}$

c. $52 \times 40 = \underline{\quad}$

3. Look for a pattern in these multiplications. Copy and complete.

a. $75 \times 50 = (75 \times 5) \times 10$
$$= 375 \times 10$$
$$= \underline{\quad}$$

$$\begin{array}{r} 75 \\ \times 5 \\ \hline 375 \end{array} \qquad \begin{array}{r} 75 \\ \times 50 \\ \hline 3{,}750 \end{array}$$

b. $38 \times 40 = (38 \times 4) \times 10$
$$= 152 \times 10$$
$$= \underline{\quad}$$

$$\begin{array}{r} 38 \\ \times 4 \\ \hline 152 \end{array} \qquad \begin{array}{r} 38 \\ \times 40 \\ \hline 1{,}520 \end{array}$$

c. What pattern can you find for multiplying by a multiple of ten?

4. Copy and complete.

a. $138 \times 40 = (138 \times 4) \times 10$ 138   138
               $= 552 \times 10$ $\times 4$ $\times 40$
               $= \underline{\hspace{1cm}}$ 552   5,520

b. $281 \times 40 = (281 \times 4) \times 10$ 281   281
               $= \underline{\hspace{1cm}} \times 10$ $\times 4$ $\times 40$
               $= \underline{\hspace{1cm}}$

c. $192 \times 80 = (192 \times 8) \times 10$ 192   192
               $= \underline{\hspace{1cm}} \times 10$ $\times 8$ $\times 80$
               $= \underline{\hspace{1cm}}$

5. Copy and complete.

We know:	*We can find:*
a. $41 \times 2 = 82$	$41 \times 20 = \underline{\hspace{1cm}}$
b. $131 \times 3 = 393$	$131 \times 30 = \underline{\hspace{1cm}}$
c. $444 \times 4 = 1,776$	$444 \times 40 = \underline{\hspace{1cm}}$
d. $128 \times 4 = \underline{\hspace{1cm}}$	$128 \times 40 = \underline{\hspace{1cm}}$

EXERCISES

Multiply.

1.   87   2.   64   3.   79   4.   86
   $\times 20$ $\times 30$ $\times 40$ $\times 50$

5. 692   6. 286   7. 850   8. 970
   $\times 40$ $\times 60$ $\times 80$ $\times 30$

9. 287   10. 794   11. 666   12. 568
   $\times 20$ $\times 30$ $\times 70$ $\times 80$

13. 342   14. 476   15. 878   16. 784
   $\times 80$ $\times 30$ $\times 90$ $\times 90$

DO YOU REMEMBER?

Multiply.

1.	30 ×20	**2.**	30 ×30	**3.**	40 ×20	**4.**	80 ×20
5.	70 ×50	**6.**	80 ×90	**7.**	60 ×50	**8.**	90 ×40
9.	59 ×50	**10.**	36 ×60	**11.**	48 ×70	**12.**	39 ×80
13.	200 ×40	**14.**	300 ×20	**15.**	200 ×30	**16.**	800 ×50
17.	706 ×40	**18.**	507 ×90	**19.**	420 ×20	**20.**	711 ×80
21.	293 ×70	**22.**	356 ×80	**23.**	547 ×60	**24.**	829 ×70

Solve each problem.

25. If there are 144 pieces of chalk in one box, how many pieces are in 20 boxes?

26. Fifteen cars can be loaded on one railroad car. How many cars can be loaded on 30 railroad cars?

27. There are 500 sheets of paper in one package of drawing paper. How many sheets are in 60 packages? in 85 packages? in 93 packages?

MULTIPLYING TENS AND ONES

1. We can use what we have learned to find more products.

$$4 \times 36 = 4 \times (30 + 6)$$
$$= (4 \times 30) + (4 \times \underline{\quad})$$
$$= 120 + \underline{\quad}$$
$$= \underline{\quad}$$

a. How was 36 renamed?

b. What property of multiplication was used?

2. We can use what we know to multiply tens and ones by tens and ones. Complete and explain each step.

a. $48 \times 27 = 48 \times (20 + 7)$
$$= (48 \times 20) + (48 \times \underline{\quad})$$
$$= \underline{\quad} + \underline{\quad}$$
$$= \underline{\quad}$$

b. $76 \times 24 = 76 \times (20 + \underline{\quad})$
$$= (76 \times 20) + (76 \times \underline{\quad})$$
$$= \underline{\quad} + \underline{\quad}$$
$$= \underline{\quad}$$

3. We can also use the distributive property this way. Copy and complete.

a. $48 \times 27 = (40 + 8) \times 27$
$$= (40 \times 27) + (8 \times \underline{\quad})$$
$$= \underline{\quad} + \underline{\quad}$$
$$= \underline{\quad}$$

b. $76 \times 24 = (70 + 6) \times 24$
$$= (70 \times \underline{\quad}) + (6 \times \underline{\quad})$$
$$= \underline{\quad} + \underline{\quad}$$
$$= \underline{\quad}$$

USING A SHORT FORM

1. Multiply 27 and 48.

$$27 \times 48 = (20 + 7) \times 48$$
$$= (20 \times 48) + (7 \times 48)$$
$$= 960 + \underline{\quad}$$
$$= \underline{\quad}$$

2. We can use a shorter form.

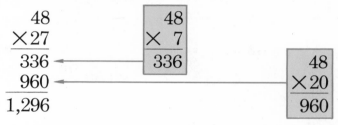

```
  48
×27
 336
 960
1,296
```

a. Compare the short form with the form in Item 1. What are the partial products?

b. What is the sum of the partial products?

3. Consider 76 × 24.

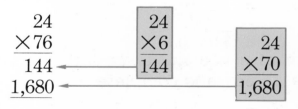

```
  24
×76
 144
1,680
```

a. Explain the partial products.

b. Find their sum.

4. Multiply.

a. 32
   ×22

b. 46
   ×34

c. 97
   ×86

d. 80
   ×94

EXERCISES

Multiply.

1. $\begin{array}{r} 44 \\ \times 11 \\ \hline \end{array}$
2. $\begin{array}{r} 44 \\ \times 22 \\ \hline \end{array}$
3. $\begin{array}{r} 44 \\ \times 33 \\ \hline \end{array}$
4. $\begin{array}{r} 47 \\ \times 44 \\ \hline \end{array}$

5. $\begin{array}{r} 82 \\ \times 83 \\ \hline \end{array}$
6. $\begin{array}{r} 49 \\ \times 37 \\ \hline \end{array}$
7. $\begin{array}{r} 38 \\ \times 41 \\ \hline \end{array}$
8. $\begin{array}{r} 97 \\ \times 86 \\ \hline \end{array}$

9. $\begin{array}{r} 98 \\ \times 89 \\ \hline \end{array}$
10. $\begin{array}{r} 47 \\ \times 41 \\ \hline \end{array}$
11. $\begin{array}{r} 68 \\ \times 12 \\ \hline \end{array}$
12. $\begin{array}{r} 97 \\ \times 84 \\ \hline \end{array}$

13. $\begin{array}{r} 11 \\ \times 99 \\ \hline \end{array}$
14. $\begin{array}{r} 47 \\ \times 88 \\ \hline \end{array}$
15. $\begin{array}{r} 67 \\ \times 49 \\ \hline \end{array}$
16. $\begin{array}{r} 84 \\ \times 36 \\ \hline \end{array}$

17. $\begin{array}{r} 69 \\ \times 55 \\ \hline \end{array}$
18. $\begin{array}{r} 28 \\ \times 22 \\ \hline \end{array}$
19. $\begin{array}{r} 17 \\ \times 18 \\ \hline \end{array}$
20. $\begin{array}{r} 22 \\ \times 43 \\ \hline \end{array}$

Let's Practice

Find the sum, difference, or product.

1. $\begin{array}{r} 4{,}786 \\ -2{,}198 \\ \hline \end{array}$
2. $\begin{array}{r} 834 \\ +297 \\ \hline \end{array}$
3. $\begin{array}{r} 409 \\ \times 8 \\ \hline \end{array}$
4. $\begin{array}{r} 3{,}492 \\ \times 3 \\ \hline \end{array}$

5. $\begin{array}{r} \$87.64 \\ \times 6 \\ \hline \end{array}$
6. $\begin{array}{r} \$100.08 \\ -89.49 \\ \hline \end{array}$
7. $\begin{array}{r} 349 \\ 476 \\ 1{,}284 \\ \hline \end{array}$
8. $\begin{array}{r} 982 \\ 476 \\ 287 \\ \hline \end{array}$

Make each sentence true. Use $>$, $<$, or $=$.

9. $7 \times 2 \equiv 15$

10. $10 \div 2 \equiv 5$

11. $8 \times 49 \equiv 9 \times 48$

12. $6 \times 48 \equiv 48 \div 6$

13. $372 \times 9 \equiv 9 \times 372$

14. $7 + 6 \equiv 6 \times 7$

15. $405 \div 5 \equiv 5 \times 405$

16. $7 + 8 \equiv 8 + 9$

HUNDREDS, TENS, AND ONES.

1. We have multiplied with multiples of ten. Copy and complete.

   a. $238 \times 20 = (238 \times 2) \times 10$
                  $= \underline{\hspace{1.5em}} \times 10$
                  $= \underline{\hspace{1.5em}}$

   b. $421 \times 40 = (421 \times 4) \times 10$
                  $= \underline{\hspace{1.5em}} \times 10$
                  $= \underline{\hspace{1.5em}}$

   c. 324×50 **d.** 821×30

2. Multiply 22 and 412.

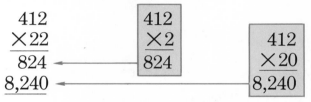

   a. Name the partial products.

   b. Find the sum of the partial products.

3. Multiply. Use the form in Item 2.

$$\begin{array}{r} 827 \\ \times 5 \\ \hline \end{array} \qquad \begin{array}{r} 827 \\ \times 40 \\ \hline \end{array} \qquad \begin{array}{r} 827 \\ \times 45 \\ \hline \end{array}$$

4. Explain each of these. Copy and complete.

   a.
$$\begin{array}{r} 238 \\ \times 44 \\ \hline 952 \\ 9{,}520 \\ \hline 10{,}472 \end{array} \quad \begin{array}{l} (\underline{\hspace{1em}} \times 238) \\ (40 \times \underline{\hspace{1em}}) \end{array}$$

   b.
$$\begin{array}{r} 984 \\ \times 86 \\ \hline 5{,}904 \\ 78{,}720 \\ \hline 84{,}624 \end{array} \quad \begin{array}{l} (\underline{\hspace{1em}} \times \underline{\hspace{1em}}) \\ (\underline{\hspace{1em}} \times 984) \end{array}$$

5. Find these products.

   a. 481
      ×12

   b. 690
      ×49

   c. 900
      ×49

   d. 807
      ×35

EXERCISES

Multiply.

  1. 481
     ×22

  2. 643
     ×33

  3. 829
     ×34

  4. 673
     ×24

  5. 481
     ×11

  6. 894
     ×39

  7. 478
     ×28

  8. 628
     ×37

  9. 426
     ×24

  10. 27
     ×22

  11. 39
     ×44

  12. 67
     ×88

Solve each problem.

13. Mrs. Davis boxes candles in a factory. She puts 12 candles in each box. How many candles does she pack in each of the following?

  a. 6 boxes   **b.** 12 boxes   **c.** 36 boxes

  d. 72 boxes   **e.** 144 boxes   **f.** 380 boxes

14. Mr. Greene baked 980 loaves of bread. By the end of the day he had 22 loaves left. How many loaves of bread did he sell?

15. Mr. Greene baked 15 dozen chocolate cupcakes and 24 dozen cream-filled cupcakes. How many cupcakes did he bake?

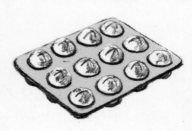

DO YOU REMEMBER?

Multiply.

1. 43 ×22	2. 31 ×23	3. 24 ×12	4. 12 ×26
5. 76 ×54	6. 92 ×47	7. 67 ×38	8. 96 ×38
9. 212 ×34	10. 132 ×23	11. 112 ×35	12. 411 ×27
13. 832 ×38	14. 432 ×85	15. 743 ×76	16. 568 ×43

Solve these problems.

17. There are 6 bottles of soda in a carton. How many bottles are in 84 cartons?

18. If there are 4 cartons of soda in a case, how many cartons are in 28 cases?

19. There are 24 bottles of soda in a case. How many bottles are in 28 cases?

20. For a party Mrs. Perry bought 8 cases and 3 cartons of soda. How many bottles did she buy in all?

21. Mr. Williams bakes 48 cookies on each cookie sheet. How many cookies can he bake on 27 cookie sheets?

USING MONEY

1. Mr. Smith bought 26 books. Each book cost $2.63. What was the total cost?

2. Multiply. Remember to express the product in dollars and cents.

   a. $6.32
    ×27

   b. $2.25
    ×44

   c. $3.68
    ×79

   d. $.89
    ×32

3. Mr. Jones, the coach, buys supplies for the elementary school basketball team.

$12.87 $10.98 $8.95 $.65

   a. He needs 7 pairs of socks. Estimate the cost. Think: $.65 is about $.70. Find the exact cost of 7 pairs of socks.

   b. Estimate the cost of 4 basketballs. Think: $12.87 is about $13.00.
   Find the exact cost of the basketballs.

   c. Estimate the cost of 7 pairs of shoes. Find the exact cost.

   d. Mr. Jones has 7 players. He bought a suit, shoes, and socks for each boy. What was the total cost?

4. Mr. Jarvis bought 8 tickets for the movies. Each ticket cost $2.50. How much did 8 tickets cost?

Estimate.

1. 7 × $4.95   **2.** 10 × $17.01   **3.** 15 × $9.99

4.-6. Find the exact answers for Exercises 1–3.

Multiply.

7. $7.69   **8.** $8.07   **9.** $4.69   **10.** $17.04
   ×24   ×98   ×89   ×23

UNEXPLORED TERRITORY

Sometimes we find interesting patterns when working with numbers. Look for a pattern as you find these products.

1. a. 37   **b.** 37   **c.** 37   **d.** 37   **e.** 37
      ×3   ×6   ×9   ×12   ×15

2. Use the pattern you found in Item 1 to make these sentences true. Check.

   a. 18 × 37 = □   **b.** □ × 37 = 777
   c. 24 × □ = 888   **d.** □ × 37 = 999

3. Find these products. Can you use the pattern?

   a. 37   **b.** 37   **c.** 37   **d.** 37
      ×33   ×36   ×39   ×42

4. Guess this product: 45 × 37

5. Look for a pattern as you multiply.

   a. 12,345,679   **b.** 12,345,679   **c.** 12,345,679
            ×9   ×18   ×27

DO YOU REMEMBER?

Divide.

1. $9\overline{)81}$ 2. $8\overline{)32}$ 3. $7\overline{)56}$ 4. $7\overline{)42}$

5. $9\overline{)72}$ 6. $7\overline{)28}$ 7. $9\overline{)36}$ 8. $8\overline{)56}$

9. $6\overline{)48}$ 10. $8\overline{)32}$ 11. $8\overline{)64}$ 12. $9\overline{)45}$

13. $8\overline{)48}$ 14. $5\overline{)35}$ 15. $8\overline{)40}$ 16. $9\overline{)63}$

17. $6\overline{)54}$ 18. $9\overline{)54}$ 19. $8\overline{)16}$ 20. $8\overline{)72}$

21. $6\overline{)36}$ 22. $7\overline{)49}$ 23. $6\overline{)42}$ 24. $7\overline{)63}$

25. $9\overline{)27}$ 26. $3\overline{)24}$ 27. $6\overline{)30}$ 28. $6\overline{)18}$

Solve each problem.

29. Find the cost of 4 tires at $32.10 a tire.

30. There are 485 cartons of milk sold in the school lunchroom each day. How many cartons are sold in 5 days?

31. Mr. Davis packs apples in gift packages. He puts 24 apples in each box. How many apples does he pack in each of the following?

a. 10 boxes

b. 20 boxes

c. 32 boxes

d. 100 boxes

e. 200 boxes

f. 500 boxes

CHAPTER REVIEW

Multiply.

1. $3 \times 40 = 3 \times (4 \times \underline{})$
   $= (3 \times 4) \times \underline{}$
   $= 12 \times \underline{}$
   $= \underline{}$

2. 8×80 3. 9×800 4. 4×600

5. 80×8 6. 800×9 7. 600×4

Use the commutative and associative properties.

8. $30 \times 400 = (3 \times 10) \times (4 \times \underline{})$
   $= (3 \times \underline{}) \times (10 \times 100)$
   $= \underline{} \times \underline{}$
   $= \underline{}$

9. 40×50 10. 40×500 11. 900×30

12. Multiply. What property is used?

   $7 \times 435 = 7 \times (400 + \underline{} + 5)$
   $= (7 \times 400) + (7 \times \underline{}) + (7 \times 5)$
   $= \underline{} + \underline{} + \underline{}$
   $= \underline{}$

Use the short form.

13. $\begin{array}{r} 213 \\ \times 7 \\ \hline \end{array}$ 14. $\begin{array}{r} 39 \\ \times 8 \\ \hline \end{array}$ 15. $\begin{array}{r} 4{,}118 \\ \times 2 \\ \hline \end{array}$ 16. $\begin{array}{r} 629 \\ \times 2 \\ \hline \end{array}$

17. Find the product 343×40. What property is used?

   $343 \times 40 = (343 \times 4) \times 10$
   $= \underline{}$

Round the greater factor to the nearest ten. Estimate.

18. 5 × 49   **19.** 8 × 64   **20.** 4 × 98

Round the greater factor to the nearest hundred. Estimate.

21. 5 × 492   **22.** 8 × 627   **23.** 2 × 945

24.-29. Find the exact products in Items 18–23.

30. Find the product 96 × 35. What property of multiplication is used?

$$96 \times 35 = (90 + 6) \times 35$$
$$= (90 \times \underline{\quad}) + (6 \times \underline{\quad})$$
$$= \underline{\quad} + \underline{\quad}$$
$$= \underline{\quad}$$

Multiply.

31. 87	**32.** 921	**33.** 476	**34.** $12.47
×22	×33	×94	×9

Solve the problem.

35. Jose's father bought 3 shirts and 2 neckties. Each shirt cost $6.98. How much did he pay for the 3 shirts?

Terms You Should Know

factor   product
estimate   partial product
associative property of multiplication
commutative property of multiplication
distributive property of multiplication
    over addition

CHAPTER TEST

Find each product or missing factor. Then name the property that is used.

1. $7 \times 90 = (7 \times \underline{\quad}) \times 10$
   $= \underline{\quad}$

2. $30 \times 30 = (3 \times 3) \times (10 \times \underline{\quad})$
   $= \underline{\quad}$

3. $8 \times 247 = 8 \times (200 + 40 + \underline{\quad})$
   $= (8 \times 200) + (8 \times 40) + (8 \times \underline{\quad})$
   $= 1600 + \underline{\quad} + \underline{\quad}$
   $= \underline{\quad}$

4. $921 \times 30 = (921 \times 3) \times \underline{\quad}$
   $= \underline{\quad}$

5. $76 \times 98 = 98 \times \underline{\quad}$

Multiply.

6. $46 \atop \times 3$	7. $909 \atop \times 8$	8. $3{,}472 \atop \times 4$	9. $68 \atop \times 7$
10. $87 \atop \times 22$	11. $399 \atop \times 80$	12. $768 \atop \times 95$	13. $542 \atop \times 66$

Solve each problem.

14. There are 4 quarts in one gallon. How many quarts are in 20 gallons?

15. There are 96 seats in each section of the stadium. There are 48 sections. How many seats are in the stadium?

16. How much will 95 lunches cost at $.45 each?

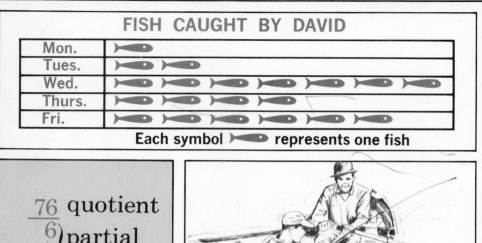

FISH CAUGHT BY DAVID

Mon.	🐟
Tues.	🐟 🐟
Wed.	🐟 🐟 🐟 🐟 🐟 🐟 🐟
Thurs.	🐟 🐟 🐟 🐟
Fri.	🐟 🐟 🐟 🐟 🐟 🐟

Each symbol 🐟 represents one fish

$$
\begin{array}{r}
76 \\
6 \\
20 \\
50 \\
\hline
3 \overline{)228} \\
150 \\
\hline
78 \\
60 \\
\hline
18 \\
18 \\
\hline
0
\end{array}
$$

76 quotient

6 ⎫
20 ⎬ partial
50 ⎭ quotients

CHAPTER SEVEN

Division of Whole Numbers

REMEMBERING DIVISION

1. A checkerboard has 64 squares. It has 8 squares in each row. How many rows are there?

   Think: $64 \div 8 = \triangle$ or $8 \times \triangle = 64$

2. The unknown quotient in a division sentence is the same as what number in a related multiplication sentence? Make these sentences true.

   Quotient

   Missing Factor

   $$64 \div 8 = \triangle \qquad\qquad 8 \times \triangle = 64$$

3. Make each pair of number sentences true.

   a. $6 \times \triangle = 42$ $42 \div 6 = \triangle$

   b. $7 \times \triangle = 42$ $42 \div 7 = \triangle$

   c. $9 \times \triangle = 63$ $63 \div 9 = \triangle$

   d. $8 \times \triangle = 48$ $48 \div 8 = \triangle$

4. Divide. Think of a missing factor.

   a. $48 \div 6$ **b.** $48 \div 8$ **c.** $54 \div 9$

   d. $28 \div 7$ **e.** $56 \div 8$ **f.** $24 \div 4$

5. There are 36 boys in the park. How many baseball teams of 9 boys each can be formed?

   a. Subtract to find the number of teams.

   b. Make the sentences $9 \times \triangle = 36$ and $36 \div 9 = \triangle$ true.

Divide.

1. $6\overline{)48}$ 2. $7\overline{)42}$ 3. $8\overline{)32}$ 4. $9\overline{)27}$

5. $4\overline{)36}$ 6. $3\overline{)24}$ 7. $7\overline{)21}$ 8. $4\overline{)32}$

9. $3\overline{)18}$ 10. $8\overline{)64}$ 11. $6\overline{)36}$ 12. $4\overline{)24}$

13. $5\overline{)35}$ 14. $7\overline{)28}$ 15. $9\overline{)36}$ 16. $6\overline{)24}$

Solve each problem.

17. Six bottles of soda will fill a carton.

   a. How many cartons can you fill if you have 18 bottles?

   b. How many cartons can you fill if you have 30 bottles?

   c. How many cartons can you fill if you have 54 bottles?

18. Sue has 42 postcards in her collection. She can put 7 postcards on each page of her book. How many pages can she fill?

19. Mr. Lawler has 28 pupils in his science class. How many groups of 7 pupils can he form?

20. The police department is packing 81 badges in boxes. How many boxes are needed if 9 badges fit in each box?

21. Mrs. West has 49 buttons to sew on shirts. She plans to sew 7 buttons on each shirt. She has enough buttons for how many shirts?

DO YOU REMEMBER?

Multiply.

1. 7×40 2. 10×48 3. 10×87

4. 15×10 5. 60×10 6. 10×321

7. 20×8 8. 300×2 9. 4×900

10. 4×800 11. 80×5 12. 40×9

Find the missing factors.

13. $\square \times 3 = 90$ 14. $\square \times 2 = 600$

15. $5 \times \triangle = 50$ 16. $\square \times 5 = 500$

17. $4 \times \triangle = 240$ 18. $7 \times \triangle = 4{,}200$

19. $\triangle \times 6 = 300$ 20. $\triangle \times 9 = 630$

21. $8 \times \triangle = 5{,}600$ 22. $6 \times \triangle = 420$

23. $9 \times \triangle = 540$ 24. $4 \times \triangle = 3{,}600$

Make each sentence true.

25. $3 \times \triangle = 60$ 26. $7 \times \triangle = 280$
    $60 \div 3 = \triangle$ $280 \div 7 = \triangle$

27. $5 \times \triangle = 300$ 28. $6 \times \triangle = 360$
    $300 \div 5 = \triangle$ $360 \div 6 = \triangle$

29. $4{,}800 \div 8 = \triangle$ 30. $560 \div 8 = \triangle$

31. $180 \div 6 = \triangle$ 32. $630 \div 9 = \triangle$

33. $3{,}200 \div 4 = \triangle$ 34. $490 \div 7 = \triangle$

USING SUBTRACTION TO DIVIDE

The children in Mrs. Moore's room were showing how they divided 70 by 7.

1. Pat showed her work.

    a. How is Pat finding the quotient?

    b. Complete Pat's work. Subtract one seven at a time.

    c. What is 70 ÷ 7?

2. Sue and Mary showed their work like this.

Sue		Mary	
		10	
7)70		7)70	
42	6 sevens	70	10 sevens
28		0	
28	4 sevens		
0	10 sevens		

    a. How many sevens did Sue subtract each time?

    b. Explain Mary's work.

    c. How does the sentence $7 \times \triangle = 70$ help us find the quotient?

    d. Who made the better use of her knowledge of multiplication?

3. Divide. Show two different ways for each.

    a. 4)80   **b.** 2)400   **c.** 5)300

USING MULTIPLICATION TO DIVIDE

Think of $108 \div 6 = \square$ and $6 \times \square = 108$. Can you think of the missing factor easily? Study each pupil's work for $108 \div 6$.

1. Bob started to subtract one six at a time.

   Bob

   $$6\overline{)108}$$
   $$\underline{6} \quad \text{1 six}$$
   $$102$$
   $$\underline{6} \quad \text{1 six}$$

   a. Copy and complete his work.

   b. How many sixes can you subtract?

2. Stan said that subtracting one six at a time takes too long.

   Stan

   $$6\overline{)108}$$
   $$\underline{30} \quad \text{5 sixes}$$
   $$78$$
   $$\underline{30} \quad \text{5 sixes}$$
   $$48$$
   $$\underline{48} \quad \text{8 sixes}$$
   $$0 \quad \text{18 sixes}$$

   a. How many sixes did he subtract at first? the second time? the third time?

   b. How many sixes did he subtract in all?

3. Dale said that he guessed. He knew that $10 \times 6 = 60$ and that $20 \times 6 = 120$.

   Dale

   $$6\overline{)108}$$
   $$\underline{60} \quad \text{10 sixes}$$
   $$48$$
   $$\underline{48} \quad \text{8 sixes}$$
   $$0 \quad \text{18 sixes}$$

   a. Why did he start by subtracting 10 sixes instead of 20 sixes?

   b. $108 - 60 = \underline{}$

   c. $48 \div 6 = \underline{}$

   d. How many sixes did he subtract in all?

4. Did all students find the same quotient? Who made the best use of multiplication?

5. Mary and Alice showed their work for 168 ÷ 7. Copy and complete their work.

Mary

```
7)168
   70    10 sevens
   ──
   98
   70    ___ sevens
   ──
   28
   28    ___ sevens
   ──
    0    ___ sevens
```

Alice

```
7)168
  140    ___ sevens
  ───
   28
   28    ___ sevens
   ──
    0    ___ sevens
```

a. How many times did Mary subtract? What was her first guess?

b. How many times did Alice subtract? What was her first guess?

c. Which girl's first guess was closer to the quotient?

d. What is the quotient?

e. Check. Multiply 7 and 24.

EXERCISES

Find the quotient.

1. 6)96	**2.** 3)261	**3.** 2)184	**4.** 7)350
5. 8)120	**6.** 2)84	**7.** 2)92	**8.** 8)728
9. 6)360	**10.** 7)427	**11.** 3)153	**12.** 4)264
13. 8)424	**14.** 4)336	**15.** 6)498	**16.** 9)297

PARTIAL QUOTIENTS

We often need to guess more than once when we divide.

1. Study Mary's work for $228 \div 3$.

   a. What was her first guess? We can say her first partial quotient was 50.

   b. What was her second guess?

   c. What was her third guess?

   d. Add the partial quotients.

   e. What is $228 \div 3$?

```
        76  quotient
         6 ⎫
        20 ⎬ partial
        50 ⎭ quotients
   3)228
       150    50 threes
        78
        60    20 threes
        18
        18    6 threes
         0
```

2. Study Bill's work for $228 \div 3$.

   a. What was Bill's first partial quotient?

   b. What was Bill's second partial quotient?

   c. Add to find the quotient.

   d. Check: $3 \times 76 =$ ____

```
           quotient
         6 ⎫ partial
        70 ⎭ quotients
   3)228
       210    70 threes
        18
        18    6 threes
         0
```

3. Whose first guess was better?

4. Divide and check.

   a. $7)\overline{483}$ b. $4)\overline{304}$ c. $6)\overline{186}$ d. $9)\overline{711}$

DO YOU REMEMBER?

Add.

1. 23
   +49

2. 649
   +287

3. 398
   +4,769

4. 888
   +234

5. 1,987
   4,860
   7,948

6. 3,879
   4,693
   8,748
   2,863

7. $8.64
   9.86
   10.47

8. 34,986
   +98,049

Subtract.

9. 87
   −54

10. 87
    −59

11. 829
    −486

12. 387
    −198

13. $13.86
    −7.34

14. 4,000
    −3,621

15. 9,007
    −8,765

16. 14,982
    −3,694

Multiply.

17. 48
    ×2

18. 54
    ×6

19. 27
    ×9

20. 83
    ×4

21. 63
    ×45

22. 470
    ×35

23. 570
    ×81

24. 394
    ×82

Solve each problem.

25. Mr. Larson has 60 boxes of canned fruit in his store. Each box contains 24 cans. How many cans are in the 60 boxes?

26. Jane is 24 years old. Her father is 60 years old. What is the difference in their ages?

27. A gas station sold 46 new tires and 57 used tires. How many tires were sold in all?

We can make better guesses as we learn more about dividing.

1. Think of $6\overline{)84}$.

   a. The quotient is greater than 10 because $10 \times 6 < 84$.

   b. Is the quotient greater than 100? Why?

2. The quotient is between 10 and 100.

   a. Is the quotient greater than 20? Why?

   b. We choose 10 as our first guess. Multiply:
   $$10 \times 6 = \underline{\quad}.$$

$$\begin{array}{r} 10 \\ 6\overline{)84} \\ 60 \end{array}$$ 10 sixes

   c. Subtract.
   $$84 - 60 = \underline{\quad}.$$

$$\begin{array}{r} 4 \\ 10 \\ 6\overline{)84} \\ 60 \\ \hline 24 \\ 24 \\ \hline 0 \end{array}$$ 10 sixes

4 sixes

3. a. Think: $6 \times \underline{\quad} = 24$ What is the second partial quotient?

   b. What is the quotient? Check.

4. We used multiples of ten. Name the first 9 multiples of ten.

5. Copy and complete each division.

   a.
   $$\begin{array}{r} 10 \\ 2\overline{)36} \\ 20 \end{array}$$ 10 twos

   b.
   $$\begin{array}{r} 10 \\ 8\overline{)96} \\ 80 \end{array}$$ 10 eights

6. Consider $7\overline{)168}$.

a. Is the quotient greater than 10? Why?

b. Is the quotient greater than 100? Why?

7. Now think of multiples of ten that are less than 100.

a. 10 × 7 = 70. Is 70 greater than 168?

$$\begin{array}{r} 20 \\ 7\overline{)168} \\ 140 \\ \hline 28 \end{array}$$ 20 sevens

b. 20 × 7 = 140. Is 140 greater than 168?

c. 30 × 7 = 210. Is 210 greater than 168?

d. Our first guess is 20. Why?

8. Complete the division.

a. Think: 28 ÷ 7 = ____

b. Add the partial quotients.

c. Check. 7 × 24 = ____

$$\begin{array}{r} 24 \\ \hline 4 \\ 20 \\ 7\overline{)168} \\ 140 \\ \hline 28 \\ 28 \\ \hline 0 \end{array}$$
20 sevens

4 sevens

9. Copy and complete each division.

a. $\begin{array}{r} 30 \\ 8\overline{)256} \\ 240 \end{array}$ 30 eights

b. $\begin{array}{r} 80 \\ 6\overline{)516} \\ 480 \end{array}$ 80 sixes

EXERCISES

Divide.

1. $2\overline{)176}$ **2.** $4\overline{)376}$ **3.** $9\overline{)252}$ **4.** $5\overline{)445}$

5. $6\overline{)276}$ **6.** $3\overline{)222}$ **7.** $8\overline{)592}$ **8.** $7\overline{)504}$

DIVIDING TENS AND ONES

1. Think of $155 \div 5$. Guess the first partial quotient. Is the first partial quotient:

   a. Greater than 10? What is 10×5?

   b. Greater than 100? What is 100×5?

2. Which multiple of ten should we choose? 10? 20? 30? 40? Why?

3. Complete the division.

   a. What is 30×5?

   b. Subtract.

   c. What is $5 \div 5$?

   d. What is the quotient? Check.

$$
\begin{array}{r}
\underline{} \text{ quotient} \\
30 \\
5\overline{)155} \\
\underline{150} \quad 30 \text{ fives} \\
5 \\
\underline{5} \quad \underline{} \text{ five} \\
0
\end{array}
$$

4. We follow several steps each time we divide. We guess, we multiply, and we subtract. Use these steps to find $256 \div 8$.

EXERCISES

Divide.

1. $2\overline{)96}$ 2. $2\overline{)48}$ 3. $4\overline{)48}$ 4. $6\overline{)486}$

5. $6\overline{)528}$ 6. $4\overline{)364}$ 7. $9\overline{)225}$ 8. $8\overline{)360}$

9. $2\overline{)184}$ 10. $4\overline{)184}$ 11. $7\overline{)448}$ 12. $9\overline{)261}$

13. $8\overline{)160}$ 14. $7\overline{)476}$ 15. $5\overline{)275}$ 16. $6\overline{)276}$

17. $4\overline{)256}$ 18. $5\overline{)370}$ 19. $7\overline{)273}$ 20. $8\overline{)584}$

DIVIDING HUNDREDS

1. Think of $848 \div 2$.

   a. Is the quotient greater than 10?

$$10 \times 2 < 848$$

   b. Is the quotient greater than 100?

$$100 \times 2 < 848$$

   c. Is the quotient greater than 1,000? Why?

   d. Is the quotient between 100 and 1,000?

2. Guess the first partial quotient.

   a. Should we use 100? 200? 300? 400? 500?

   b. Think: $400 \times 2 =$ ___

   c. Subtract.

```
    400
2)848
    800      400 twos
     48
```

```
     20
    400
2)848
    800      400 twos
     48
     40      20 twos
```

3. Guess the second partial quotient.

   a. Is it greater than 10? 20? 30?

   b. Think: $20 \times 2 =$ ___

   c. Subtract.

```
    424      quotient
      4
     20
    400
2)848
    800      400 twos
     48
     40      20 twos
      8
      8      4 twos
      0      424 twos
```

4. Complete the division.

   a. Think: $8 \div 2 =$ ___

   b. Subtract.

5. What is $848 \div 2$? Check.

6. Consider 849 ÷ 3.

    a. Guess the first partial quotient. Is it greater than 10? 100? 1,000?

    b. What is the first partial quotient? Why?

    c. Complete the division.

$$\begin{array}{r} 3\overline{)849} \\ 600 \\ \hline 249 \end{array} \quad \underline{\hspace{1cm}} \text{ threes}$$

    d. Check.

7. Guess the first partial quotient for each division. Do not divide.

    a. $5\overline{)785}$ **b.** $2\overline{)680}$ **c.** $9\overline{)963}$ **d.** $8\overline{)920}$

EXERCISES

Divide.

    1. $3\overline{)720}$ **2.** $3\overline{)735}$ **3.** $6\overline{)828}$ **4.** $8\overline{)896}$

    5. $4\overline{)648}$ **6.** $3\overline{)639}$ **7.** $2\overline{)724}$ **8.** $5\overline{)635}$

    9. $7\overline{)805}$ **10.** $8\overline{)912}$ **11.** $9\overline{)999}$ **12.** $5\overline{)965}$

Solve each problem.

13. Mr. Post has 732 cartons of oranges. He must deliver 6 cartons to each of the stores on his list. To how many stores can he deliver the oranges?

14. There are 417 people at the parents' meeting at our school. They are divided equally into 3 groups. How many people are in each group?

USING MULTIPLES OF 100

1. Mr. Miller is putting 3 tennis balls in each can. How many cans does he need for 618 tennis balls?

   a. Is the quotient greater than 10? greater than 100? greater than 1,000?

$$\begin{array}{r} 200 \\ 3\overline{)618} \\ 600 \\ \hline 18 \end{array}$$ 200 threes

   b. What multiple of 100 should we use? 100? 200? 300?

   c. What is 200 × 3? Subtract.

   d. What is the second partial quotient?

   e. What is 618 ÷ 3?

$$\begin{array}{r} 206 \\ \hline 6 \\ 200 \\ 3\overline{)618} \\ 600 \\ \hline 18 \\ 18 \\ \hline 0 \end{array}$$

   200 threes

   6 threes

   206 threes

2. Consider 1,275 ÷ 3. Is the quotient greater than 10? 100? 1,000?

   a. What multiple of 100 should we use?

   b. What is 400 × 3? Subtract.

$$\begin{array}{r} 400 \\ 3\overline{)1,275} \\ 1,200 \end{array}$$ 400 threes

226

c. Guess the second partial quotient. Is it greater than 10? greater than 100? Why?

d. What multiple of ten should we use? 10? 20? 30?

e. Complete the division. Check.

$$
\begin{array}{r}
20 \\
400 \\
3\overline{)1{,}275} \\
1{,}200 \quad \text{400 threes} \\
\overline{75} \\
60 \quad \underline{}\text{ threes} \\
\overline{15}
\end{array}
$$

3. Guess the first partial quotient. Do not divide.

a. $3\overline{)1{,}104}$ **b.** $5\overline{)385}$ **c.** $2\overline{)1{,}852}$ **d.** $9\overline{)873}$

EXERCISES

Divide and check.

1. $4\overline{)824}$ **2.** $8\overline{)3{,}392}$ **3.** $6\overline{)4{,}548}$ **4.** $8\overline{)4{,}376}$

5. $3\overline{)903}$ **6.** $6\overline{)2{,}292}$ **7.** $5\overline{)1{,}540}$ **8.** $9\overline{)1{,}071}$

9. $5\overline{)1{,}710}$ **10.** $9\overline{)5{,}643}$ **11.** $7\overline{)686}$ **12.** $7\overline{)2{,}569}$

Let's Practice

Solve each problem.

1. Mr. Baker wants to put a fence around his garden. It is 40 feet long and 30 feet wide. How many feet of fencing does he need?

2. Linda's mother plans to put wall-to-wall carpeting in the living room. The room is 20 feet long and 15 feet wide. What is the area of the room?

PROBLEM SOLVING

1. Benjamin has 448 sea shells. He puts 8 shells in each box. How many boxes does he need?
Think: $448 \div 8 = \triangle$ or $8 \times \triangle = 448$.

2. Mr. Smith buys 3,750 pounds of meat in 5 weeks for the school lunchroom. He buys the same amount each week. How many pounds does he buy each week?

3. There were 336 children on the playground. The coach had them line up in rows in different ways. Find the number of rows that were formed each time. Complete the chart.

Children in Each Row	Number of Rows
8	_____
7	_____
6	_____
4	_____
3	_____

Let's Practice

Divide. Check.

1. $2\overline{)56}$ 2. $2\overline{)88}$ 3. $3\overline{)96}$ 4. $6\overline{)72}$

5. $7\overline{)91}$ 6. $4\overline{)52}$ 7. $5\overline{)65}$ 8. $8\overline{)136}$

9. $9\overline{)819}$ 10. $9\overline{)738}$ 11. $8\overline{)152}$ 12. $3\overline{)186}$

LOOKING FOR A QUOTIENT

1. Look at the related sentences $6 \div 2 = \square$ and $\triangle \times 2 = 6$. What whole number makes the sentences true?

2. Write a related multiplication sentence for each division sentence. Then make the sentences true.

   a. $14 \div 7 = \square$ b. $18 \div 9 = \square$

   c. $12 \div 3 = \square$ d. $16 \div 2 = \square$

   e. $18 \div 3 = \square$ f. $4 \div 4 = \square$

3. Write a related multiplication sentence for $7 \div 2 = \square$. Does any whole number make the sentence true?

The division $7 \div 2$ does not have a whole number for a quotient.

4. Consider $8 \div 3 = \square$. Write a related multiplication. Does any whole number make the sentence true?

EXERCISES

Tell whether there is a whole number for a quotient. If there is one, find it.

1. $8 \div 1$ 2. $8 \div 2$ 3. $19 \div 6$

4. $8 \div 4$ 5. $8 \div 5$ 6. $8 \div 8$

7. $5 \div 2$ 8. $24 \div 6$ 9. $7 \div 2$

10. $14 \div 3$ 11. $16 \div 4$ 12. $24 \div 5$

REMAINDERS

1. There were 7 boys in the park. They were standing in teams with 2 boys on each team.

   a. How many teams were there?

   b. How many boys were not on a team of 2?

   c. Explain the subtraction that shows this.

$$
\begin{array}{rl}
7 & \\
-2 & \text{1 two} \\
\hline
5 & \\
-2 & \text{1 two} \\
\hline
3 & \\
-2 & \text{1 two} \\
\hline
1 & \text{3 twos}
\end{array}
$$

2. We can also use division. Explain the work at the right. The 1 is called a *remainder*.

$$
\begin{array}{r}
3 \\
2\overline{)7} \\
6 \quad (3 \times 2) \\
\hline
1
\end{array}
$$

3. We can also write $7 = (3 \times 2) + 1$ to describe the problem.

   a. How many sets of 2 are shown?

   b. How many members are left over?

   c. Are there enough members left over to make another set of two?

4. There were 8 girls. They were divided into teams of 3.

    a. How many teams were there?

    b. How many girls were not on a team of 3?

    c. Copy and complete.
       Check your answer. $3\overline{)8}$

    d. Make this sentence true.
       $\dfrac{6}{2}$ ___ threes remainder

       (___ × 3) + 2 = 8

5. Copy and complete each division. Write a true sentence to show a check.

    a. $7\overline{)32}$ **b.** $3\overline{)19}$ **c.** $4\overline{)26}$ **d.** $9\overline{)49}$

6. Is the remainder greater than or less than the number you divided by? Why?

EXERCISES

Divide. Write a true sentence to show a check.

    1. $9\overline{)48}$ **2.** $7\overline{)25}$ **3.** $3\overline{)13}$ **4.** $6\overline{)49}$

    5. $8\overline{)27}$ **6.** $8\overline{)49}$ **7.** $9\overline{)74}$ **8.** $9\overline{)84}$

    9. $6\overline{)45}$ **10.** $4\overline{)34}$ **11.** $7\overline{)29}$ **12.** $5\overline{)18}$

Solve each problem.

13. How many baseball teams of 9 boys each can be formed with 23 boys? How many boys will not be on a team?

14. How many nickels can you get in exchange for 32 pennies? How many extra pennies will you have?

PROBLEM SOLVING

1. There are 32 boys in the gym. How many teams with 5 boys each can be formed? How many extra boys will there be?

   a. What is the remainder?

   b. Check. Make this sentence true.

   $(6 \times 5) +$ ___ $= 32$

$$\begin{array}{r} 6 \\ 5\overline{)32} \\ 30 \\ \hline 2 \end{array}$$

___ fives

2. How many teams with 3 children each can be formed with 17 children?

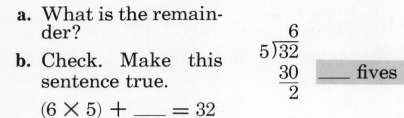

Mary

$$\begin{array}{r} 4 \\ 3\overline{)17} \\ 12 \\ \hline 5 \end{array}$$

4 threes

Bob

$$\begin{array}{r} 5 \\ 3\overline{)17} \\ 15 \\ \hline 2 \end{array}$$

5 threes

   a. Study Mary's work.
      Does $17 = (4 \times 3) + 5$?

   b. Study Bob's work.
      Does $17 = (5 \times 3) + 2$?

   c. Compare Mary's remainder with the divisor 3. What was wrong with her answer?

3. Mary corrected her work. It is shown at the right. Explain what she did.

$$\begin{array}{r} 5 \\ \overline{1} \\ 4 \\ 3\overline{)17} \\ 12 \\ \hline 5 \\ 3 \\ \hline 2 \end{array}$$

4 threes

1 three

5 threes

232

4. How many teams with 9 boys each can be formed from a group of 68 boys? How many extra boys will there be?

Solve each problem.

1. Al has 38 pennies.

    a. How many nickels can he get for his 38 pennies?

    b. How many pennies will he have left?

2. A carton holds 6 bottles of soda. How many cartons can you fill with 45 bottles? How many extra bottles will you have?

3. John had 45 marbles and some sacks. He put 5 marbles in each sack. How many sacks did he use? How many marbles were left?

4. There are 29 new bicycle tires in the store. There are enough tires for how many bicycles? How many extra tires are there?

5. There are 62 boys in the park. How many baseball teams of 9 boys each can be made? How many boys will be left?

6. There are 20 boys in the gym. How many teams of 6 boys each can be made? How many boys would not be on a team?

7. The teacher asked 32 children to line up in rows of 5 children each. How many rows did they make? How many children were left? Check your answer.

DO YOU REMEMBER?

Add.

1. 8	**2.** 20	**3.** 47	**4.** 680
7	30	81	290
6	80	96	460
9	90	48	390
4	70	27	170

5. 397	**6.** 3,490	**7.** 3,876	**8.** 87,643
286	2,860	4,987	27,891
498	8,700	4,089	38,761
347	9,490	9,999	34,989

Subtract.

9. 348	**10.** 382	**11.** 382	**12.** 382
−176	−193	−183	−173

13. 10,000	**14.** 40,007	**15.** $128.76	**16.** $379.48
−8,763	−3,089	−98.89	−189.39

Multiply.

17. 74	**18.** 987	**19.** 207	**20.** 4,170
×6	×4	×9	×5

21. 487	**22.** 389	**23.** 479	**24.** 1,435
×40	×43	×97	×88

Divide.

25. 7)42   **26.** 4)45   **27.** 7)560   **28.** 8)574

29. 4)347   **30.** 2)189   **31.** 6)564   **32.** 5)405

33. 3)295   **34.** 5)478   **35.** 9)759   **36.** 7)528

37. 6)567   **38.** 8)499   **39.** 4)393   **40.** 3)197

234

When we divide can we tell how many different remainders are possible?

1. Divide each of these numbers by 4.

   0, 1, 12, 13, 14, 15, 16, 21, 23, 26

   a. What is the smallest remainder?

   b. What is the largest remainder?

   c. How many different remainders are possible when dividing by 4? Name them.

2. Divide each number by 5.

   10, 11, 12, 13, 14, 15, 16, 17, 18, 19, 20

   a. What is the smallest remainder?

   b. What is the largest remainder?

   c. How many different remainders are possible when dividing by 5? Name them.

3. Divide 7, 8, 9, 10, 11, 12, 13, and 14 by 6. Find all the different remainders. What is the smallest possible remainder? the largest?

4. a. What different remainders are possible when we divide by 3? by 7? by 9?

   b. How many different remainders did you find for each?

   c. Can you guess how many different remainders are possible when we divide by 8?

5. Divide.

   a. $8\overline{)265}$ b. $7\overline{)325}$ c. $2\overline{)911}$ d. $8\overline{)850}$

PRACTICE IN FINDING REMAINDERS

1. Consider $409 \div 7 = \square$. Study the work below.

   a. Why is 50 a good first guess?

   b. Find 50×7.

   c. Consider $59 \div 7$. Is there a whole number quotient?

   d. $7 \times \underline{\hspace{1cm}}$ is close to 59.

$$
\begin{array}{r}
58 \text{ r } 3 \\
\hline
8 \\
50 \\
7\overline{)409} \\
350 \\
\hline
59 \\
56 \\
\hline
3 \\
\end{array}
$$

2. Check the answer. Is this a true sentence?
   $409 = (58 \times 7) + 3$

EXERCISES

Divide and check.

1. $8\overline{)435}$ 2. $4\overline{)226}$ 3. $4\overline{)375}$ 4. $4\overline{)186}$

5. $5\overline{)461}$ 6. $6\overline{)104}$ 7. $8\overline{)281}$ 8. $7\overline{)400}$

9. $2\overline{)199}$ 10. $8\overline{)407}$ 11. $9\overline{)400}$ 12. $5\overline{)402}$

Solve the problem.

13. Dick divided his collection of 305 stamps equally among 4 of his friends. How many did each friend get? How many were left over?

DIVIDING BY MULTIPLES OF TEN

1. Make the pairs of related sentences true.

   a. $10 \times \triangle = 90$ **b.** $30 \times \triangle = 120$
   $90 \div 10 = \triangle$ $120 \div 30 = \triangle$

   In each division we divided by a multiple of ten.

2. Consider $267 \div 40$.

   a. Make your first guess.

   Try 40×1.
   Try 40×10.

   $$\begin{array}{r} 6 \\ 40\overline{)267} \\ 240 \end{array}$$

   b. Our first guess is between 1 and 10. Why?

   c. Should we choose 2? 3? 4? 5? 6? 7?

   d. Multiply: 40×6 ___.

   e. Subtract.

   f. What is the remainder?

   $$\begin{array}{r} 6 \\ 40\overline{)267} \\ 240 \\ \hline 27 \end{array}$$

   g. Check:
   $(6 \times 40) + 27 = \square$

3. Divide and check.

   a. $30\overline{)259}$ **b.** $50\overline{)439}$ **c.** $90\overline{)624}$ **d.** $70\overline{)124}$

EXERCISES

Divide and check.

1. $20\overline{)189}$ 2. $30\overline{)296}$ 3. $50\overline{)412}$ 4. $30\overline{)248}$

5. $40\overline{)315}$ 6. $60\overline{)360}$ 7. $90\overline{)721}$ 8. $80\overline{)493}$

9. $90\overline{)672}$ 10. $60\overline{)558}$ 11. $90\overline{)651}$ 12. $70\overline{)348}$

MORE DIVISION

1. Make these pairs of related sentences true.

   a. $40 \times \square = 2,000$ **b.** $50 \times \triangle = 1,000$
   $2,000 \div 40 = \square$ $1,000 \div 50 = \triangle$

2. Think of $882 \div 80$.

   a. Make your first guess.

   Try 80×1.
   Try 80×10.

$$\begin{array}{r} 10 \\ 80\overline{)882} \\ 800 \\ \hline 82 \end{array}$$

   b. Is 800 close to 882?
   What is 80×20?

3. **a.** Make your second guess.

   Try 80×1.
   Subtract.

   b. Add: $10 + 1$.

   c. What is the remainder?

$$\begin{array}{r} 1 \\ 10 \\ 80\overline{)882} \\ 800 \\ \hline 82 \\ 80 \\ \hline 2 \end{array}$$

4. Divide and check. Explain each step.

   a. $60\overline{)1,732}$ **b.** $50\overline{)1,821}$ **c.** $20\overline{)328}$

EXERCISES

Divide and check.

1. $70\overline{)910}$ 2. $10\overline{)396}$ 3. $90\overline{)993}$ 4. $80\overline{)874}$

5. $20\overline{)478}$ 6. $30\overline{)493}$ 7. $50\overline{)1,632}$ 8. $60\overline{)1,320}$

9. $50\overline{)843}$ 10. $70\overline{)982}$ 11. $60\overline{)784}$ 12. $40\overline{)691}$

DO YOU REMEMBER?

Do each exercise.

1. 87	**2.** 960	**3.** $68.74	**4.** 68,492
96	380	98.76	48,764
49	249	39.84	39,876

5. 758
  $\times 9$

6. 849
  $\times 23$

7. 1,001
  -899

8. 1,010
  -899

9. 40,760
  $-31,598$

10. 6,482
  $\times 17$

11. $28.37
  $\times 49$

12. $684.27
  -149.38

13. 1,000
  -166

14. 74
  $\times 8$

15. $3\overline{)147}$

16. $30\overline{)147}$

Make each sentence true. Use $>$, $<$, or $=$.

17. $8 \times (12 \times 28) \equiv (8 \times 12) \times 284$

18. $1,284 + 3,987 \equiv 3,897 + 1,284$

19. $(687 + 943) + 349 \equiv 687 + (943 + 349)$

20. $82 \times (10 + 8) \equiv (82 \times 10) + (82 \times 8)$

21. $(3 \times 7) + 8 \equiv 3 \times (7 + 8)$

UNEXPLORED TERRITORY

Copy the table below. Compare the numbers in Row A and Row B. How are they related?

Name the missing numbers using multiplication and addition.

Row A	1	2	3	4	5	6	7	8
Row B	3	5	7	9				

USING MONEY

1. Mr. Smith paid $1.25 for 5 bags of popcorn. How much did each bag cost?
Think of $1.25 as 125 cents. $125 \div 5 = \square$ or $5 \times \square = 125$.

$$\begin{array}{r} 25 \\ \underline{5} \\ 20 \\ 5\overline{)125} \\ \underline{100} \\ 25 \\ \underline{25} \\ 0 \end{array}$$

a. Divide as you do with whole numbers.

25 cents or $.25

b. Write the answer using a dollar sign.

2. David paid $.35 for 7 candy bars. How much did each one cost?
Think: $35 \div 7 = \square$ or $7 \times \square = 35$.
Divide and check.

$$\begin{array}{r} 5 \\ 7\overline{)35} \\ \underline{35} \\ 0 \end{array}$$

5 cents or $.05

3. If $1.00 is shared equally among 3 people, how much will each person receive? Will there be any extra money that cannot be shared?

$$\begin{array}{r} 33 \\ \underline{3} \\ 30 \\ 3\overline{)100} \\ \underline{90} \\ 10 \\ \underline{9} \\ 1 \end{array}$$

a. Check the answer for the division.

b. Does the remainder mean dollars or cents?

33 cents, r 1 cent or $.33, r $.01

4. Divide and check.

    a. $4.88 ÷ 2   **b.** $.72 ÷ 9   **c.** $.38 ÷ 7

Divide and check.

  1. $8.40 ÷ 4   **2.** $3.24 ÷ 6   **3.** $4.25 ÷ 5

  4. $2.38 ÷ 7   **5.** $3.16 ÷ 4   **6.** $.48 ÷ 7

  7. $.68 ÷ 7   **8.** $10.00 ÷ 4   **9.** $37.48 ÷ 8

10. $6.50 ÷ 5   **11.** $7.20 ÷ 9   **12.** $98.99 ÷ 8

Solve each problem.

13. Chris bought 3 notebooks for $.60. How much did each notebook cost?

14. If 6 baseballs cost $13.50, what does one baseball cost?

15. Charlie's father paid $56.00 to rent a car for 7 days. How much did it cost to rent the car for one day?

16. Look at the ad at the right. How much would each of the following items cost?

  a. 1 pear

  b. 1 apple

  c. 1 orange

  d. 1 can of soda

  e. 2 pears

  f. 2 apples

  g. 3 oranges

SPECIAL

Pears	3 for $.39
Apples	3 for $.33
Oranges	2 for $.38
Cans of soda	2 for $.20

AVERAGES

Mary had an average score of 8 on her tests. What is an average?

1. Mary's family used these cans of soda.

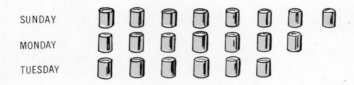

SUNDAY
MONDAY
TUESDAY

a. How many cans were used in 3 days?

$$8 + 7 + 6 = \triangle$$

b. If they used the same amount each day, how many cans would have been used in one day?

$$21 \div 3 = \square$$

We say that an *average* of 7 cans was used each day.

2. Mary had scores of 9, 8, and 7 on 3 different tests.

a. What was the total score on all 3 tests?

b. Find her average score. $9 + 8 + 7 = 24$

$$24 \div 3 = 8$$

average score

number of tests

total score

3. Compare the addends and sum in each sentence. What do you find?

$$9 + 8 + 7 = 24 \qquad 8 + 8 + 8 = 24$$

242

4. Jack took 4 tests. He got the following scores: 5, 7, 4, 12.

    a. What was his total score?

    b. What can replace each $\square$ to make the second sentence true?

$$5 + 7 + 4 + 12 = 28$$
$$\square + \square + \square + \square = 28$$

    c. We can think: $4 \times \square = 28$ or $28 \div 4 = \square$. What is the average?

5. Find the average of the numbers in each set.

    a. 9, 4, 5   **b.** 8, 8, 3, 1   **c.** 8, 7, 3, 2, 0

EXERCISES

Find the average.

1. 4, 7, 3, 2   **2.** 8, 7, 3   **3.** 14, 18

4. 18, 9, 36   **5.** 0, 2, 4   **6.** 8, 7, 6

7. 16, 20, 30, 34   **8.** 0, 1, 2, 3, 4, 5, 6

9. 4, 9, 9, 9, 9, 8   **10.** 5, 6, 7, 8, 9

Solve each problem.

11. Dave played fullback on the football team. He carried the ball 8 times for a total gain of 56 yards. What was his average gain?

12. The students in the fourth grade had a used-book sale. Twenty students brought in 140 books. What was the average number of books each student brought?

PICTURE GRAPHS

A graph can be used for organizing facts. There are many different kinds of graphs. One kind of graph is called a picture graph.

1. David and his dad went on a fishing trip. This graph tells us about the number of fish David caught.

Days	FISH CAUGHT by DAVID
Mon.	🐟
Tues.	🐟 🐟
Wed.	🐟 🐟 🐟 🐟 🐟 🐟 🐟
Thurs.	🐟 🐟 🐟 🐟
Fri.	🐟 🐟 🐟 🐟 🐟 🐟

Each symbol 🐟 represents 1 fish

a. What does each fish in the graph represent?

b. How many fish did David catch on Monday?

c. Which day did he catch the most fish? How many did he catch that day?

d. Which day did David catch the least number of fish? How many did he catch that day?

e. How many fish did he catch on each of the other days?

f. What was the average number of fish caught on these five days?

2. David caught 10 fish on Saturday. How many pictures of fish should be drawn on a graph for Saturday?

3. This picture graph shows how many fish David's dad caught.

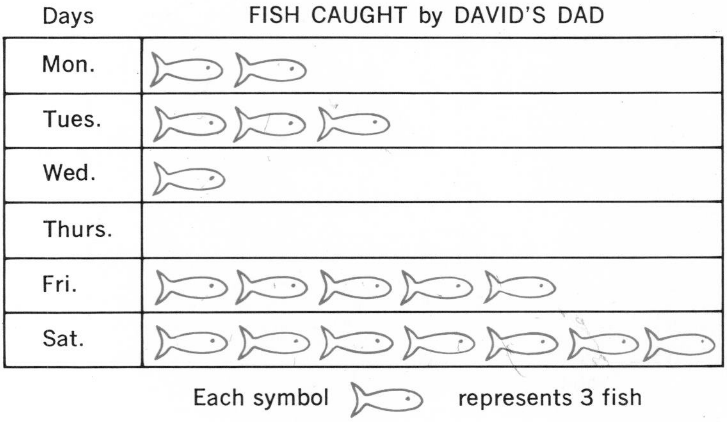

Days   FISH CAUGHT by DAVID'S DAD

Mon.	🐟 🐟
Tues.	🐟 🐟 🐟
Wed.	🐟
Thurs.	
Fri.	🐟 🐟 🐟 🐟 🐟
Sat.	🐟 🐟 🐟 🐟 🐟 🐟 🐟

Each symbol 🐟 represents 3 fish

a. How many fish did he catch on Monday?

b. How many did he catch on each of the other days?

c. What was the average number of fish he caught each day?

d. If he caught 12 fish on Sunday, how would it be shown on the graph?

4. Compare the number of fish that David caught on Tuesday with the number of fish his dad caught on Tuesday.

a. How many did David catch?

b. How many did David's dad catch?

c. How many more fish did David's dad catch (on Tuesday) than David?

BAR GRAPHS

Another kind of graph is a bar graph.

1. This graph shows the number of hours David fished each day.

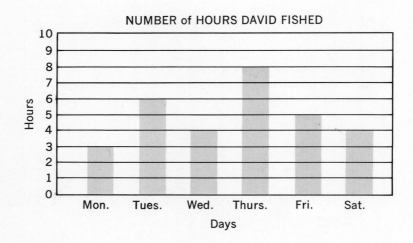

NUMBER of HOURS DAVID FISHED

a. Which day did David fish for the longest amount of time?

b. Which day did David fish for the least amount of time?

c. David fished three hours on Monday. How many hours did he fish on Tuesday?

d. How many hours did he fish on each of the other days?

e. What was the average number of hours that he fished each day?

f. How many more hours did he spend fishing on Thursday than Wednesday?

g. If David fished for seven hours on Sunday, how would it be shown on the graph?

2. This bar graph tells how many hours David's dad fished.

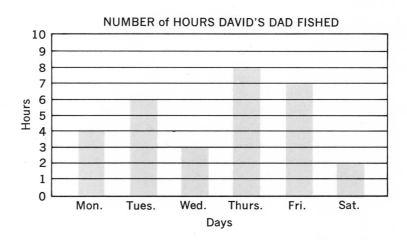

NUMBER of HOURS DAVID'S DAD FISHED

a. Which day did David's dad fish the longest amount of time?

b. Which day did he fish the least amount of time?

c. David's dad fished 4 hours on Monday. How many hours did he fish on Tuesday?

d. How many hours did he fish on Wednesday?

e. How many hours did he fish on each of the other days?

f. What was the average number of hours that David's dad fished each day?

g. How many more hours did he spend fishing on Friday than Saturday?

h. For how many hours did David fish without his dad on Saturday? Look at the graphs for Item 1 and Item 2.

247

DO YOU REMEMBER?

Divide.

1. $2\overline{)28}$ 2. $2\overline{)76}$ 3. $4\overline{)148}$ 4. $8\overline{)784}$

5. $6\overline{)840}$ 6. $8\overline{)848}$ 7. $4\overline{)840}$ 8. $6\overline{)726}$

9. $5\overline{)4,285}$ 10. $7\overline{)3,920}$ 11. $9\overline{)7,236}$

12. $7\overline{)5,453}$ 13. $50\overline{)250}$ 14. $40\overline{)480}$

15. $30\overline{)660}$ 16. $80\overline{)960}$ 17. $20\overline{)273}$

18. $80\overline{)473}$ 19. $60\overline{)582}$ 20. $90\overline{)352}$

21. $70\overline{)821}$ 22. $40\overline{)457}$ 23. $50\overline{)666}$

24. $30\overline{)1,564}$ 25. $\$.84 \div 3$ 26. $\$.98 \div 7$

Solve each problem.

27. There were 15 children at a party. To play a game, they had to form 3 equal groups. How many children were in each group?

28. If a train travels at 50 miles an hour, how long will it take to go 550 miles?

29. Mrs. Morris bought a bag of 128 candies for children on Halloween. She wanted to give each child 8 candies. How many children could she treat?

30. Two fourth-grade classes are going on a trip together. There are 56 students. How many groups of 10 students are there? How many students will be in a smaller group?

248

PROBLEM SOLVING

1. Jim's mother bought a cap for $1.98, a shirt for $2.98, and a pair of shoes for $9.98. How much did the clothing cost?

2. Frank had 156 baseball cards. He gave his best friend 27 of them. How many cards did Frank keep?

3. Mr. Reed ordered 27 boxes of colored paper for his bookstore. There were 12 packs of paper in each box. How many packs of colored paper did he order?

4. Mr. Reed has 125 notebooks to put on the counter. He puts them into 7 equal stacks. How many notebooks will be left over?

5. Martha saw 18 rows of girl scouts marching in a parade. There were 7 girl scouts in each row. How many girl scouts were in the parade?

6. The forestry department wants to plant 157 trees in a field. They plant 9 trees in a row.

   a. How many full rows can they plant?

   b. Will they have a row that is not full? How many trees will be in that row?

CHAPTER REVIEW

Think of the division $8\overline{)784}$.

1. Is the quotient greater than 10? Is it less than 100? Why?

2. The quotient is between what two multiples of ten?

3. Divide. What is the quotient?

Study the example at the right.

$$\begin{array}{r} 6 \\ 70\overline{)452} \\ 420 \\ \hline 32 \end{array}$$

4. $70 \times \triangle = 420$

5. What is the remainder?

6. Check. $(70 \times 6) + \square = 452$

Find the averages.

7. 19, 17   8. 46, 92, 24   9. 7, 6, 7, 4

Divide.

10. $2\overline{)12}$ 11. $4\overline{)27}$ 12. $6\overline{)50}$ 13. $8\overline{)96}$

14. $30\overline{)240}$ 15. $40\overline{)278}$ 16. $50\overline{)625}$ 17. $70\overline{)224}$

Solve the problem.

18. A storekeeper has 528 bottles of soda in cartons. There are 6 bottles in each carton. How many cartons does he have?

Terms You Should Know

average	quotient	remainder
graph	division	partial quotient

Divide.

1. $4\overline{)276}$ 2. $7\overline{)847}$ 3. $9\overline{)1,818}$

4. $8\overline{)240}$ 5. $5\overline{)327}$ 6. $6\overline{)287}$

7. $7\overline{)832}$ 8. $3\overline{)4,321}$ 9. $20\overline{)520}$

10. $50\overline{)4,720}$ 11. $.96 \div 4$ 12. $2.45 \div 5$

13. Find the average: 4, 6, 7, 8, 5.

Solve each problem.

14. Mike's parents paid $375.00 for 3 months' rent. How much is the rent each month?

15. Angelo rode his bike 18 miles in 3 hours. How far did he go in one hour?

16. If a train travels 60 miles in an hour, how long will it take to go 420 miles?

17. Mary rode 6 miles in the first hour of her trip. She rode 6 miles in the second hour, and 3 miles in the third hour. How many miles did she average each hour?

18. Miss Rogers bought a piece of meat for $4.74. If the meat weighed 6 pounds, how much did each pound of meat cost?

19. Sam is sharing his 140 marbles equally with Roy. How many marbles will each boy have?

20. A school buys 175 books for 6 classes to share equally. How many books does each class receive? How many are left over?

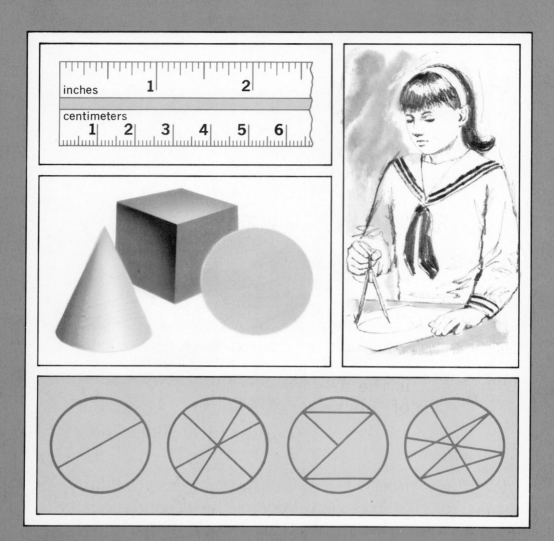

CHAPTER EIGHT

Geometry

AREA

This square and its inside is called a square centimeter (sq cm).

1. How many square centimeters will the inside of this rectangle hold?

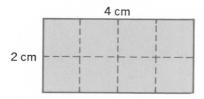

The **area** tells how big the inside of the rectangle is. The area is 8 square centimeters.

2. What is the area of the inside of this rectangle?

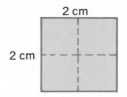

EXERCISES

Find the areas.

1.
5 cm
3 cm

2.
5 cm
2 cm

3.
2 cm   4 cm

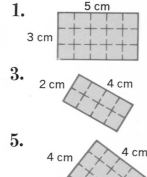

4.
6 cm
3 cm

5.
4 cm   4 cm

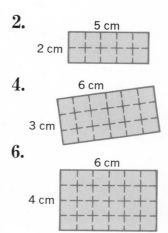

6.
6 cm
4 cm

FINDING AREAS BY MULTIPLYING

How can we find areas without counting squares?

1. a. How long is this rectangle? How wide?

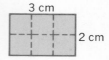

3 cm
2 cm

  b. What is the area?

2. a. How long is this rectangle? How wide?

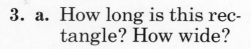

4 cm
5 cm

  b. How many squares are in each row?

  c. How many rows are there?

  d. What is the area?

3. a. How long is this rectangle? How wide?

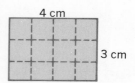

4 cm
3 cm

  b. Multiply your answers.

  c. What is the area?

4. a. How long is this rectangle? How wide?

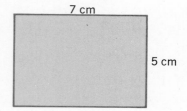

7 cm
5 cm

  b. What is the area?

5. How can you find an area without counting squares?

254

> To find the area of a rectangle we can multiply the **length** by the **width**.

6. What is the area?

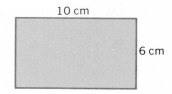

Find the areas.

1.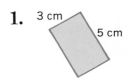

2.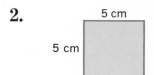

3.

4.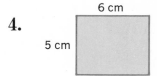

5.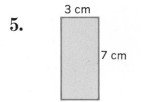

6.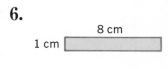

UNEXPLORED TERRITORY

Write addition sentences using 1, 2, 4, and 8 as addends. Use 3, 5, 6, 7, 9, 10, 11, 12, 13, 14, and 15 as sums. Do not repeat any addends in a sentence.

Example $2 + 4 = 6$
$1 + 2 + 4 + 8 = 15$

AREAS

This square and its inside is called a square inch (sq in.).

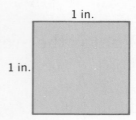

1. What is the area of each in square inches?

a.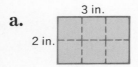

b.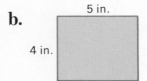

2. What is the area in square feet (sq ft)?

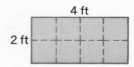

3. The top of John's desk is 3 feet long and 2 feet wide. Find the area of the top of his desk in square feet.

4. What is the area in square yards (sq yd)?

5. John's rock garden is 6 yards long and 3 yards wide. What is the area of the garden?

256

PROBLEM SOLVING

Write a number sentence for each problem. Make each sentence true.

1. The paperboy delivered 89 papers to an apartment house each day. How many papers would he deliver in 31 days?

2. There are 24 bottles of pop in a case. How many bottles are in 88 cases?

3. Mr. Lyon is packing 12 pears in each box. How many pears will there be in 60 boxes?

4. Mr. Carlson sold 45 tires at $27 each. How much did he receive for all the tires?

5. Bill sold 25 papers. Jerry sold 49 papers. How many did the boys sell altogether?

6. Twelve fourth-grade boys each collected 150 leaves for an art project. How many leaves did they collect in all?

7. Mr. Jensen earns $225 each week. How much money does Mr. Jensen earn in 52 weeks?

8. The clerk in the school cafeteria collects about $350 each day. About how much does she collect in 20 days?

9. For a play 1,289 adults' tickets and 345 children's tickets were sold. How many tickets were sold in all?

10. Mr. Ritt pays $95 each month to rent his house. How much rent would he pay during 24 months?

PERIMETERS AND AREAS

What can we discover about perimeters and areas?

1. What is the perimeter of this rectangle? What is the area?

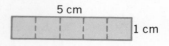

5 cm
1 cm

2. What is the perimeter? What is the area?

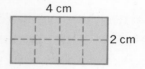

4 cm
2 cm

3. What is the perimeter? What is the area?

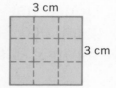

3 cm
3 cm

4. What is the perimeter of each rectangle?

a.
7 cm
1 cm

b.
6 cm
2 cm

c.
5 cm
3 cm

d.
4 cm
4 cm

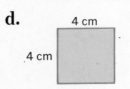

What is the area of each? Which has the greatest area?

5. Draw 5 rectangles with perimeters of 20 cm. Which has the greatest area?

EXERCISES

1. Draw all the rectangles you can think of with a perimeter of 24 cm. Which has the greatest area?

2. Think of rectangles with perimeter 28 cm. Which has the greatest area? Draw it. Find the area.

3. Bob has 36 feet of wire fence for a rectangular-shaped dog pen. He wants the pen to have the largest area possible. How long and how wide should he make the pen?

4. Mr. Jones has 40 feet of fence for a rectangular-shaped garden. The biggest garden he can enclose has how much area?

Find the areas of these rectangles.

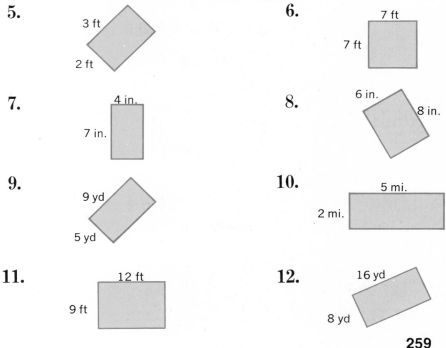

5. 3 ft, 2 ft

6. 7 ft, 7 ft

7. 4 in., 7 in.

8. 6 in., 8 in.

9. 9 yd, 5 yd

10. 5 mi., 2 mi.

11. 12 ft, 9 ft

12. 16 yd, 8 yd

DOUBLING RECTANGLES

What happens when we double the sides of a rectangle?

1. **a.** Draw a rectangle 2 cm wide and 3 cm long.

   b. Find the perimeter.

   c. What is the area?

   d. Draw a rectangle twice as long and twice as wide.

   e. What is its perimeter? its area?

2. **a.** Draw a square 3 cm on a side.

   b. What is its perimeter?

   c. What is its area?

   d. Draw a square 6 cm on a side.

   e. What is its perimeter? its area?

3. When you double the sides of a rectangle, what happens to the perimeter?

4. When you double the sides of a rectangle, what happens to the area?

When the sides of a rectangle are doubled, the perimeter doubles. The area doubles twice, or the area is multiplied by 4.

260

What is the perimeter of each rectangle? What is the area? Double the length and width of each rectangle. Find the new perimeter and area.

1.

5 cm

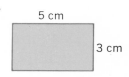

3 cm

2.

6 in.

3 in.

3.

5 yd

5 yd

4.

3 yd

7 yd

UNEXPLORED TERRITORY

Find the areas.

1.

3 cm

2 cm

5 cm

3 cm

2 cm

2.

3 yd

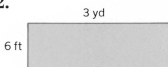

6 ft

Let's Practice

Multiply.

1. 24	**2.** 483	**3.** 627	**4.** 807
×2	×3	×5	×46

Divide.

5. 2)13 **6.** 3)20 **7.** 6)49 **8.** 4)31

9. 7)15 **10.** 8)35 **11.** 9)60 **12.** 9)62

Make each sentence true. Use > and <.

13. 379 + 865 ≡ 1134   **14.** 6002 − 5896 ≡ 1216

RECTANGULAR BOXES

Here is a picture of a box. It is made of rectangle shapes.

If a box is made of square shapes, it is called a *cube*.

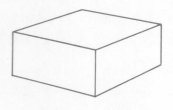

1. Draw a rectangle.

2. Draw parallel segments, like this.

3. Draw segments, like this.

4. What did you draw?

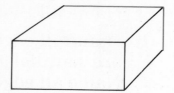

5. Letter your drawing, like this.

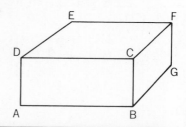

Each corner point is called a **vertex** (plural, **vertices**).

6. Name each vertex.

Each line segment is called an **edge**.

7. The rectangle *ABCD* and its inside is a *face.* Name some other faces.

1. Draw a cube. Start by drawing a square, like this.

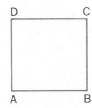

2. Name the vertices of your cube.

3. Name some edges of your cube.

4. Name some faces of your cube.

5. a. This drawing shows hidden parts dotted. Name all the faces.

b. Name all edges that are parallel to $\overline{QV}$. Name all edges that are parallel to $\overline{PQ}$.

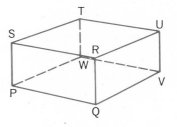

6. A cube or rectangular box has how many faces? how many edges? how many vertices?

Let's Practice

1. The Empire State Building in New York City is 1,250 feet tall. The Chrysler Building is 1,046 feet tall. How much taller is the Empire State Building?

2. There were 4,568 adults and 3,788 children at the circus. How many people were there?

CIRCLES

1. Mark a point in the middle of your paper. Name it *B*.

2. Mark a point 1 cm from *B*.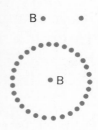

3. Mark 10 more points 1 cm from *B*.

4. Connect the points, like this.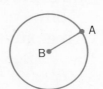

5. What did you draw?

All points of a circle are the same distance from a certain point. That point is called the **center.**

6. Mark point *A* as shown. Is *A* inside, outside, or on the circle? Is *B*?

7. Draw $\overline{BA}$. How long is it?

A segment from the center to a point of the circle is called a **radius.**

8. Draw some more segments like $\overline{BA}$. How long are they?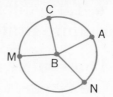

9. Draw a circle with a 2-cm radius. Name the center *P*.

10. Draw segment $\overline{MN}$, like this. How long is it?

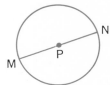

A segment like $\overline{MN}$ is called a **diameter**.

11. Draw some more segments like $\overline{MN}$. How long are they?

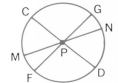

EXERCISES

1. Name each radius.

2. How long is $\overline{BN}$? $\overline{BC}$?

3. Name each diameter.

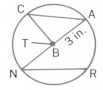

4. Radius $\overline{BN}$ is 4 in. long. How long is $\overline{BX}$? $\overline{BT}$? $\overline{PX}$? $\overline{MQ}$? $\overline{TN}$?

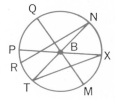

5. a. Draw a circle with a 6-cm radius.

   b. Draw a radius.

   c. Draw a diameter.

   d. How long is the diameter?

6. A circle has a 9-in. radius. How long is a diameter of the circle?

DO YOU REMEMBER?

Name or describe each figure.

1.

2.

3.

4.

5.

6.

7.

8.

9.

10.

11.

12.

13.

14.

15.

16.

17.

18.

Find each sum or difference.

19. $\begin{array}{r} 3{,}146 \\ +4{,}197 \\ \hline \end{array}$ 20. $\begin{array}{r} 87{,}120 \\ -8{,}198 \\ \hline \end{array}$ 21. $\begin{array}{r} 3{,}009 \\ -359 \\ \hline \end{array}$ 22. $\begin{array}{r} 40{,}102 \\ +93{,}905 \\ \hline \end{array}$

Find each product or quotient.

23. $\begin{array}{r} 406 \\ \times 37 \\ \hline \end{array}$ 24. $80\overline{)209}$ 25. $\begin{array}{r} 628 \\ \times 40 \\ \hline \end{array}$ 26. $45\overline{)2{,}047}$

Solve the problem.

27. Mr. Landers paid $.95 each for 9 tickets to the basketball game. How much did he spend?

266

DRAWING CIRCLES

Here are two ways to draw circles.

1. Use a strip of cardboard. Punch two holes 2 inches apart. Stick a pin through one hole. Put your pencil in the other hole and draw a circle. Your circle will have a 2-inch radius.

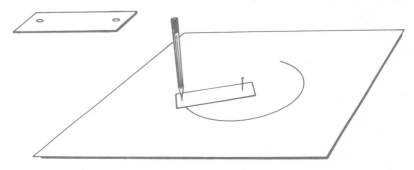

2. Use a *compass*. Put cardboard under your paper. Stick the point into the paper. Let the pencil point touch the paper lightly. Hold the compass between your thumb and finger and twirl it. Draw a circle. A radius is $\overline{EF}$.

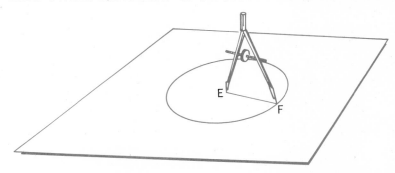

3. Use a strip of cardboard or compass. Draw a circle with a 1-inch radius. Draw a circle with a 3-inch radius.

4. Use a compass. Draw a circle with a 2-inch radius. Draw a circle with a 4-inch radius.

1. Draw a circle with a 2-inch radius.

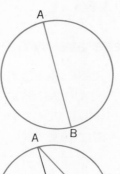

2. With your ruler, draw diameter $\overline{AB}$.

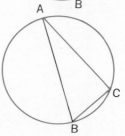

3. Mark point C on the circle. Draw $\overline{AC}$ and $\overline{BC}$.

4. What kind of angle is ∠ACB? Use your drawing triangle to check.

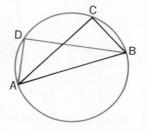

5. Mark another point D. Draw $\overline{AD}$ and $\overline{BD}$. What kind of angle is ∠ADB?

6. Repeat for some other points.

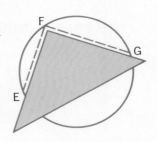

7. Draw another circle with a 2-inch radius.

8. With your drawing triangle, draw right angle EFG.

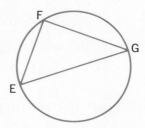

9. Use your ruler. Draw $\overline{EG}$.

10. What kind of segment is $\overline{EG}$?

11. What kind of triangle is EFG?

CONES

Here are some *cones*.

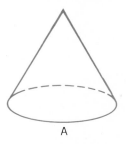

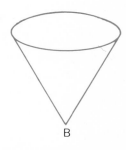

A

B

The flat part of a cone is called the **base**. The point is called the **vertex**.

1. The base is a circle. From one side it looks like this when we draw it. Make a drawing like it.

2. Now draw two segments like this. They should be the same length. What did you draw?

3. In drawing A above, the base is hidden. Draw a base. Now draw two segments. Erase part of the base and make it dashed.

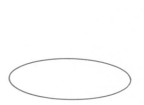

1. Draw a cone like this.

2. Draw a cone like this. Color the base. Name the vertex *P*.

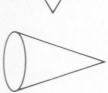

3. Name some objects that are cone-shaped.

Let's Practice

What is the meaning of the underlined digit symbol?

Example　947　9 × 100 or 900

1. 6̲84　　2. 7,2̲18　　3. 14̲,689　　4. 3̲84,147

Add.

5.	309	6.	$36.09	7.	3,048	8.	$4.63
	26		2.46		946		.98
	437		19.12		5,008		7.15

Solve each problem.

9. The school cafeteria has 7 dozen hamburgers. How many children can buy 1 hamburger for lunch?

10. A gym teacher paid $34.89 for 3 basketballs. How much did one basketball cost?

11. In July a family's telephone bill was $14.87. In August the telephone bill was $27.35. How much more was the bill in August?

MATCHING AND COMPARING

How are these alike? Which one is different?
How is it different?

	a.	b.	c.	d.

1. square, quadrilateral, triangle, trapezoid

2. 4 cm by 3 cm; 6 cm by 2 cm; 3 cm by 4 cm; 5 cm by 4 cm

3. circles with radius/diameter marks

4. circles with inscribed figures

5. circle, partial figure, triangle, half-circle

6. square, cube, rectangle, rectangle

7. cone, triangle, quadrilateral, circle

8. parallel lines, diagonal lines

9. square (6,6,6,6); triangle (8,8,8); rectangle (7,3,3,7); hexagon (4,4,4,4,4,4)

PROBLEM SOLVING

1. **a.** Mammoth Cave in Kentucky covers about 51,354 acres. Carlsbad Caverns in New Mexico covers about 46,753 acres. How many more acres are in Mammoth Cave than in the Carlsbad Caverns?

   b. Wind Cave in South Dakota covers about 28,059 acres. How many more acres are in the Carlsbad Caverns than in Wind Cave?

2. On their vacation the Parker family traveled 324 miles the first day, 420 miles the second day, and 248 miles the third day. How many miles did they travel in the three days?

3. The Parker family went camping. Mr. Parker paid $18.95 for a lantern, $24.95 for a heater, and $18.95 for a gas burner. What was the total cost of these three items?

4. A large tent costs $129.89. A smaller tent costs $89.95. How much more does the larger tent cost?

5. Mr. Parker rented a small trailer for $65 a week. A large trailer rents for $110 a week. How much less is the rent for the smaller trailer?

6. When Sam and Bill went to summer camp they traveled 4 hours by train and 2 hours by bus. How long did it take them to get to camp?

7. Sam and Bill hiked 10 miles the first day, 12 miles the second day, and 8 miles the third day. How many miles did they hike in the three days?

8. Sam buys a camping magazine every month for $.35. How much does he spend for the magazine during 12 months?

9. When Sam went to camp he weighed 69 pounds. When he came home he weighed 72 pounds. How many pounds did Sam gain?

10. When Bill arrived at camp he weighed 80 pounds. When he came home he weighed 78 pounds. How many pounds did Bill lose?

11. a. Arlan worked on Mr. Dale's vegetable farm. Mr. Dale paid him $15.75 the first week, $25.00 the second week, and $32.00 the third week. How much money did Arlan earn?

    b. How much more money did Arlan earn the third week than during the first week?

    c. What was the average amount of money Arlan earned in one week?

CHAPTER REVIEW

1. Find the areas and perimeters.

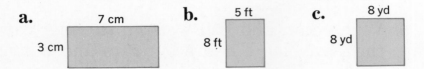

a. 7 cm, 3 cm   **b.** 5 ft, 8 ft   **c.** 8 yd, 8 yd

2. When the sides are doubled in picture 1a, what is the perimeter? the area?

3. a. Name three vertices, three edges, three faces.

b. Name <u>two</u> edges parallel to $\overline{AB}$.

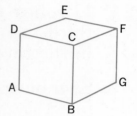

4. Which segment is a radius? a diameter?

5. Segment $\overline{MN}$ is 6 yd long. How long is $\overline{AB}$? How long is $\overline{PQ}$?

6. Draw a cube. Letter the vertices.

7. Draw a cone with the base hidden.

8. Draw a cone with the base in view. Name the vertex P. Color the base.

Terms You Should Know

area	perimeter	cube	circle
vertex	edge	face	cone
radius	diameter	center	base

274

CHAPTER TEST

1. Find the perimeter.

2. Find the area.

6 in.

4 in.

3. If the sides are doubled, what is the perimeter?

4. If the sides are doubled, what is the area?

5. Draw a cube and letter it.

6. How many faces has a cube?

7. How many edges has a cube?

8. How many vertices has a cube?

Look at the circle.

9. Which segment is a radius?

10. Which segment is a diameter?

In this circle a radius is 3 cm long.

11. How long is $\overline{PQ}$?

12. How long is $\overline{MN}$?

13. How long is $\overline{AB}$?

14. Draw a cone with the base in view.

15. Draw a cone with the base hidden.

16. How many vertices has a cone?

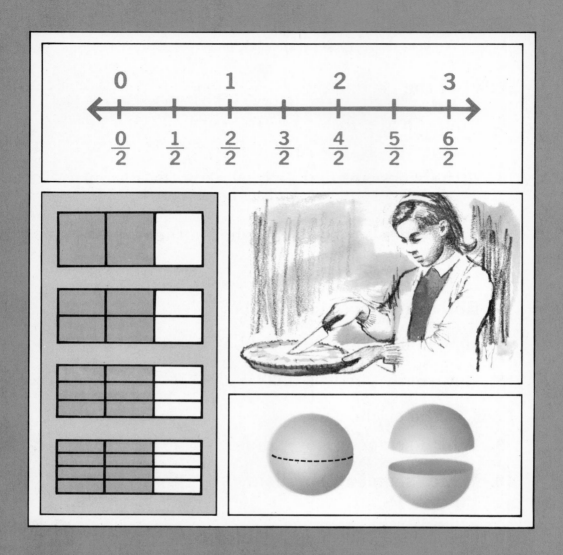

CHAPTER NINE

Fractions

A NEW KIND OF NUMBER

We can use a number to tell about a part of something.

1. Charles is sawing the board into 2 parts of the same size. Each part is one-half of the board.

   We write: $\frac{1}{2}$ or one-half.

2. Bill marked his board to show 3 parts of the same size. What is each part called?

   We write: $\frac{1}{3}$ or one-third.

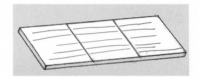

3. How many parts of the same size did Jack show? What part is colored?

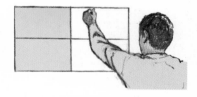

4. Which picture does not show $\frac{1}{2}$ shaded? Why?

   a.    b.   c.

5. Which pictures do not show $\frac{1}{4}$ shaded?

   a.    b. 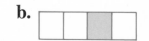   c.

Numbers like $\frac{1}{2}$, $\frac{1}{3}$, $\frac{1}{4}$, and $\frac{3}{4}$ are **fractions**. We use fractions to tell about parts of things.

6. Sometimes we use a fraction to tell about a part of a set.

   a. Two of the 3 animals are lions. $\frac{2}{3}$ of the animals are lions.

   b. What part of the animals are bears?

EXERCISES

What part of each shape is shaded?

1.    2.   3.

4.   5.   6.

What part of each set is shaded?

7.    8.    9.

10.    11.    12.

Draw a picture for each fraction.

13. $\frac{1}{4}$ 14. $\frac{3}{5}$ 15. $\frac{1}{6}$ 16. $\frac{2}{3}$

READING FRACTIONAL NUMERALS

1. Jack drew this picture.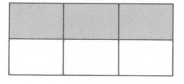

   a. How many parts of the same size did he show?

   b. How many parts are colored?

   c. What part of the whole shape is colored?

   d. A name for three-sixths is $\frac{3}{6}$. The numeral $\frac{3}{6}$ is called a *fractional numeral*.

   $\frac{3}{6}$ 3←——Number of parts that are shaded.
   6←——Number of parts in all.

   e. Draw a picture to show sixths. Shade $\frac{4}{6}$.

$\frac{5}{7}$ ←—— **numerator**
←—— **denominator**

The number named above the bar is called the **numerator**. The number named below the bar is called the **denominator**.

---

2. Name the numerators.
   Name the denominators.

   a. $\frac{3}{5}$ b. $\frac{4}{7}$ c. $\frac{9}{11}$ d. $\frac{13}{11}$ e. $\frac{24}{91}$

3. Study these fractional numerals.

Fractional Numerals	We Read
$\frac{2}{3}$	two-thirds
$\frac{1}{5}$	one-fifth

4. Read these numerals.

a. $\frac{3}{5}$ **b.** $\frac{4}{7}$ **c.** $\frac{1}{8}$ **d.** $\frac{5}{9}$

Write a fractional numeral to tell what part of each shape is shaded.

1. 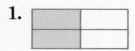 **2.** **3.**

4. Draw a picture and shade $\frac{2}{3}$ of it.

Write fractional numerals.

5. one-eighth **6.** two-tenths

7. seven-sixteenths **8.** four-twelfths

9. three-fifteenths **10.** one-half

11. five-twentieths **12.** six-twelfths

Write word names.

13. $\frac{1}{2}$ **14.** $\frac{3}{4}$ **15.** $\frac{3}{5}$ **16.** $\frac{1}{9}$

17. $\frac{7}{10}$ **18.** $\frac{2}{3}$ **19.** $\frac{1}{6}$ **20.** $\frac{1}{3}$

21. Name the numerators in Exercises 13–20.

22. Name the denominators in Exercises 13–20.

Copy and complete.

23. $\frac{7}{48}$ is ____ forty-eighths.

24. $\frac{5}{2}$ is ____ halves.

280

PARTS OF A WHOLE

1. Mrs. Cox cut the cake into 2 pieces of the same size.

    a. Each piece is what part of the cake?

    b. The numerator 1 in $\frac{1}{2}$ tells the number of parts we are considering. What does the denominator mean?

2. She then cut each piece in half. Are all pieces the same size? Each piece is what part of the whole cake? Write the numeral that shows this.

3. Mother again cut each piece in half. Each piece is what part of the cake?

4. The shaded part of this picture shows how much of the cake was eaten.

    a. What part of the cake was eaten?

    b. What part was left?

    c. In $\frac{7}{8}$, what does the numerator tell us?

EXERCISES

Name the fraction for each picture.

1.   2.   3.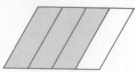

4.   5.   6.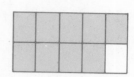

Draw pictures for these fractions.

7. $\frac{3}{4}$ 8. $\frac{3}{5}$ 9. $\frac{3}{10}$ 10. $\frac{4}{6}$

11. $\frac{5}{6}$ 12. $\frac{4}{5}$ 13. $\frac{1}{2}$ 14. $\frac{4}{8}$

Let's Practice

Do each of the following exercises.

1. $\begin{array}{r} 64,981 \\ -39,999 \\ \hline \end{array}$
2. $\begin{array}{r} 1,049 \\ -768 \\ \hline \end{array}$
3. $\begin{array}{r} 7,684 \\ +6,684 \\ \hline \end{array}$
4. $\begin{array}{r} 1,000 \\ -100 \\ \hline \end{array}$

5. $\begin{array}{r} 398 \\ -287 \\ \hline \end{array}$
6. $\begin{array}{r} 827 \\ \times 36 \\ \hline \end{array}$
7. $\begin{array}{r} 695 \\ +847 \\ \hline \end{array}$
8. $\begin{array}{r} 714 \\ \times 28 \\ \hline \end{array}$

9. $5\overline{)875}$ 10. $6\overline{)984}$ 11. $60\overline{)723}$ 12. $7\overline{)273}$

13. Divide.

   a. $9 \div 9$ b. $12 \div 12$

   c. $86 \div 86$ d. $226 \div 226$

   e. If you divide any number by itself, what is the quotient?

PARTS OF SETS

1. Al has this set of marbles.

   a. How many marbles does Al have?

   b. Are all of Al's marbles the same size?

   c. How many marbles are colored?

   d. We say that $\frac{7}{11}$ of Al's marbles are colored. What is the numerator in $\frac{7}{11}$? What is the denominator?

   e. What part of Al's marbles are not colored?

2. **a.** The bats are $\frac{3}{13}$ of this set.

   b. The baseballs are what part of the set?

   c. What part of $\frac{6}{13}$ tells us the number of baseballs?

   d. What part of $\frac{6}{13}$ tells us the number of members in the whole set?

   e. The apples are what part of the set?

   f. Write a fractional numeral for this.

We can use fractional numerals to tell about parts of sets.

$$\frac{6}{13}$$ Numerator: Number of members we are thinking of.

Denominator: Number of members in the whole set.

What part of each set is colored? Write a fractional numeral.

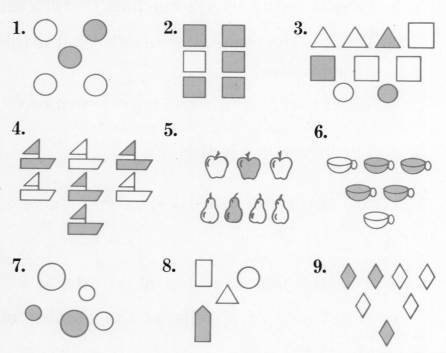

1. 2. 3.

4. 5. 6.

7. 8. 9.

For each fractional numeral, draw a set and color part of it.

10. $\frac{3}{5}$ 11. $\frac{5}{7}$ 12. $\frac{1}{6}$ 13. $\frac{7}{12}$

14. $\frac{3}{4}$ 15. $\frac{1}{3}$ 16. $\frac{1}{2}$ 17. $\frac{2}{3}$

284

ONE-HALF

1. When we divide an object into two parts of the same size, each part is one-half of the object. Which pictures show halves?

   a. **b.** **c.** **d.**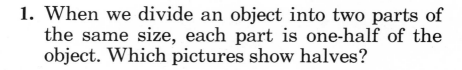

2. When we divide a set into halves, each half has the same number of members.

   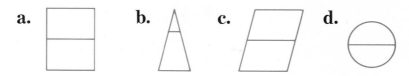

   The number of members in each part of the set is $\frac{1}{2}$ of the number of members in the whole set. What is $\frac{1}{2}$ of 8?

3. Which of these sets are divided into halves?

   a. **b.** **c.** **d.**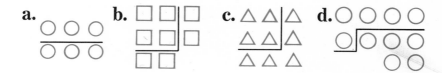

4. What is $\frac{1}{2}$ of 10?

5. What is $\frac{1}{2}$ of 6?

6. Draw 12 sticks. What is $\frac{1}{2}$ of 12?

7. Draw 18 balls. What is $\frac{1}{2}$ of 18?

EXERCISES

Draw a picture to show each of the following.

1. $\frac{1}{2}$ of 4   2. $\frac{1}{2}$ of 16   3. $\frac{1}{2}$ of 8

4. $\frac{1}{2}$ of 2   5. $\frac{1}{2}$ of 10   6. $\frac{1}{2}$ of 14

Copy and complete. Use the pictures you drew to help you.

7. $\frac{1}{2}$ of 2 is ___   8. $\frac{1}{2}$ of 14 is ___

9. $\frac{1}{2}$ of 10 is ___   10. $\frac{1}{2}$ of 4 is ___

11. $\frac{1}{2}$ of 8 is ___   12. $\frac{1}{2}$ of 16 is ___

Let's Practice

1. Mrs. Burns bought Peggy a new spring hat for $3.98, a dress for $6.50, and gloves for $1.29. How much did Peggy's clothes cost?

2. This year the city telephone directory has 1,848 pages. Last year the directory had 1,749 pages. How much larger is the directory for this year?

3. The moving company charges $21.50 an hour to move a family's furniture. If the men take 6 hours, how much will the moving cost?

4. Mr. Pappas sells pizza pie. On Saturday his sales were $31.50. On Sunday the sales were $43.75. What was the total?

ONE-THIRD, ONE-FOURTH

1. Which pictures show thirds?

   a.   b.   c.

2. How many eggs are in $\frac{1}{3}$ dozen?

3. When we divide a set into thirds, each set has the same number of members.

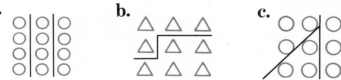

   What is $\frac{1}{3}$ of 6?

4. Which of these sets are divided into thirds?

   a.   b.   c.

5. Study the pictures in Items 4a and 4c.

   a. What is $\frac{1}{3}$ of 9?

   b. What is $\frac{1}{3}$ of 12?

6. Which pictures show fourths?

   a.   b.    c.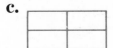

7. What is $\frac{1}{4}$ of 12?

8. One fourth of a dollar is sometimes called a quarter. How many quarters make one dollar?

EXERCISES

Study each picture. Make each sentence true.

1.

⚬ ● ⚬ ⚬

$\frac{1}{4}$ of 4 is ___ .

2.

● ⚬ ● ⚬
● ⚬ ⚬ ⚬

$\frac{1}{4}$ of 8 is ___ .

3.

● ● ●
⚬ ⚬ ⚬
⚬ ⚬ ⚬

$\frac{1}{3}$ of 9 is ___ .

Copy and complete. Draw a picture to help you.

4. $\frac{1}{3}$ of 6 is ____   5. $\frac{1}{3}$ of 9 is ____

6. $\frac{1}{3}$ of 15 is ____   7. $\frac{1}{4}$ of 12 is ____

8. $\frac{1}{4}$ of 20 is ____   9. $\frac{1}{4}$ of 16 is ____

10. $\frac{1}{3}$ of 27 is ____   11. $\frac{1}{3}$ of 24 is ____

Let's Practice

1. What is the perimeter of a square if the length of a side is 8 inches?

2. The rent for an apartment is $135 a month. How much is the rent for one year?

3. One ping pong ball cost $.33. How much must Jeanie pay for 15 balls?

PROBLEM SOLVING

1. Jack, Joe, and Bill have to carry 21 books to the library.

   a. Bill said, "If each of us takes $\frac{1}{3}$ of them, we will each carry the same number of books." Is he right?

   b. Joe said, "If I divide 21 by 3, the quotient is 7. We can each carry 7 books." Is Joe right?

   c. Which sentences are true?

   $$\frac{1}{3} \text{ of } 21 = 7 \qquad 21 \div 3 = 7$$

2. Father gave $18 to Dan and Ron. If they share the money equally, how much will each boy receive?

   Think: $\frac{1}{2}$ of 18 is ____ $18 \div 2 = \square$

3. Mary took 20 sandwiches to the picnic. The children ate $\frac{1}{2}$ of them. How many sandwiches were eaten?

   Think: $\frac{1}{2}$ of 20 is ____ $20 \div 2 = \square$

4. Jane gave Mary $\frac{1}{2}$ of her cookies. If Mary got 7 cookies, how many cookies did Jane have?

289

5. Grandfather had $24 in his pocket.

   a. He gave Jack $\frac{1}{2}$ of it. How much money did Jack receive?

   b. He gave Mary $\frac{1}{3}$ of the $24. How much money did Mary receive?

6. How many minutes are in $\frac{1}{4}$ hour?

   $\frac{1}{4}$ of 60 is ____

7. How many minutes are in $\frac{1}{2}$ hour?

8. How many ounces are in $\frac{1}{2}$ pound?

9. How many eggs are in $\frac{1}{3}$ dozen?

10. Mrs. Roberts bought an 18-foot roll of wax paper. She used $\frac{1}{3}$ of it. How many feet of wax paper did she use?

11. There are 26 students in Miss White's class. One-half of them voted for Paul for class president. How many voted for Paul?

12. The top of Mrs. Booth's kitchen table is in the shape of a circle. A diameter measures 6 feet. How long is a radius?

13. On a spelling test of 56 words, Sally misspelled $\frac{1}{4}$ of the words. How many words did she misspell?

14. How many words did she spell correctly?

DO YOU REMEMBER?

Use $=$, $>$, or $<$. Make each sentence true.

1. $10 \times 10 \times 10 \equiv 1{,}000$

2. $10 \times 10 \times 100 \equiv 100 \times 100$

3. $10 \times 1{,}000 \equiv 10 \times 100 \times 10$

4. $10{,}000 - 1 \equiv 99{,}999 + 1$

5. $624 \times 27 \equiv 208 \times 81$

Add.

6.	**7.**	**8.**	**9.**
27	308	8,746	$8.27
38	904	2,493	3.04
49	602	2,986	9.07
27	907	3,487	6.32

Subtract.

10.	**11.**	**12.**	**13.**
34	340	342	$12.48
−9	−90	−87	−9.47

Find the sums or differences.

14. $1{,}892 + 1{,}476 + 2{,}184$ **15.** $24{,}287 - 6{,}319$

16. $84{,}900 - 28{,}370$ **17.** $\$190.00 - \$188.41$

18. $16 + 19 + 28 + 4{,}287$ **19.** $\$1.63 + \$4.76 + \$9.87$

Solve each problem.

20. There are 24 hours in a day. How many hours are there in 365 days?

21. How many weeks are in a year?

COMPARING FRACTIONS

Which is greater, $\frac{1}{2}$ or $\frac{1}{3}$?

1. Which is more, $\frac{1}{2}$ of a bar or $\frac{1}{3}$ of it?

2. Which is more, $\frac{1}{3}$ of a bar or $\frac{1}{4}$ of it?

3. Draw 2 pictures like this.

   a. Color $\frac{1}{3}$ of one picture.

   b. Color $\frac{1}{5}$ of the other picture.

   c. Which is greater, $\frac{1}{3}$ or $\frac{1}{5}$?

4. Which is greater? Draw a picture for help.

   a. $\frac{1}{4}$ or $\frac{1}{5}$ b. $\frac{1}{6}$ or $\frac{1}{5}$ c. $\frac{1}{4}$ or $\frac{1}{3}$ d. $\frac{1}{5}$ or $\frac{1}{7}$

5. What did you discover?

$\frac{1}{4} > \frac{1}{5}$ When the numerators are one, the numeral with the greater denominator names the smaller number.

6. Mother baked a pie. Jack ate $\frac{1}{6}$ of it, and Mary ate $\frac{1}{8}$ of it. Who ate more pie?

292

Use $>$ or $<$ to make true sentences.

1. $\frac{1}{5} \equiv \frac{1}{4}$ **2.** $\frac{1}{7} \equiv \frac{1}{9}$ **3.** $\frac{1}{9} \equiv \frac{1}{7}$

4. $\frac{1}{3} \equiv \frac{1}{2}$ **5.** $\frac{1}{8} \equiv \frac{1}{5}$ **6.** $\frac{1}{10} \equiv \frac{1}{4}$

LET'S EXPLORE

Which is greater, $\frac{1}{6}$ or $\frac{2}{6}$?　$\frac{1}{3}$ or $\frac{2}{3}$?

1. Which is more, $\frac{1}{4}$ of a bar or $\frac{3}{4}$ of it?

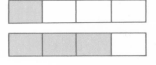

2. Which is more, $\frac{2}{5}$ of a bar or $\frac{3}{5}$ of it?

3. Draw a picture to show $\frac{2}{4}$. Draw another to show $\frac{3}{4}$. Which is greater, $\frac{3}{4}$ or $\frac{2}{4}$?

4. Which fraction is greater? Draw pictures if you need help.

　a. $\frac{3}{5}$ or $\frac{4}{5}$ **b.** $\frac{3}{7}$ or $\frac{5}{7}$ **c.** $\frac{5}{8}$ or $\frac{3}{8}$ **d.** $\frac{2}{7}$ or $\frac{6}{7}$

5. What did you discover?

$\frac{5}{9} > \frac{4}{9}$ When the denominators are the same, the numeral with the greater numerator names the greater number.

EXERCISES

Use $>$ or $<$ to make true sentences.

1. $\frac{1}{3} \equiv \frac{2}{3}$ 2. $\frac{7}{10} \equiv \frac{5}{10}$ 3. $\frac{4}{9} \equiv \frac{2}{9}$

4. $\frac{3}{4} \equiv \frac{1}{4}$ 5. $\frac{0}{5} \equiv \frac{4}{5}$ 6. $\frac{3}{7} \equiv \frac{6}{7}$

7. $\frac{8}{11} \equiv \frac{0}{11}$ 8. $\frac{18}{21} \equiv \frac{20}{21}$ 9. $\frac{9}{10} \equiv \frac{7}{10}$

10. $\frac{7}{8} \equiv \frac{5}{8}$ 11. $\frac{7}{15} \equiv \frac{11}{15}$ 12. $\frac{1}{8} \equiv \frac{3}{8}$

13. $\frac{6}{7} \equiv \frac{2}{7}$ 14. $\frac{5}{12} \equiv \frac{7}{12}$ 15. $\frac{3}{10} \equiv \frac{2}{10}$

16. $\frac{10}{11} \equiv \frac{9}{11}$ 17. $\frac{4}{5} \equiv \frac{2}{5}$ 18. $\frac{7}{8} \equiv \frac{3}{8}$

LET'S EXPLORE

1. Which is greater, $\frac{1}{3}$ or $\frac{1}{4}$?

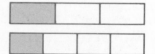

2. Which is greater, $\frac{2}{3}$ or $\frac{2}{4}$?

3. a. Which is greater, $\frac{1}{5}$ or $\frac{1}{4}$?

   b. $\frac{2}{5}$ is twice as much as ———.

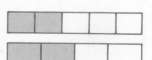

   c. $\frac{2}{4}$ is twice as much as ———.

   d. Which is greater, $\frac{2}{5}$ or $\frac{2}{4}$?

4. **a.** Which is greater, $\frac{1}{5}$ or $\frac{1}{6}$?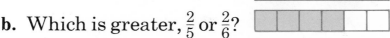

   b. Which is greater, $\frac{2}{5}$ or $\frac{2}{6}$?

   c. Which is greater, $\frac{4}{5}$ or $\frac{4}{6}$?

5. Which is greater?

   a. $\frac{3}{5}$ or $\frac{3}{4}$ **b.** $\frac{5}{6}$ or $\frac{5}{7}$ **c.** $\frac{5}{9}$ or $\frac{5}{11}$ **d.** $\frac{5}{11}$ or $\frac{5}{7}$

6. What did you discover?

> $\frac{3}{5} < \frac{3}{4}$ When the numerators are the same, the numeral with the greater denominator names the smaller number.

Use $>$ or $<$ to make true sentences.

1. $\frac{3}{8} \equiv \frac{3}{5}$ 2. $\frac{4}{9} \equiv \frac{4}{13}$ 3. $\frac{6}{9} \equiv \frac{6}{7}$

4. $\frac{3}{5} \equiv \frac{3}{4}$ 5. $\frac{5}{10} \equiv \frac{5}{9}$ 6. $\frac{3}{8} \equiv \frac{3}{23}$

7. $\frac{4}{7} \equiv \frac{4}{11}$ 8. $\frac{6}{9} \equiv \frac{7}{9}$ 9. $\frac{3}{10} \equiv \frac{3}{8}$

10. $\frac{3}{7} \equiv \frac{3}{16}$ 11. $\frac{8}{12} \equiv \frac{8}{13}$ 12. $\frac{5}{9} \equiv \frac{5}{6}$

13. $\frac{5}{8} \equiv \frac{5}{7}$ 14. $\frac{8}{11} \equiv \frac{8}{9}$ 15. $\frac{4}{7} \equiv \frac{6}{7}$

16. $\frac{6}{9} \equiv \frac{6}{7}$ 17. $\frac{6}{11} \equiv \frac{6}{8}$ 18. $\frac{4}{9} \equiv \frac{4}{5}$

LET'S EXPLORE

Fractions are numbers that are not whole numbers. They can be greater than one.

1. **a.** The cake is cut into halves.

   b. How many halves are there?

   c. How many halves make 1?

   $$\frac{2}{2} = 1$$

2. **a.** Each cake is cut into halves.

   b. How many halves are there in the 2 cakes?

   $$\frac{4}{2} = 2$$

The fractional numeral $\frac{4}{2}$ names the whole number 2.

3. How many thirds are in 2?

   $$\frac{\triangle}{3} = 2$$

4. How many halves are in 3?

   $$\frac{\triangle}{2} = 3$$

5. **a.** How many thirds are in one candy bar? $1 = \frac{\triangle}{3}$

   b. How many fourths? $1 = \frac{\triangle}{4}$

   c. How many fifths? $1 = \frac{\triangle}{5}$

6. What did you discover in Items 5a, b, and c?

$\frac{3}{3} = 1$ When the numerator and the denominator are the same, a fractional numeral names the number one.

7. a. How many halves are in 2? $2 = \frac{\triangle}{2}$

   b. How many thirds are in 2? $2 = \frac{\triangle}{3}$

   c. How many fourths are in 2? $2 = \frac{\triangle}{4}$

   d. How many fifths are in 2? $2 = \frac{\triangle}{5}$

   e. What did you discover?

$\frac{6}{3} = 2$ When the numerator is twice the denominator, a fractional numeral names the number 2.

8. a. What number is named by $\frac{6}{2}$? by $\frac{9}{3}$? by $\frac{12}{4}$?

   b. What did you discover about fractional numerals for the number 3?

EXERCISES

Write 5 fractional numerals for each number.

1. 1   **2.** 2   **3.** 3   **4.** 4   **5.** 7

Write standard numerals.

6. $\frac{3}{3}$ **7.** $\frac{12}{3}$ **8.** $\frac{10}{5}$ **9.** $\frac{6}{3}$ **10.** $\frac{6}{6}$

11. $\frac{12}{4}$ **12.** $\frac{4}{2}$ **13.** $\frac{8}{4}$ **14.** $\frac{10}{2}$ **15.** $\frac{15}{5}$

FRACTIONS GREATER THAN 1

How does $\frac{3}{2}$ compare with one?

LET'S EXPLORE

1. a. Each bar is cut to show halves.

   We know: $\frac{\triangle}{2} = 1$.

   b. How many parts in all are colored?

   c. Three halves make more than 1, so $\frac{3}{2} > 1$.

2. a. Write a fractional numeral for the colored part of each shape.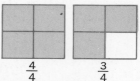

   $\frac{4}{4}$ $\frac{3}{4}$

   b. Does it name a number greater than, or less than 1?

   c. Which is greater, the numerator or the denominator?

3. Draw a picture to show $\frac{5}{4}$.

   a. Is $\frac{5}{4}$ less than 1, or greater than 1?

   b. Which is greater, the numerator or the denominator?

4. If a fractional numeral names a number greater than 1, how do the numerator and denominator compare?

$\frac{5}{3} > 1$ In $\frac{5}{3}$ the numerator is greater than the denominator.

5. If the numerator and denominator are the same, what number is named?

6. If the numerator is less than the denominator, is the number named greater than 1, or less than 1?

7. Use $<$, $>$, or $=$. Make true sentences.

    a. $\frac{5}{3} \equiv 1$ **b.** $1 \equiv \frac{2}{3}$ **c.** $\frac{5}{5} \equiv 1$ **d.** $\frac{4}{3} \equiv 1$

EXERCISES

1. Write 5 fractional numerals for fractions greater than 1.

2. Write 5 fractional numerals for fractions less than 1.

Draw a picture for each fraction.

3. $\frac{5}{4}$ **4.** $\frac{5}{3}$ **5.** $\frac{6}{4}$ **6.** $\frac{7}{5}$

Use $>$, $<$, or $=$. Make true sentences.

7. $\frac{3}{5} \equiv 1$ **8.** $\frac{5}{3} \equiv 1$ **9.** $\frac{7}{7} \equiv 1$

10. $\frac{2}{3} \equiv 1$ **11.** $1 \equiv \frac{3}{3}$ **12.** $\frac{4}{5} \equiv 1$

13. $1 \equiv \frac{5}{4}$ **14.** $\frac{5}{8} \equiv 1$ **15.** $1 \equiv \frac{5}{2}$

16. $\frac{8}{3} \equiv 1$ **17.** $1 \equiv \frac{9}{11}$ **18.** $\frac{9}{1} \equiv 1$

19. $\frac{9}{9} \equiv 1$ **20.** $\frac{6}{3} \equiv 1$ **21.** $1 \equiv \frac{1}{2}$

EQUIVALENT FRACTIONAL NUMERALS

1. **a.** What part is shaded?

   b. Cut each part in half. How many fourths are formed?

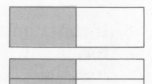

The sentence $\frac{1}{2} = \frac{2}{4}$ means that $\frac{1}{2}$ and $\frac{2}{4}$ name the same number. If fractional numerals name the same number, we say they are **equivalent**.

2. Draw a picture to show two-fourths. Cut each fourth in half.

   a. Two-fourths is how many eighths?

   b. $\frac{2}{4} = \frac{\triangle}{8}$

3. **a.** Draw the picture to show $\frac{4}{8}$ again. Cut each part in half.

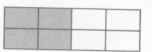

   b. How many parts are there in all? How many parts are shaded?

   c. Write another fractional numeral equivalent to $\frac{4}{8}$.

4. Make each sentence true.

   a. $\frac{1}{2} = \frac{\triangle}{4}$ **b.** $\frac{2}{4} = \frac{\triangle}{8}$ **c.** $\frac{1}{2} = \frac{\triangle}{8}$

5. Draw a picture to show $\frac{1}{2}$. Cut each part into three parts.

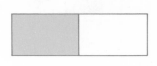

a. One-half is how many sixths?

b. $\frac{1}{2} = \frac{\triangle}{6}$

6. Draw a picture to show $\frac{3}{4}$. Cut each part in half.

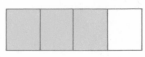

a. Three-fourths is how many eighths?

b. $\frac{3}{4} = \frac{\triangle}{8}$

7. Draw a picture to show $\frac{3}{4}$. Cut each part into three parts. $\frac{3}{4} = \frac{9}{\triangle}$

EXERCISES

For each picture, write two fractional numerals.

1.  **2.**   **3.**  **4.**

Draw a picture to show each fraction. Tell whether the fractional numerals are equivalent.

5. $\frac{3}{5}$ and $\frac{6}{10}$ **6.** $\frac{1}{2}$ and $\frac{2}{5}$ **7.** $\frac{3}{4}$ and $\frac{9}{12}$

Copy and complete.

8. $\frac{1}{3}, \frac{}{6}, \frac{}{9}, \frac{}{12}, \frac{5}{15}, \frac{}{18}$ **9.** $\frac{1}{4}, \frac{}{8}, \frac{}{12}, \frac{}{16}, \frac{5}{20}$

BUILDING A SET OF EQUIVALENT NUMERALS

1. Draw a picture for $\frac{2}{3}$. Show each part cut into halves.

   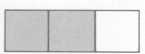

   a. How many sixths are shaded?

   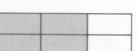

   b. Write a fractional numeral equivalent to $\frac{2}{3}$.

2. Draw another picture for $\frac{2}{3}$. Show each part cut into three parts.

   a. How many ninths are shaded?

   b. $\frac{2}{3} = \frac{\triangle}{9}$

   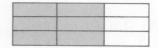

3. Draw a picture for $\frac{2}{3}$. Show each part cut into fourths.

   a. This is how many twelfths?

   b. How many twelfths are shaded?

   c. $\frac{2}{3} = \frac{\triangle}{12}$

4. Draw a picture for $\frac{2}{3}$. Show each part cut into five parts.

   $\frac{2}{3} = \frac{\triangle}{15}$

1. Draw a picture for $\frac{3}{4}$.

2. Show each piece cut in half. Write a fractional numeral equivalent to $\frac{3}{4}$.

3. Write 5 fractional numerals equivalent to $\frac{3}{4}$. Draw pictures if you need help.

4. Write 5 fractional numerals equivalent to each of these numerals.

   a. $\frac{2}{5}$ **b.** $\frac{3}{5}$ **c.** $\frac{4}{5}$ **d.** $\frac{1}{2}$ **e.** $\frac{1}{3}$

Let's Practice

1. A car is traveling at 60 miles an hour. A jet plane overhead is traveling 10 times as fast. How fast is the jet plane traveling?

2. What is the area of a room that is 13 feet long and 8 feet wide?

3. The Highway Department plans to repair 288 miles of roads. If workmen can repair 6 miles each day, how many days will the work take?

4. Kathy took a bicycle trip. She rode 5 miles the first hour, 2 miles the second hour, and 2 miles the third hour. What was the average number of miles she rode in an hour?

5. At the movies Joey bought 4 bags of popcorn which cost $.35 a bag. How much did he spend?

USING SETS

1. How many blocks are in this set? How many are colored?

We know that $\frac{5}{10}$ of them are colored.

We can also say that $\frac{1}{2}$ of them are colored.

$$\frac{1}{2} = \frac{5}{10}$$

2. Which two fractional numerals tell what part of each set is colored?

a. $\frac{1}{3}$, $\frac{1}{2}$, $\frac{3}{9}$ b. $\frac{7}{12}$, $\frac{2}{3}$, $\frac{8}{12}$ c. $\frac{3}{4}$, $\frac{1}{8}$, $\frac{6}{8}$

EXERCISES

Write two or more equivalent fractional numerals to tell what part of the set is colored.

1. 2. 3.

4. 5. 6.

7. Make each sentence true.

a. $\frac{1}{8} = \frac{\triangle}{16}$ b. $\frac{4}{5} = \frac{\square}{10}$ c. $\frac{1}{6} = \frac{\triangle}{24}$

DO YOU REMEMBER?

Do each of the following exercises.

1. 8,724
   276
   83

2. $23.82
   .56
   5.01

3. 1,432
   2,846
   365

4. 572,101
   8,430
   76,496

5. $714
   −29

6. $84.20
   −5.14

7. 8,700,000
   −34,926

8. 875,118
   −874,198

9. 4,723
   ×5

10. $27.94
    ×8

11. 576
    ×18

12. 927
    ×39

13. $3\overline{)762}$ 14. $9\overline{)587}$ 15. $40\overline{)596}$ 16. $60\overline{)999}$

Copy and complete.

17. $\frac{1}{2}$ of 4 = ____

18. $\frac{1}{3}$ of 6 = ____

19. $\frac{1}{4}$ of 16 = ____

20. $\frac{1}{8}$ of 32 = ____

Solve each problem.

21. There are 378 people at the Parents' Meeting at our school. They are divided evenly into 7 groups. How many people are in each group?

22. Greenville has a population of 28,463. In the election 10,411 people voted. How many people did not vote?

23. A garden measures 27 feet long and 16 feet wide. How many feet of fencing is needed to put around the garden?

THE NUMBER LINE

1. **a.** Draw a number line like this.

   b. Think of cutting each part in half. Mark your line to show halves.

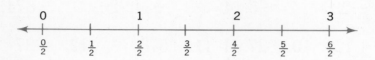

2. Make each sentence true. Use the number line to help you.

   a. $\dfrac{2}{\triangle} = 1$ **b.** $\dfrac{\triangle}{2} = 2$ **c.** $\dfrac{\triangle}{2} = 4$

3. Draw another number line. Mark it to show thirds.

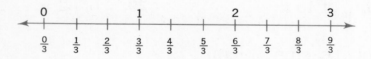

4. Make each sentence true. Use the number line to help you.

   a. $\dfrac{3}{\triangle} = 1$ **b.** $\dfrac{\triangle}{3} = 2$ **c.** $\dfrac{\triangle}{3} = 3$

5. Make each sentence true. Use $>$ or $<$.

   a. $\dfrac{4}{3} \equiv \dfrac{2}{3}$ **b.** $\dfrac{0}{3} \equiv \dfrac{2}{3}$ **c.** $\dfrac{7}{3} \equiv 2$

   d. $\dfrac{3}{3} \equiv \dfrac{6}{3}$ **e.** $\dfrac{1}{3} \equiv \dfrac{5}{3}$ **f.** $\dfrac{6}{3} \equiv \dfrac{9}{3}$

   g. $\dfrac{5}{3} \equiv \dfrac{3}{3}$ **h.** $\dfrac{8}{3} \equiv \dfrac{6}{3}$ **i.** $\dfrac{2}{3} \equiv \dfrac{1}{3}$

USING THE NUMBER LINE

1. Fractional numerals which name the same number are equivalent.

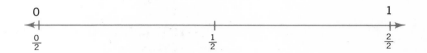

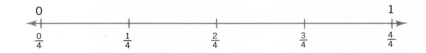

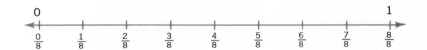

a. Find the fractional numerals $\frac{1}{2}$, $\frac{2}{4}$, and $\frac{4}{8}$ on the number line. What do you discover?

b. Find two fractional numerals that name 0.

c. Find two names for 1.

2. Make each sentence true. Use the number lines to help you.

a. $\frac{3}{4} = \frac{\triangle}{8}$ **b.** $\frac{0}{8} = \frac{\triangle}{2}$ **c.** $\frac{2}{8} = \frac{\triangle}{4}$

d. $\frac{6}{8} = \frac{\triangle}{4}$ **e.** $\frac{2}{2} = \frac{\triangle}{8}$ **f.** $\frac{8}{8} = \frac{\triangle}{4}$

g. $\frac{1}{2} = \frac{\triangle}{4}$ **h.** $\frac{0}{4} = \frac{\triangle}{2}$ **i.** $\frac{1}{2} = \frac{\triangle}{8}$

j. $\frac{2}{4} = \frac{\triangle}{8}$ **k.** $\frac{4}{8} = \frac{\triangle}{2}$ **l.** $\frac{2}{2} = \frac{\triangle}{4}$

3. Find equivalent fractional numerals on the number line. Make each sentence true.

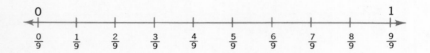

a. $\frac{1}{3} = \frac{\triangle}{9}$ **b.** $\frac{2}{3} = \frac{\triangle}{9}$ **c.** $\frac{4}{6} = \frac{\triangle}{3}$

d. $\frac{6}{6} = \frac{\triangle}{3}$ **e.** $\frac{1}{3} = \frac{\triangle}{6}$ **f.** $\frac{6}{6} = \frac{\triangle}{9}$

g. $\frac{0}{6} = \frac{\triangle}{3}$ **h.** $\frac{3}{9} = \frac{\triangle}{3}$ **i.** $\frac{2}{6} = \frac{\triangle}{9}$

j. $\frac{4}{6} = \frac{\triangle}{9}$ **k.** $\frac{0}{6} = \frac{\triangle}{9}$ **l.** $\frac{6}{9} = \frac{\triangle}{3}$

EXERCISES

Make each sentence true.

1. $\frac{1}{2} = \frac{\square}{4}$ **2.** $\frac{3}{3} = \frac{\triangle}{9}$ **3.** $\frac{1}{4} = \frac{\triangle}{8}$

4. $\frac{6}{8} = \frac{\triangle}{4}$ **5.** $\frac{8}{8} = \frac{\triangle}{2}$ **6.** $\frac{2}{4} = \frac{\triangle}{8}$

7. $\frac{8}{8} = \frac{\triangle}{4}$ **8.** $1 = \frac{\square}{6}$ **9.** $\frac{2}{8} = \frac{\triangle}{4}$

10. $\frac{4}{8} = \frac{\triangle}{2}$ **11.** $\frac{\triangle}{4} = 1$ **12.** $\frac{1}{3} = \frac{\triangle}{9}$

EQUIVALENT FRACTIONAL NUMERALS

You know these names for one-half.

$$\frac{1}{2}, \frac{2}{4}, \frac{3}{6}, \frac{4}{8}$$

1. Find other equivalent fractional numerals for $\frac{1}{2}$.

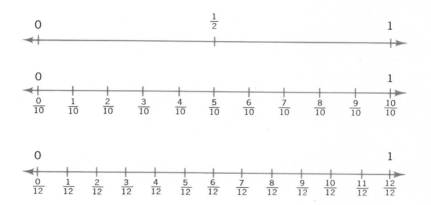

a. Study the numerators and denominators. Look for a pattern.

$$\frac{1}{2}, \frac{2}{4}, \frac{3}{6}, \frac{4}{8}, \frac{5}{10}, \frac{6}{12}$$

b. What equivalent fractional numeral comes next?

c. Write 4 more fractional numerals for $\frac{1}{2}$.

2. You know that $\frac{1}{4}$ and $\frac{2}{8}$ are names for one-fourth. What fractional numeral comes next in the pattern?

$$\frac{1}{4}, \frac{2}{8}, \frac{3}{12}, \cdots$$

3. You know that $\frac{1}{3}$, $\frac{2}{6}$, and $\frac{3}{9}$ are names for one-third.

a. The number line shows that $\frac{1}{3} = \frac{\triangle}{12}$.

b. Look for a pattern.

$$\frac{1}{3}, \frac{2}{6}, \frac{3}{9}, \frac{4}{12}, \cdots$$

What comes next after $\frac{4}{12}$?

c. Write 3 more equivalent fractional numerals that fit the pattern.

EXERCISES

Write the next 3 equivalent fractional numerals for each set.

1. $\frac{1}{4}, \frac{2}{8}, \frac{3}{12}, \frac{4}{16}, \cdots$ **2.** $\frac{4}{5}, \frac{8}{10}, \frac{12}{15}, \cdots$

3. $\frac{1}{6}, \frac{2}{12}, \frac{3}{18}, \cdots$ **4.** $\frac{5}{6}, \frac{10}{12}, \frac{15}{18}, \cdots$

5. $\frac{1}{10}, \frac{2}{20}, \frac{3}{30}, \cdots$ **6.** $\frac{7}{8}, \frac{14}{16}, \frac{21}{24}, \cdots$

7. $\frac{2}{3}, \frac{4}{6}, \frac{6}{9}, \cdots$ **8.** $\frac{3}{4}, \frac{6}{8}, \frac{9}{12}, \cdots$

9. $\frac{2}{5}, \frac{4}{10}, \frac{6}{15}, \cdots$ **10.** $\frac{3}{5}, \frac{6}{10}, \frac{9}{15}, \cdots$

LET'S EXPLORE

How can we tell if two fractional numerals are equivalent?

1. Complete these equivalent fractional numerals.

$$\frac{2}{3}, \frac{4}{6}, \frac{\triangle}{9}, \frac{\triangledown}{12}, \frac{\square}{15}$$

2. We know $\frac{2}{3} = \frac{4}{6}$. $\dfrac{2}{3} = \dfrac{4}{6}$

   a. Multiply the numerator 2 by the denominator 6.

   b. Multiply the numerator 4 by the denominator 3.

   c. How do your answers compare?

3. We know $\frac{4}{6} = \frac{8}{12}$. $\dfrac{4}{6} = \dfrac{8}{12}$

   a. Multiply the numerator 4 by the denominator 12.

   b. Multiply the numerator 8 by the denominator 6.

   c. How do your answers compare?

4. Test $\frac{6}{9}$ and $\frac{8}{12}$ to see if they are equivalent.

   For $\frac{6}{9}$ and $\frac{8}{12}$, we multiply like this.

   $$\dfrac{6}{9} = \dfrac{8}{12} \qquad\qquad 6 \times 12 = 8 \times 9$$
   $$\text{so } \frac{6}{9} = \frac{8}{12}$$

5. Test $\frac{3}{5}$ and $\frac{9}{15}$.

6. Test $\frac{1}{2}$ and $\frac{2}{3}$.

a. Multiply the numerator 1 by the denominator 3.

b. Multiply the numerator 2 by the denominator 2.

c. Is 1×3 equal to 2×2?
We find that 1×3 is not equal to 2×2, so $\frac{1}{2}$ is not equivalent to $\frac{2}{3}$.

Which pairs of numerals are equivalent?

1. $\frac{3}{4}, \frac{6}{8}$ 2. $\frac{2}{3}, \frac{5}{6}$ 3. $\frac{4}{8}, \frac{8}{16}$

4. $\frac{3}{8}, \frac{4}{9}$ 5. $\frac{6}{8}, \frac{9}{12}$ 6. $\frac{4}{7}, \frac{8}{14}$

7. $\frac{5}{9}, \frac{6}{10}$ 8. $\frac{3}{10}, \frac{9}{12}$ 9. $\frac{1}{2}, \frac{4}{6}$

Make each sentence true.

10. $\frac{2}{3} = \frac{\triangle}{12}$ 11. $\frac{9}{12} = \frac{\triangle}{4}$

12. $\frac{4}{5} = \frac{16}{\triangle}$ 13. $\frac{\triangle}{4} = \frac{6}{24}$

14. $\frac{12}{\triangle} = \frac{2}{3}$ 15. $\frac{2}{3} = \frac{\triangle}{18}$

16. $\frac{\triangle}{20} = \frac{3}{4}$ 17. $\frac{3}{4} = \frac{6}{\triangle}$

18. $\frac{6}{\triangle} = \frac{9}{12}$ 19. $\frac{3}{7} = \frac{9}{\triangle}$

CHAPTER REVIEW

What part of each object or set is shaded? Write a fractional numeral.

1.    2.   3.

4.    5.   6.

7. Draw a picture and shade $\frac{3}{4}$ of it.

8. Draw a picture of a set of objects and shade $\frac{3}{4}$ of them.

Copy and complete.

9. $\frac{1}{4}$ of 8 = ___   10. $\frac{1}{4}$ of 1 = ___

11. $\frac{1}{2}$ of 10 = ___   12. $\frac{1}{3}$ of 9 = ___

Make each sentence true. Use $>$ or $<$.

13. $\frac{1}{4} \equiv \frac{1}{3}$ 14. $\frac{3}{8} \equiv \frac{3}{7}$ 15. $\frac{9}{10} \equiv 1$

16. $\frac{2}{3} \equiv \frac{2}{4}$ 17. $1 \equiv \frac{10}{3}$ 18. $\frac{5}{4} \equiv \frac{4}{9}$

19. $\frac{3}{8} \equiv \frac{5}{8}$ 20. $\frac{1}{2} \equiv \frac{1}{3}$ 21. $\frac{3}{3} \equiv \frac{4}{5}$

Write standard numerals.

22. $\frac{10}{5}$ 23. $\frac{3}{3}$ 24. $\frac{12}{2}$

Which pairs of fractional numerals are equivalent?

25. $\frac{2}{3}, \frac{4}{6}$　　**26.** $\frac{5}{10}, \frac{6}{11}$　　**27.** $\frac{6}{8}, \frac{3}{4}$　　**28.** $\frac{3}{9}, \frac{4}{12}$

Write 5 fractional numerals equivalent to each.

29. $\frac{1}{2}$　　**30.** $\frac{1}{3}$　　**31.** $\frac{1}{4}$　　**32.** $\frac{2}{3}$

Make each sentence true.

33. $\frac{4}{8} = \frac{\triangle}{4}$ 　　　　　　　**34.** $\frac{3}{4} = \frac{\triangle}{12}$

35. $\frac{2}{3} = \frac{8}{\triangle}$ 　　　　　　　**36.** $\frac{1}{2} = \frac{\triangle}{6}$

37. $\frac{5}{6} = \frac{\triangle}{12}$ 　　　　　　　**38.** $\frac{1}{7} = \frac{\triangle}{21}$

39. $\frac{1}{8} = \frac{\triangle}{16}$ 　　　　　　　**40.** $\frac{2}{7} = \frac{\triangle}{21}$

Solve each problem.

41. Johnny gave $\frac{1}{4}$ of 12 cookies to his sister. How many cookies did he give away?

42. Mr. Reed had 21 rabbits in his pet shop. He sold $\frac{1}{7}$ of them. How many rabbits did he sell?

Terms You Should Know

fractional numeral　　　denominator

numerator　　　fraction

equivalent fractional numeral

CHAPTER TEST

Write 2 equivalent fractional numerals that tell what part of each is shaded. Circle the simpler name.

1.   **2.** 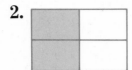   **3.**

Write 5 fractional numerals equivalent to each.

4. $\frac{2}{5}$ **5.** $\frac{3}{5}$ **6.** $\frac{3}{4}$ **7.** $\frac{2}{3}$

Tell whether these are equivalent.

8. $\frac{3}{8}, \frac{12}{32}$ **9.** $\frac{6}{8}, \frac{2}{3}$ **10.** $\frac{9}{18}, \frac{6}{9}$ **11.** $\frac{4}{10}, \frac{6}{12}$

Make each sentence true.

12. $\frac{1}{2} = \frac{\triangle}{10}$ **13.** $\frac{2}{3} = \frac{\triangle}{12}$ **14.** $\frac{2}{5} = \frac{\triangle}{10}$ **15.** $\frac{3}{4} = \frac{\triangle}{12}$

Use $>$, $=$, or $<$ to make true sentences.

16. $1 \equiv \frac{5}{5}$ **17.** $\frac{3}{5} \equiv 1$ **18.** $\frac{1}{10} \equiv \frac{1}{11}$ **19.** $\frac{2}{3} \equiv \frac{2}{5}$

20. $\frac{6}{5} \equiv 1$ **21.** $\frac{2}{5} \equiv \frac{3}{5}$ **22.** $\frac{3}{4} \equiv \frac{3}{5}$ **23.** $\frac{5}{4} \equiv 1$

Write standard numerals.

24. $\frac{7}{7}$ **25.** $\frac{14}{7}$ **26.** $\frac{21}{7}$ **27.** $\frac{10}{2}$

28. $\frac{24}{8}$ **29.** $\frac{63}{9}$ **30.** $\frac{72}{8}$ **31.** $\frac{40}{8}$

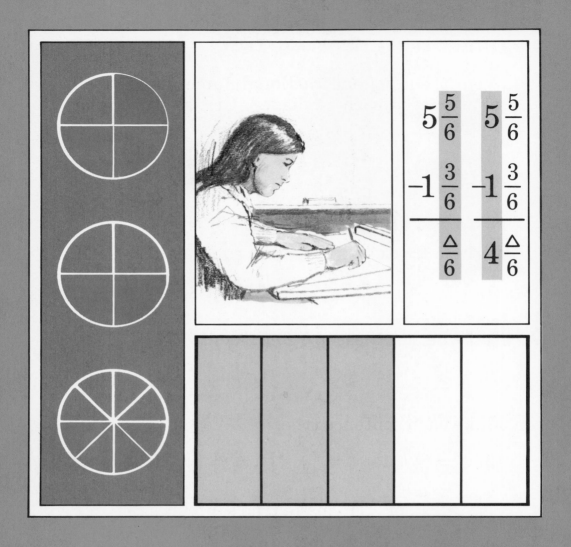

CHAPTER TEN

Addition and Subtraction of Fractions

ADDING FRACTIONS—
DENOMINATORS ALIKE

How can we add two fractions, such as $\frac{3}{8}$ and $\frac{2}{8}$?

1. The glass in picture A below is $\frac{3}{8}$ full of water. The glass in picture B is $\frac{2}{8}$ full.

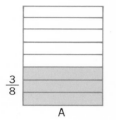
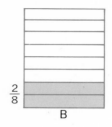
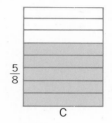

a. If you pour the water from B into A, how full will A be? Picture C shows this.

$$\frac{3}{8} + \frac{2}{8} = \frac{3+2}{8}$$
$$= \frac{\triangle}{8}$$

b. If you pour the water from A into B, how full will B be?

$$\frac{2}{8} + \frac{3}{8} = \frac{2+3}{8}$$
$$= \frac{\triangle}{8}$$

c. Add. Use pictures A, B, and C to help you.

$$\begin{array}{c} \frac{3}{8} \\ +\frac{2}{8} \\ \hline \end{array} \qquad \begin{array}{c} \frac{2}{8} \\ +\frac{3}{8} \\ \hline \end{array}$$

317

2. Now look at these glasses of water.

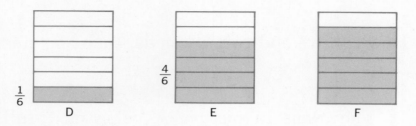

$\frac{1}{6}$ D $\frac{4}{6}$ E   F

a. If the water in D is poured into E, how full will E be? Picture F shows this.

$$\frac{4}{6} + \frac{1}{6} = \frac{4+1}{6}$$

$$= \frac{\triangle}{6}$$

b. If the water in E is poured into D, how much will be in D?

Add: $\frac{1}{6} + \frac{4}{6} = \frac{\triangle}{6}$

3. Add. Draw pictures to help you if you wish.

    a. $\frac{1}{5} + \frac{3}{5}$ **b.** $\frac{2}{4} + \frac{1}{4}$ **c.** $\frac{4}{7} + \frac{2}{7}$

4. What have you discovered?

When the denominators are the same, we add the numerators. We keep the same denominator.

Example $\frac{4}{7} + \frac{2}{7} = \frac{4+2}{7}$ $\frac{4}{7}$

$$= \frac{6}{7} \qquad\qquad +\frac{2}{7}$$

$$\frac{6}{7}$$

Add.

1. $\frac{1}{4}+\frac{1}{4}$ 2. $\frac{1}{3}+\frac{1}{3}$ 3. $\frac{2}{5}+\frac{2}{5}$

4. $\frac{3}{8}+\frac{4}{8}$ 5. $\frac{2}{7}+\frac{4}{7}$ 6. $\frac{3}{9}+\frac{2}{9}$

7. $\frac{1}{7}+\frac{4}{7}$ 8. $\frac{3}{10}+\frac{4}{10}$ 9. $\frac{6}{12}+\frac{5}{12}$

10. $\frac{3}{5}$ $+\frac{1}{5}$ 11. $\frac{3}{7}$ $+\frac{2}{7}$ 12. $\frac{5}{9}$ $+\frac{2}{9}$ 13. $\frac{4}{11}$ $+\frac{5}{11}$ 14. $\frac{6}{12}$ $+\frac{5}{12}$

Let's Practice

Solve each problem.

1. A jet airplane traveled 727 miles to Chicago, then 1,875 miles to San Francisco, then 345 miles to Los Angeles. How many miles did it travel in all?

2. An orange grower packed 792 crates of oranges on each truck. He shipped 18 truckloads. How many crates did he ship?

3. Carol spent $4.50 for 5 records. Each record cost the same. How much did each cost?

4. Bob ate 12 pancakes. His little sister ate $\frac{1}{3}$ as many. How many did she eat?

5. Karl is counting shirts in the stockroom. He counts 300 white shirts and 198 blue shirts. How many more white shirts are there?

SUBTRACTING

1. Gene has $\frac{5}{8}$ of a cake. He eats $\frac{3}{8}$ of the cake. How much cake is left?

  a. Copy and complete.

  $$\frac{5}{8} - \frac{3}{8} = \frac{\triangle}{8}$$

$\frac{5}{8}$

  b. Remember, addition and subtraction are opposite operations. Check your answer by adding.

  $$\frac{3}{8} + \frac{\triangle}{8} = \frac{5}{8}$$

$\frac{2}{8}$

2. Bob has $\frac{3}{4}$ of a candy bar. He eats $\frac{1}{4}$ of the candy bar. How much is left?

  a. Copy and complete.

  $$\frac{3}{4} - \frac{1}{4} = \frac{3-1}{4}$$

  $$= \frac{\triangle}{4}$$

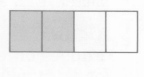

$$\begin{array}{r} \frac{3}{4} \\ -\ \frac{1}{4} \\ \hline \frac{\triangle}{4} \end{array}$$

  b. Check: $\frac{1}{4} + \frac{\triangle}{4} = \frac{3}{4}$

When the denominators are the same, we subtract the numerators. We keep the same denominator.

Example $\frac{3}{8} - \frac{2}{8} = \frac{3-2}{8}$

$$= \frac{1}{8}$$

Subtract. Check by adding.

1. $\frac{5}{8} - \frac{1}{8}$ 2. $\frac{3}{8} - \frac{1}{8}$ 3. $\frac{11}{12} - \frac{9}{12}$

4. $\frac{6}{7} - \frac{2}{7}$ 5. $\frac{13}{21} - \frac{11}{21}$ 6. $\frac{6}{7} - \frac{6}{7}$

Subtract.

7. $\begin{array}{r} \frac{7}{8} \\ -\frac{2}{8} \\ \hline \end{array}$ 8. $\begin{array}{r} \frac{8}{9} \\ -\frac{3}{9} \\ \hline \end{array}$ 9. $\begin{array}{r} \frac{5}{11} \\ -\frac{1}{11} \\ \hline \end{array}$ 10. $\begin{array}{r} \frac{10}{13} \\ -\frac{5}{13} \\ \hline \end{array}$

11. $\begin{array}{r} \frac{3}{4} \\ -\frac{1}{4} \\ \hline \end{array}$ 12. $\begin{array}{r} \frac{6}{8} \\ -\frac{6}{8} \\ \hline \end{array}$ 13. $\begin{array}{r} \frac{7}{9} \\ -\frac{6}{9} \\ \hline \end{array}$ 14. $\begin{array}{r} \frac{4}{8} \\ -\frac{1}{8} \\ \hline \end{array}$

Solve the problem.

15. Mother served $\frac{3}{8}$ of her apple pie and $\frac{5}{8}$ of her peach pie. How much more peach pie than apple pie did she serve?

UNEXPLORED TERRITORY

The sign for a fraction used by the Egyptians was a flattened circle. The circle meant a part and the numeral below told the size of the part.

One-third was shown by .

What fraction is shown by each symbol?

1.   2.   3.

DO YOU REMEMBER?

Write 5 equivalent fractional numerals for each.

1. $\frac{1}{4}$ 2. $\frac{2}{3}$ 3. $\frac{3}{4}$ 4. $\frac{1}{5}$

5. $\frac{2}{3}$ 6. $\frac{1}{8}$ 7. $\frac{3}{8}$ 8. $\frac{3}{5}$

Which pairs of fractional numerals are equivalent?

9. $\frac{2}{3}, \frac{4}{6}$ 10. $\frac{3}{9}, \frac{1}{3}$ 11. $\frac{2}{3}, \frac{8}{15}$ 12. $\frac{2}{3}, \frac{6}{9}$

13. $\frac{4}{6}, \frac{8}{12}$ 14. $\frac{6}{12}, \frac{1}{3}$ 15. $\frac{3}{8}, \frac{6}{16}$ 16. $\frac{5}{10}, \frac{1}{3}$

Make each sentence true.

17. $\frac{1}{4} = \frac{\square}{8}$ 18. $\frac{1}{3} = \frac{\square}{9}$ 19. $\frac{1}{4} = \frac{\square}{16}$

20. $\frac{1}{2} = \frac{\square}{12}$ 21. $\frac{1}{3} = \frac{\square}{12}$ 22. $\frac{1}{4} = \frac{\square}{20}$

23. $\frac{1}{5} = \frac{\square}{10}$ 24. $\frac{2}{5} = \frac{\square}{15}$ 25. $\frac{2}{3} = \frac{\square}{18}$

26. $\frac{3}{5} = \frac{\square}{10}$ 27. $\frac{2}{3} = \frac{\square}{6}$ 28. $\frac{3}{4} = \frac{\square}{8}$

29. $\frac{4}{5} = \frac{\square}{10}$ 30. $\frac{2}{3} = \frac{\square}{9}$ 31. $\frac{3}{4} = \frac{\square}{16}$

32. $\frac{1}{5} = \frac{\square}{15}$ 33. $\frac{2}{3} = \frac{\square}{12}$ 34. $\frac{3}{4} = \frac{\square}{12}$

35. $\frac{3}{5} = \frac{\square}{15}$ 36. $\frac{1}{3} = \frac{\square}{15}$ 37. $\frac{1}{4} = \frac{\square}{20}$

38. $\frac{4}{5} = \frac{\square}{15}$ 39. $\frac{2}{3} = \frac{\square}{15}$ 40. $\frac{3}{4} = \frac{\square}{20}$

PROBLEM SOLVING

1. Mr. Cast has 732 crates of apples. He must deliver 6 crates to each store on his list. To how many stores can he deliver the apples?

2. On the family trip Dad spent $81.00 for motels, $32.50 for gasoline, $132.67 for food, and $97.63 for extra things. How much did he spend in all?

3. Allentown is 42 miles from Norwalk. Waterville is 18 times as far from Norwalk. How far is Waterville from Norwalk?

4. There are 60 minutes in one hour. Ginny spent 180 minutes doing her homework. How many hours is that?

5. Terry can type 60 words in one minute. If she types at the same speed, how many words can she type in 7 minutes?

6. A rancher had 5,247 head of cattle. He sold 300 of them. How many did he have left?

7. A waiter received $12.50 in tips on Monday, $11.70 on Tuesday, $7.55 on Wednesday, and $20.05 on Thursday. What was the average amount he received?

8. What is the area of a field 624 feet long by 97 feet wide?

9. There are 2,095 seats in an auditorium. Students sold 1,608 tickets for a concert. How many seats were empty during the concert?

DIFFERENT DENOMINATORS

How can we add fractions when the denominators are different?

1. If you pour the water from A and B into C, how full will C be?

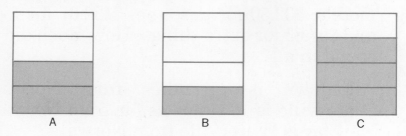

   A   B   C

    a. We know from the picture of glass C that $\frac{1}{2} + \frac{1}{4}$ is how many fourths? $\frac{1}{2} + \frac{1}{4} = \frac{\triangledown}{4}$

    b. We need to use names for $\frac{1}{2}$ and $\frac{1}{4}$ which have the same denominator. $\frac{1}{2}$ is how many fourths? $\frac{1}{2} = \frac{\triangle}{4}$

    c. We rename $\frac{1}{2}$ as $\frac{2}{4}$ and then add.

$$\frac{2}{4} + \frac{1}{4} = \frac{2 + 1}{4}$$
$$= \frac{\triangle}{4}$$

2. Consider $\frac{1}{3} + \frac{3}{6}$. Are the denominators alike?

    a. Here are some fractional numerals equivalent to $\frac{1}{3}$: $\frac{1}{3}, \frac{2}{6}, \frac{3}{9}, \frac{4}{12}, \frac{5}{15}$

    b. What name for $\frac{1}{3}$ has the denominator 6?

c. Copy and complete.

$$\frac{1}{3} + \frac{3}{6} = \frac{2}{6} + \frac{3}{6}$$
$$= \frac{2+3}{6}$$
$$= \frac{\square}{6}$$

Add.

1. $\frac{1}{4} + \frac{3}{12}$ 2. $\frac{1}{2} + \frac{1}{8}$ 3. $\frac{1}{2} + \frac{1}{6}$ 4. $\frac{1}{4} + \frac{5}{8}$

5. $\frac{1}{2} + \frac{3}{8}$ 6. $\frac{4}{5} + \frac{1}{10}$ 7. $\frac{1}{5} + \frac{3}{10}$ 8. $\frac{2}{7} + \frac{3}{14}$

9. $\begin{array}{r} \frac{3}{5} \\ +\frac{2}{10} \\ \hline \end{array}$ 10. $\begin{array}{r} \frac{5}{6} \\ +\frac{1}{3} \\ \hline \end{array}$ 11. $\begin{array}{r} \frac{3}{8} \\ +\frac{1}{4} \\ \hline \end{array}$ 12. $\begin{array}{r} \frac{1}{2} \\ +\frac{3}{10} \\ \hline \end{array}$ 13. $\begin{array}{r} \frac{3}{10} \\ +\frac{2}{5} \\ \hline \end{array}$

14. $\begin{array}{r} \frac{3}{8} \\ +\frac{1}{16} \\ \hline \end{array}$ 15. $\begin{array}{r} \frac{1}{4} \\ +\frac{1}{8} \\ \hline \end{array}$ 16. $\begin{array}{r} \frac{1}{4} \\ +\frac{3}{12} \\ \hline \end{array}$ 17. $\begin{array}{r} \frac{1}{2} \\ +\frac{3}{8} \\ \hline \end{array}$ 18. $\begin{array}{r} \frac{1}{2} \\ +\frac{1}{6} \\ \hline \end{array}$

Solve the problem.

19. **a.** Bonnie ate $\frac{1}{3}$ of a bag of candy. Candice ate $\frac{1}{9}$ of the candy. How much of the bag of candy did they both eat?

    b. There were 27 pieces of candy in the bag. How many pieces did Bonnie eat? How many pieces did Candice eat?

FINDING LIKE DENOMINATORS

How can we add $\frac{1}{2}$ and $\frac{1}{3}$?

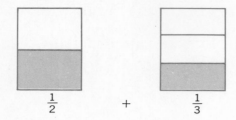

$$\frac{1}{2} \qquad + \qquad \frac{1}{3}$$

1. **a.** List 6 fractional numerals equivalent to $\frac{1}{2}$.

   b. Can you find one with the denominator 3?

2. **a.** List 6 fractional numerals equivalent to $\frac{1}{3}$.

   b. Can you find one with the denominator 2?

3. Study your list of numerals.

$$\frac{1}{2}, \frac{2}{4}, \frac{3}{6}, \frac{4}{8}, \frac{5}{10}, \frac{6}{12}, \frac{7}{14} \qquad \frac{1}{3}, \frac{2}{6}, \frac{3}{9}, \frac{4}{12}, \frac{5}{15}, \frac{6}{18}, \frac{7}{21}$$

   a. Find names for $\frac{1}{2}$ and $\frac{1}{3}$ with the same denominator.

   b. What name for $\frac{1}{2}$ has the denominator 6?

   c. What name for $\frac{1}{3}$ has the denominator 6?

   d. Use these to add.

$$\frac{1}{2} + \frac{1}{3} = \frac{3}{6} + \frac{2}{6}$$
$$= \frac{3+2}{6}$$
$$= \frac{\triangle}{6}$$

4. Consider $\frac{1}{3} + \frac{1}{4}$.

    a. List several fractional numerals for $\frac{1}{3}$.

    b. List several fractional numerals for $\frac{1}{4}$.

    c. Find two names with the same denominator. Add.

$$\frac{1}{3} + \frac{1}{4} = \frac{4}{12} + \frac{3}{12}$$
$$= \frac{4 + 3}{12}$$
$$= \frac{\triangle}{12}$$

To add $\frac{2}{3}$ and $\frac{1}{4}$ we rename both numbers. We list names for $\frac{2}{3}$ and $\frac{1}{4}$. We choose names with the same denominator and add.

EXERCISES

Add. List equivalent fractional numerals to help you.

1. $\frac{1}{2} + \frac{1}{3}$ **2.** $\frac{1}{2} + \frac{1}{5}$ **3.** $\frac{3}{4} + \frac{2}{3}$ **4.** $\frac{2}{5} + \frac{1}{3}$

5. $\frac{2}{3} + \frac{1}{2}$ **6.** $\frac{1}{4} + \frac{1}{5}$ **7.** $\frac{1}{3} + \frac{3}{4}$ **8.** $\frac{3}{5} + \frac{1}{4}$

9. $\frac{1}{3} + \frac{3}{5}$ **10.** $\frac{2}{5} + \frac{1}{4}$ **11.** $\frac{2}{5} + \frac{2}{3}$ **12.** $\frac{3}{4} + \frac{4}{5}$

13. $\frac{1}{7}$ **14.** $\frac{2}{4}$ **15.** $\frac{1}{3}$ **16.** $\frac{2}{5}$ **17.** $\frac{1}{3}$

      $+\frac{1}{2}$ $+\frac{1}{3}$ $+\frac{2}{8}$ $+\frac{1}{2}$ $+\frac{1}{4}$

PROPERTIES OF ADDITION

1. We know that $2 + 3 = 3 + 2$. Why?

2. **a.** Add.

$$\tfrac{1}{8} + \tfrac{4}{8} = \frac{1 + 4}{8} \qquad\qquad \tfrac{4}{8} + \tfrac{1}{8} = \frac{4 + 1}{8}$$
$$= \frac{\triangle}{8} \qquad\qquad\qquad\quad = \frac{\triangle}{8}$$

   b. Does $\tfrac{1}{8} + \tfrac{4}{8} = \tfrac{4}{8} + \tfrac{1}{8}$?

   c. What property of addition does this show?

3. Consider $\tfrac{1}{8} + \tfrac{2}{8} + \tfrac{4}{8}$.

   a. $\left(\tfrac{1}{8} + \tfrac{2}{8}\right) + \tfrac{4}{8} = \tfrac{3}{8} + \tfrac{4}{8}$
   $$= \frac{\square}{8}$$

   b. $\tfrac{1}{8} + \left(\tfrac{2}{8} + \tfrac{4}{8}\right) = \tfrac{1}{8} + \tfrac{6}{8}$
   $$= \frac{\square}{8}$$

   c. Then $\left(\tfrac{1}{8} + \tfrac{2}{8}\right) + \tfrac{4}{8} = \tfrac{1}{8} + \left(\tfrac{2}{8} + \tfrac{4}{8}\right)$.

   d. What property of addition is shown?

4. Make each sentence true.

   a. $\tfrac{1}{3} + \tfrac{1}{6} = \square + \tfrac{1}{3}$ **b.** $\tfrac{3}{8} + \tfrac{2}{8} = \tfrac{2}{8} + \square$

   c. $\left(\tfrac{1}{3} + \tfrac{2}{8}\right) + \tfrac{1}{8} = \tfrac{1}{3} + \left(\tfrac{2}{8} + \square\right)$

5. What property of addition is shown in Item 4a? Item 4b? Item 4c?

MORE SUBTRACTION

How can we subtract when the denominators are different?

1. Consider $\frac{2}{3} - \frac{1}{4}$.

   a. List some fractional numerals for $\frac{2}{3}$. List some for $\frac{1}{4}$.

   b. Find names for $\frac{2}{3}$ and $\frac{1}{4}$ with the same denominator.

   $$\frac{2}{3}, \frac{4}{6}, \frac{6}{9}, \boxed{\frac{8}{12}}, \frac{10}{15}$$

   $$\frac{1}{4}, \frac{2}{8}, \boxed{\frac{3}{12}}, \frac{4}{16}, \frac{5}{20}$$

   c. Subtract. Copy and complete.

   $$\frac{2}{3} - \frac{1}{4} = \frac{8}{12} - \frac{3}{12} \qquad\qquad \frac{2}{3} = \frac{8}{12}$$
   $$= \frac{8-3}{12} \qquad\qquad\quad \frac{-\frac{1}{4} = \frac{3}{12}}{}$$
   $$= \frac{\triangle}{12} \qquad\qquad\qquad \frac{\triangle}{12}$$

2. Consider $\frac{2}{3} - \frac{2}{5}$.

   a. List some fractional numerals for $\frac{2}{3}$. List some for $\frac{2}{5}$.

   b. Choose names for $\frac{2}{3}$ and $\frac{2}{5}$ with the same denominator.

   c. Complete the subtraction $\frac{2}{3} - \frac{2}{5}$.

3. Subtract. Explain each step.

a. $\dfrac{3}{6}$ $-\dfrac{1}{4}$ b. $\dfrac{6}{8}$ $-\dfrac{2}{3}$ c. $\dfrac{5}{6}$ $-\dfrac{1}{4}$ d. $\dfrac{5}{7}$ $-\dfrac{1}{2}$

EXERCISES

Subtract.

1. $\dfrac{9}{12}$ $-\dfrac{1}{2}$ 2. $\dfrac{1}{2}$ $-\dfrac{1}{5}$ 3. $\dfrac{3}{5}$ $-\dfrac{1}{4}$ 4. $\dfrac{3}{6}$ $-\dfrac{3}{8}$

5. $\dfrac{3}{8}$ $-\dfrac{1}{3}$ 6. $\dfrac{3}{7}$ $-\dfrac{1}{4}$ 7. $\dfrac{1}{2}$ $-\dfrac{3}{7}$ 8. $\dfrac{3}{4}$ $-\dfrac{1}{6}$

9. $\dfrac{5}{6}$ $-\dfrac{1}{4}$ 10. $\dfrac{1}{2}$ $-\dfrac{1}{3}$ 11. $\dfrac{1}{3}$ $-\dfrac{1}{4}$ 12. $\dfrac{3}{4}$ $-\dfrac{3}{5}$

13. $\dfrac{3}{4}$ $-\dfrac{2}{3}$ 14. $\dfrac{7}{8}$ $-\dfrac{1}{3}$ 15. $\dfrac{7}{8}$ $-\dfrac{1}{5}$ 16. $\dfrac{3}{4}$ $-\dfrac{1}{3}$

Solve the problem.

17. a. Carl has $\dfrac{1}{2}$ of a pie. Leonard has $\dfrac{2}{5}$ of a pie. How much more pie does Carl have than Leonard?

b. How much pie do both boys have in all?

DO YOU REMEMBER?

Do each of these exercises.

1. 87
   26
   48

2. 349
   267
   398

3. $62.47
   28.36
   89.05

4. 284,976
   +948,712

5. 621
   −348

6. $40.87
   −38.27

7. 87,492
   −38,762

8. 91,111
   −82,222

9. 235
   ×8

10. 227
    ×93

11. 274
    ×89

12. 235
    ×88

13. 6)492   14. 9)253   15. 40)827   16. 7)854

Solve each problem.

17. Name the three figures at the right.

18. ∠*LPM* is a right angle. What kind of triangle is triangle *LPM*?

19. Name the sides of angle *ABC*. Name the vertex.

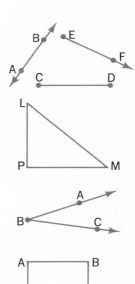

20. **a.** Copy the rectangle at the right. Draw its diagonals. Name them.

    b. What special kind of rectangle is it?

Make each sentence true. Use >, <, or =.

21. 800−399≡801−499   22. 8×72≡4×144

331

MIXED NUMERALS

1. Each bar is cut into halves.

   a. How many halves are shaded?
   b. One whole bar and how many halves are shaded?
   c. We write $\frac{3}{2}$ or $1\frac{1}{2}$. (We say "one and one-half.")

2. Each bar is cut into fourths.

   a. How many fourths are shaded?
   b. This makes one whole bar and how many fourths? Think: $\frac{4}{4} = 1$, so $\frac{7}{4} = 1\frac{3}{4}$. A numeral like $1\frac{3}{4}$ is called a *mixed numeral*.

3. Write a fractional numeral for the shaded part in each picture.

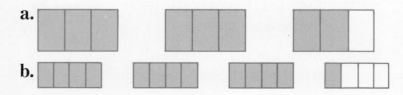

4. Write a mixed numeral for the shaded part of each picture in Item 3a and Item 3b.

5. We know $\frac{8}{4} = 2$, so $\frac{9}{4}$ is 2 and how many more fourths?

$$\frac{9}{4} = \frac{8}{4} + \frac{1}{4}$$
$$= 2 + \frac{1}{4}$$
$$= 2\frac{1}{4}$$

6. Find a pattern.

   a. $\frac{9}{3} = 3$, $\quad \frac{10}{3} = 3\frac{1}{3}$, $\quad \frac{11}{3} = $ ___

   b. $\frac{12}{6} = 2$, $\quad \frac{13}{6} = 2\frac{1}{6}$, $\quad \frac{14}{6} = $ ___, $\quad \frac{15}{6} = $ ___

   c. $\frac{10}{5} = 2$, $\quad \frac{11}{5} = $ ___, $\quad \frac{13}{5} = $ ___

7. Write mixed numerals.

   a. $\frac{4}{3}$ **b.** $\frac{10}{4}$ **c.** $\frac{13}{3}$ **d.** $\frac{7}{3}$ **e.** $\frac{5}{4}$

EXERCISES

1. Draw a picture to show $\frac{4}{3}$. Write a mixed numeral for $\frac{4}{3}$.

Write mixed numerals. Draw pictures if you need help.

   2. $\frac{5}{3}$ **3.** $\frac{9}{5}$ **4.** $\frac{11}{4}$ **5.** $\frac{11}{5}$ **6.** $\frac{7}{4}$

   7. $\frac{6}{5}$ **8.** $\frac{13}{4}$ **9.** $\frac{11}{2}$ **10.** $\frac{12}{5}$ **11.** $\frac{15}{4}$

   12. $\frac{11}{3}$ **13.** $\frac{13}{6}$ **14.** $\frac{9}{8}$ **15.** $\frac{15}{7}$ **16.** $\frac{25}{6}$

SUMS GREATER THAN ONE

1. Bonnie walked $\frac{5}{8}$ of a mile to the store. She then walked $\frac{6}{8}$ of a mile to the post office. We can show the problem on a number line.

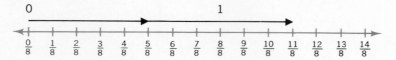

a. How far did Bonnie walk?

b. How much more than one mile did Bonnie walk?

c. Add: $\frac{5}{8} + \frac{6}{8} = \frac{\triangle}{8}$

2. Mother made 2 cakes of the same size. Jack's friends ate $\frac{1}{2}$ of one cake and $\frac{3}{4}$ of the other cake. How much cake did they eat in all?

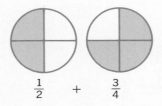

$\frac{1}{2}$ + $\frac{3}{4}$

a. Name the sum with a fractional numeral.

$$\frac{1}{2} + \frac{3}{4} = \frac{2}{4} + \frac{3}{4}$$
$$= \frac{\triangle}{4}$$

b. Name the sum with a mixed numeral.

$$\frac{4}{4} = 1, \text{ so } \frac{5}{4} = 1\frac{\square}{4}$$

3. Copy and complete. Explain each step.

$$\frac{2}{3} + \frac{3}{4} = \frac{8}{12} + \frac{9}{12}$$
$$= \frac{17}{12}$$
$$= 1\frac{\triangle}{12}$$

$$\frac{2}{3} = \frac{\triangledown}{12}$$
$$+\frac{3}{4} = \frac{\hexagon}{12}$$
$$\overline{\phantom{+\frac{3}{4}}}$$
$$\frac{\square}{12} = 1\frac{\triangle}{12}$$

Add. Name the sum with a standard numeral or a mixed numeral.

1. $\frac{1}{2}$ **2.** $\frac{4}{7}$ **3.** $\frac{2}{3}$ **4.** $\frac{4}{5}$ **5.** $\frac{6}{5}$

$+\frac{3}{6}$ $+\frac{5}{7}$ $+\frac{3}{4}$ $+\frac{1}{2}$ $+\frac{7}{5}$

6. $\frac{1}{3}$ **7.** $\frac{3}{5}$ **8.** $\frac{9}{13}$ **9.** $\frac{5}{3}$ **10.** $\frac{7}{8}$

$+\frac{5}{6}$ $+\frac{2}{5}$ $+\frac{7}{13}$ $+\frac{2}{3}$ $+\frac{9}{8}$

11. $\frac{6}{15} + \frac{10}{15}$ **12.** $\frac{7}{9} + \frac{8}{9}$ **13.** $\frac{6}{10} + \frac{9}{10}$

Solve each problem.

14. Mike spent $\frac{2}{3}$ of an hour on his scrapbook before dinner and $\frac{3}{4}$ of an hour on it after dinner. How much time did he spend on his scrapbook that evening?

15. Alice bought material for a dress. She bought $\frac{3}{8}$ of a yard of red cloth and $\frac{3}{4}$ of a yard of white cloth. How much material did she buy?

ADDITION USING MIXED NUMERALS

1. Mrs. Smith has $2\frac{3}{8}$ apple pies and $1\frac{1}{8}$ lemon pies.

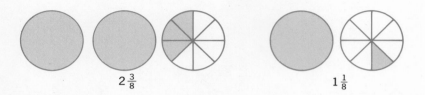

$2\frac{3}{8}$ $1\frac{1}{8}$

    a. How many whole pies does she have?

    b. Each small piece is $\frac{1}{8}$ of a pie. How many small pieces are there?

    c. How much pie does she have in all?

2. We can add $2\frac{3}{8}$ and $1\frac{1}{8}$. Explain each step.

$$
\begin{aligned}
2\tfrac{3}{8} + 1\tfrac{1}{8} &= \left(2 + \tfrac{3}{8}\right) + \left(1 + \tfrac{1}{8}\right) \\
&= \left(2 + 1\right) + \left(\tfrac{3}{8} + \tfrac{1}{8}\right) \\
&= 3 + \tfrac{4}{8} \\
&= 3\tfrac{4}{8}
\end{aligned}
$$

    a. How was $2\frac{3}{8}$ renamed?

    b. How was $1\frac{1}{8}$ renamed?

    c. Why is $\left(2 + \frac{3}{8}\right) + \left(1 + \frac{1}{8}\right) = (2 + 1) + \left(\frac{3}{8} + \frac{1}{8}\right)$ true?

3. We can use a vertical form. Explain each step.

$$2\tfrac{3}{8}$$
$$+1\tfrac{1}{8}$$
$$\overline{\tfrac{\triangle}{8}}$$

$$2\tfrac{3}{8}$$
$$+1\tfrac{1}{8}$$
$$\overline{3\tfrac{\triangle}{8}}$$

$$\tfrac{3}{8} + \tfrac{1}{8} = \tfrac{\triangle}{8} \qquad 2 + 1 = 3 \qquad 3 + \tfrac{\triangle}{8} = 3\tfrac{\triangle}{8}$$

4. Consider $6\tfrac{1}{2} + 8\tfrac{1}{3}$.

   a. List names for $\tfrac{1}{2}$ and names for $\tfrac{1}{3}$.

   b. Select names for $\tfrac{1}{2}$ and $\tfrac{1}{3}$ with the same denominator. Add.

$$6\tfrac{1}{2} = 6\tfrac{\triangle}{6}$$
$$+8\tfrac{1}{3} = 8\tfrac{\square}{6}$$

EXERCISES

Add.

1. $2\tfrac{1}{4}$ **2.** $3\tfrac{3}{8}$ **3.** $6\tfrac{1}{5}$ **4.** $7\tfrac{1}{2}$
    $+2\tfrac{1}{4}$ $+2\tfrac{1}{8}$ $+3\tfrac{2}{5}$ $+8\tfrac{1}{3}$

5. $1\tfrac{1}{2}$ **6.** $3\tfrac{3}{8}$ **7.** $8\tfrac{7}{16}$ **8.** $9\tfrac{1}{2}$
    $+1\tfrac{1}{4}$ $+2\tfrac{1}{4}$ $+12\tfrac{5}{16}$ $+6\tfrac{1}{3}$

9. $7\tfrac{2}{6}$ **10.** $3\tfrac{8}{19}$ **11.** $9\tfrac{3}{8}$ **12.** $16\tfrac{1}{4}$
  $+14\tfrac{1}{3}$ $+8\tfrac{7}{19}$ $+15\tfrac{1}{2}$ $+5\tfrac{2}{3}$

SUBTRACTION USING MIXED NUMERALS

1. Mrs. Nelson had $5\frac{5}{6}$ cakes. She sold $1\frac{3}{6}$ cakes. How much cake was left? Think: $5\frac{5}{6} - 1\frac{3}{6}$. Explain each step.

$$5\ \frac{5}{6}$$
$$-1\ \frac{3}{6}$$
$$\overline{\quad\frac{\triangle}{6}}$$

$$5\ \frac{5}{6}$$
$$-1\ \frac{3}{6}$$
$$\overline{4\ \frac{\triangle}{6}}$$

$$\frac{5}{6} - \frac{3}{6} = \frac{\triangle}{6} \qquad 5 - 1 = 4 \qquad 4 + \frac{\triangle}{6} = 4\frac{\triangle}{6}$$

2. Mr. Nolan had $15\frac{1}{2}$ yards of silk on a bolt. He sold $4\frac{1}{3}$ yards. How much silk did he have left? Think: $15\frac{1}{2} - 4\frac{1}{3}$. Explain each step.

a. $\frac{1}{2}, \frac{2}{4}, \frac{3}{6}, \frac{4}{8}, \frac{5}{10}, \frac{6}{12}$

$\frac{1}{3}, \frac{2}{6}, \frac{3}{9}, \frac{4}{12}, \frac{5}{15}$

b. $15\frac{1}{2} = 15\frac{3}{6}$

$$\underline{-4\frac{1}{3} = \quad 4\frac{2}{6}}$$
$$11\frac{1}{6}$$

338

3. Subtract. Explain each step.

a. $4\frac{2}{3}$ **b.** $7\frac{2}{8}$ **c.** $8\frac{9}{16}$ **d.** $7\frac{5}{8}$

$-\frac{1}{2}$ $-6\frac{1}{4}$ $-4\frac{1}{2}$ $-7\frac{2}{8}$

Subtract.

1. $7\frac{7}{8}$ **2.** $4\frac{2}{3}$ **3.** $10\frac{4}{8}$ **4.** $7\frac{2}{3}$

$-3\frac{2}{8}$ $-1\frac{1}{6}$ $-3\frac{1}{8}$ $-1\frac{1}{4}$

5. $5\frac{3}{7}$ **6.** $8\frac{2}{3}$ **7.** $6\frac{5}{6}$ **8.** $2\frac{1}{2}$

$-\frac{1}{7}$ $-5\frac{1}{3}$ $-2\frac{2}{3}$ $-1\frac{1}{4}$

9. $3\frac{4}{8}$ **10.** $7\frac{5}{7}$ **11.** $4\frac{5}{8}$ **12.** $6\frac{9}{10}$

$-1\frac{1}{2}$ $-7\frac{1}{14}$ $-1\frac{2}{8}$ $-4\frac{1}{10}$

Solve the problem.

13. Mr. Toth used $2\frac{3}{4}$ gallons of paint to paint one room, and $1\frac{1}{2}$ gallons of paint for a second room. How much more paint did he use in the first room?

PROBLEM SOLVING

1. Mary has $\frac{2}{3}$ yard of red ribbon and $\frac{1}{4}$ yard of white ribbon. How much ribbon does she have in all?

2. Allan rode his bicycle $1\frac{1}{8}$ miles in the morning and $3\frac{1}{2}$ miles in the afternoon. How long was Allan's bicycle trip?

3. Mother had $\frac{7}{8}$ of a cherry pie. Bill and Jerry ate $\frac{2}{8}$ of the pie. How much pie was left?

4. Mr. Adams had $15\frac{3}{4}$ feet of rope. He gave Jack $6\frac{1}{2}$ feet of rope. How much rope did Mr. Adams have left?

5. Tony's family lives $4\frac{8}{10}$ miles from Rutland. David's family lives $2\frac{1}{10}$ miles from Rutland. How much closer to Rutland does David's family live than Tony's?

6. Lou practiced on her piano for $2\frac{1}{4}$ hours. Ann practiced for 2 hours.

   a. How much longer did Lou practice?

   b. How many hours did both girls practice?

CHAPTER REVIEW

1. We know that $\frac{1}{2} + \frac{2}{3} = \frac{2}{3} + \frac{1}{2}$. Why?

2. Copy and complete.

   a. $\frac{2}{7} + \frac{4}{7} = \frac{2 + \square}{7}$

   $= \frac{\triangle}{7}$

   b. $\frac{6}{10} - \frac{2}{10} = \frac{\square - 2}{10}$

   $= \frac{\triangle}{10}$

3. Consider $\frac{1}{3} + \frac{1}{6}$.

   a. Why is it that we cannot add the numerators and use the denominator 6?

   b. $\frac{1}{3}$ is how many sixths? $\frac{1}{3} = \frac{\square}{6}$

   c. Complete the addition $\frac{1}{3} + \frac{1}{6}$.

4. Copy and complete.

   a. $\frac{1}{4} + \frac{2}{16}$

   b. $\frac{2}{5} + \frac{3}{10}$

   c. $\frac{3}{8} - \frac{1}{4}$

   d. $\frac{5}{9} - \frac{5}{18}$

5. Consider $\frac{3}{4} - \frac{1}{3}$.

   a. Find 5 fractional numerals for $\frac{3}{4}$. for $\frac{1}{3}$.

   b. Which fractional numerals for $\frac{3}{4}$ and $\frac{1}{3}$ have the same denominator?

   c. Complete the subtraction $\frac{3}{4} - \frac{1}{3}$.

6. Copy and complete.

    a. $\frac{4}{5} + \frac{2}{3}$ **b.** $\frac{1}{4} + \frac{2}{3}$ **c.** $\frac{5}{7} - \frac{1}{2}$ **d.** $\frac{2}{5} - \frac{1}{3}$

7. Al practiced his drums for $\frac{2}{4}$ of an hour, and later for $\frac{3}{4}$ of an hour. How long did he practice?

    a. Did Al practice for more than one hour?

    b. Copy and complete.

$$\frac{2}{4} + \frac{3}{4} = \frac{\square + 3}{4}$$
$$= \frac{\triangle}{4}$$
$$= 1\frac{\triangledown}{4}$$

8. Consider $4\frac{1}{8} + 9\frac{1}{8}$.

    a. Add the two fractions. What is their sum?

    b. Add the two whole numbers. What is their sum?

    c. Copy and complete. $4\frac{1}{8} + 9\frac{1}{8} = \square\frac{\triangle}{8}$.

9. Copy and complete.

    a. $6\frac{2}{3} + 5\frac{1}{3}$ **b.** $9\frac{7}{8} - 2\frac{3}{8}$ **c.** $6\frac{4}{9} + 1\frac{3}{8}$

Terms You Should Know

commutative property   mixed numerals
associative property   denominator
equivalent fractional numerals

CHAPTER TEST

Add.

1. $\dfrac{3}{8}$
$+\dfrac{3}{8}$

2. $5\dfrac{4}{10}$
$+6\dfrac{2}{5}$

3. $\dfrac{3}{9}$
$+\dfrac{6}{9}$

4. $6\dfrac{3}{8}$
$+2\dfrac{1}{4}$

Subtract.

5. $\dfrac{7}{12}$
$-\dfrac{5}{12}$

6. $4\dfrac{2}{3}$
$-1\dfrac{2}{3}$

7. $\dfrac{3}{4}$
$-\dfrac{2}{3}$

8. $\dfrac{7}{8}$
$-\dfrac{3}{4}$

9. Study these fractional numerals.

$$\dfrac{4}{6}, \dfrac{7}{14}, \dfrac{6}{8}, \dfrac{9}{15}, \dfrac{8}{16}, \dfrac{10}{15}$$

   a. Which name $\dfrac{1}{2}$?

   b. Which name $\dfrac{2}{3}$?

Write mixed numerals.

10. $\dfrac{5}{3}$ **11.** $\dfrac{9}{7}$ **12.** $\dfrac{9}{4}$ **13.** $\dfrac{12}{11}$

Solve each problem.

14. Al had $\dfrac{1}{2}$ gallon of paint. He bought $\dfrac{1}{4}$ gallon more. How much paint does he have now?

15. Mrs. Allen had $10\dfrac{3}{8}$ cups of sugar. She borrowed $3\dfrac{1}{2}$ cups. How much sugar did she have in all?

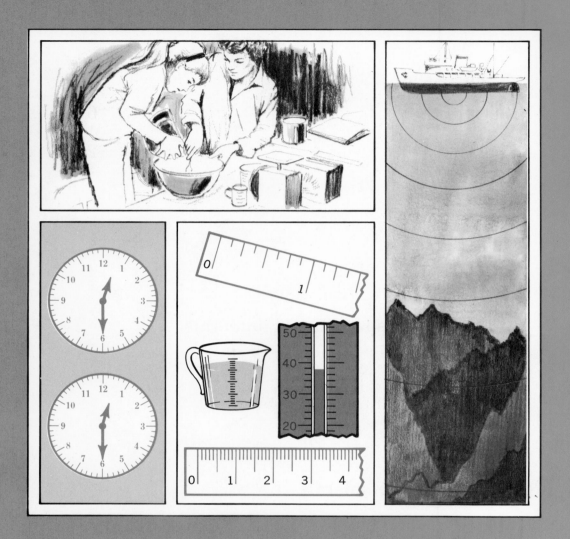

CHAPTER ELEVEN

Measurement

TIME

Man learned to tell time by the sun. If the sun is directly overhead, it is 12 o'clock noon.

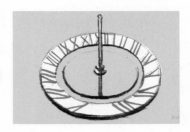

1. Where will the sun be in 24 hours?

2. The time shown is 4:15. It is read as four fifteen. It is also:

   a. a quarter past ____

   b. ____ minutes past four

3. What time is shown?

   a.    **b.**    **c.**

4. The time is 3:35.

   a. Which numeral tells the hour?

   b. Which numeral tells how many minutes past the hour?

5. Where will the minute hand be in:

   a. 5 minutes

   b. 30 minutes

6. Paul came home at 3:25. Then he played ball for 1 hour and 45 minutes. What time did he finish playing ball? We add.

3 hr 25 min	4 hr + 70 min
1 hr 45 min	4 hr + ___ hr + 10 min
4 hr 70 min	___ hr + 10 min or 5:10

7. The time is now 4:25. June went to the store 1 hour and 45 minutes ago. What time did she leave? We subtract.

4 hr + 25 min	3 hr + 85 min
1 hr + 45 min	1 hr + 45 min
	2 hr + ___ min or ___

EXERCISES

What time is shown?

1. 2. 3.

What time will it be 1 hour and 40 minutes after each time shown?

4. 5. 6.

7.-9. What was the time 1 hour and 40 minutes before each time shown above?

346

DO YOU REMEMBER?

Make each sentence true.

1. $747 + 1{,}829 = \square$ 2. $8 \times 300 = \square$

3. $\square + 384 = 796$ 4. $600 \div 6 = \square$

5. $\square - 189 = 263$ 6. $3 \times \triangle = 600$

Round to the nearest hundred.

7. 874   8. 703   9. 450   10. 1,922

Add.

11. 904	12. 2,015	13. 1,919	14. 7,492
341	386	2,828	8,503
786	1,047	3,737	9,614

Subtract.

15. 7,489	16. 3,862	17. 7,000	18. 7,003
−6,048	−1,978	−3,456	−3,498

Multiply.

19. 860	20. 348	21. 362	22. $49.84
×9	×7	×22	×23

Divide.

23. $8\overline{)96}$ 24. $10\overline{)190}$ 25. $7\overline{)423}$ 26. $20\overline{)875}$

27. $4\overline{)148}$ 28. $3\overline{)723}$ 29. $30\overline{)251}$ 30. $80\overline{)784}$

31. $50\overline{)625}$ 32. $9\overline{)6{,}458}$ 33. $40\overline{)293}$ 34. $6\overline{)5{,}125}$

35. $2\overline{)346}$ 36. $30\overline{)4{,}654}$ 37. $60\overline{)730}$ 38. $4\overline{)7{,}364}$

AM AND PM

There are 24 hours in a day. When the sun is overhead, it is 12:00 *noon*. The time 12 hours after noon is 12:00 *midnight*. The hours from midnight to noon are labeled *am*. The hours from noon to midnight are labeled *pm*.

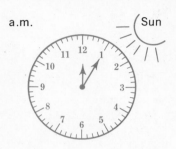

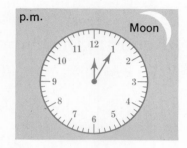

1. **a.** Would you eat dinner at 6 am or 6 pm?

   b. Are banks usually open at 10 am or 10 pm?

   c. Are you in school at 10 am or 10 pm?

   d. Are you usually asleep at 2 am or 2 pm?

2. What will the time be four hours after noon?

3. Four hours after 9 am it will be 1 pm. What will the time be four hours after:

   a. 3 am   **b.** 3 pm   **c.** 7 am

   d. 8 am   **e.** 8 pm   **f.** 7 pm

4. Three hours before 2 pm it was 11 am. What was the time three hours before:

   a. 7 am   **b.** 7 pm   **c.** 11 am

   d. 3 am   **e.** 3 pm   **f.** 11 pm

5. Bill's father leaves for work at 6 am. He gets home at 6 pm. How long is he gone?

6. While the second hand goes around once, the minute hand moves one space.

7. While the minute hand moves 1 space, the second hand moves ____ spaces.

8. How many spaces does the second hand move in 3 minutes?

There are 60 seconds in one minute.

EXERCISES

Solve each problem.

1. It takes 4 hours and 20 minutes to go from New York to Syracuse by train. The train leaves New York at 8:30 am. What time does it arrive in Syracuse?

2. Jim works for six hours. He finishes work at 4 pm. What times does he start?

What time will it be six hours after:

3. 5 am   **4.** 6 am   **5.** 7 am

6. 11 am   **7.** 2 pm   **8.** 10 pm

9. Betty went to the dentist at 11:45 am and left at 1:15 pm. How long was she there?

TEMPERATURE

What happens to water when it gets very cold?
What happens to water when it gets very hot?

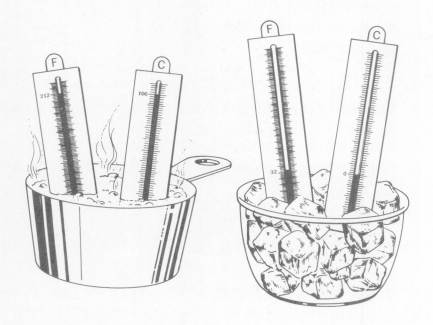

1. In the United States we usually use a thermometer with a *Fahrenheit* (F) scale. Water boils at 212°F. At what temperature does water freeze on this scale?

2. The Celsius thermometer is used in many countries. It is also used by scientists all over the world. On the *Celsius* (C) scale water freezes at 0°. At what temperature does water boil on this scale?

3. What temperature is shown on each thermometer? If the temperature dropped 10° what would each thermometer read?

a. 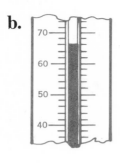 **b.** **c.**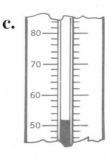

4. Which temperature shown above is the hottest? the coldest?

5. Jane kept a record of noon temperatures.

Sun.	Mon.	Tues.	Wed.	Thur.	Fri.	Sat.
40°	52°	44°	36°	20°	20°	14°

    a. Which noon was the warmest? the coldest?

    b. How many degrees difference was there between the warmest and coldest noon?

6. A temperature of 20°C is very pleasant. If it were 36°C, would it be warmer or colder?

7. About what is the hottest temperature where you live? About what is the coldest temperature?

8. At 8 am the temperature in Mexico City was 16°C. By noon it had risen 12°C. What was the temperature at noon?

9. The temperature at midnight in Mexico City was 8°C. How much lower than the 8 am temperature was this?

EIGHTH INCHES

1. Measure these.

   a. 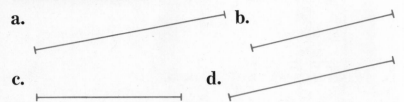 b.

   c. d.

2. **a.** How many parts between 0 and 1 are on ruler I? ruler II? ruler III?

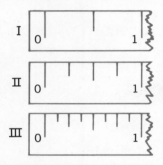

   b. What are the parts called on ruler I? ruler II?

   c. Ruler III is marked in eighths of an inch. Each part is $\frac{1}{8}$ inch.

3. How long is each segment?

   a. ├─────┤ b. ├───────────┤

4. **a.** Is the length of $\overline{AB}$ closer to $\frac{6}{8}$ in. or $\frac{7}{8}$ in.?

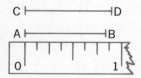

   b. Is the length of $\overline{CD}$ closer to $\frac{8}{8}$ in. or $\frac{7}{8}$ in.?

352

c. The length of each segment is $\frac{7}{8}$ inch to the nearest $\frac{1}{8}$-inch. This means the length is closer to $\frac{7}{8}$ inch than to $\frac{6}{8}$ inch or $\frac{8}{8}$ inch.

5. Measure to the nearest $\frac{1}{8}$ in.

a. 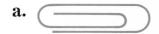   **b.**

6. Draw a line segment $2\frac{3}{8}$ in. long. Mark the endpoints A and B.

7. Mark $\overline{AB}$ in eighths of an inch.

Measure to the nearest $\frac{1}{8}$ in.

1.   **2.**

3.

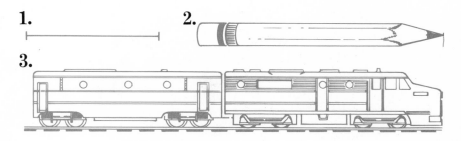

Draw line segments.

4. $\frac{4}{8}$ in. long   **5.** $2\frac{4}{8}$ in. long

6. $2\frac{1}{8}$ in. long   **7.** $4\frac{1}{8}$ in. long

8. $1\frac{6}{8}$ in. long   **9.** $3\frac{5}{8}$ in. long

FEET, YARDS, MILES

We measure the length of a book in inches.

1. What unit might we use to measure the length of a room?

1 foot is 12 inches

2. Would you measure the length of a parking lot in feet? What other unit of measure could you use?

1 yard is 3 feet

3. How many feet is:

   a. 2 yards   **b.** 10 yards   **c.** 52 yards

4. How many yards is:

   a. 15 feet   **b.** 60 feet   **c.** 156 feet

1 yard is 36 inches

5. How many inches is:

   a. 2 yards   **b.** 10 yards   **c.** 18 yards

6. What unit might we use to measure the distance between cities? the length of a river?

1 mile is 5,280 feet

7. Doris and Jean live 4 miles apart. How many feet is this?

8. The balloon is 28 miles high. How many feet is this?

9. a. In a mile, are there more than 2,000 yards? 1,500 yards?

b. How many yards are in a mile?

10. Find the perimeter?

a. ___ yd ___ ft

b. ___ ft

c. How much longer is $\overline{AD}$ than $\overline{DC}$?

C   61 yd   B
58 yd 1 ft   112 yd 2 ft
D   203 yd 1 ft   A

EXERCISES

Copy and complete.

1.

miles	feet	yards
1	5,280	
3		

2. Find the perimeter.

a. ___ yd ___ ft

b. ___ ft

c. How much shorter is $\overline{AB}$ than $\overline{DC}$?

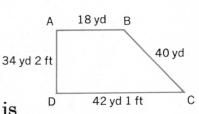

A   18 yd   B
34 yd 2 ft   40 yd
D   42 yd 1 ft   C

USING A TABLE

The following table shows how fast animals can travel.

SPEED OF ANIMALS	
Animal	*Miles Per Hour*
Cat	30
Cheetah	65
Fly	5
Golden eagle	120
Greyhound	40
Hummingbird	60
Jack rabbit	45
Man (running)	20
Man (swimming)	5
Racehorse	45
Snake	2

Use the table above to answer these questions.

1. How fast can each of these animals travel?

   a. fly   **b.** snake   **c.** cat

2. How many more miles an hour can a jack rabbit travel than a greyhound?

3. A hummingbird travels how much slower than a golden eagle?

4. What is the speed of the slowest animal named?

5. What is the speed of the fastest animal named?

6. What is the difference in speed between the fastest animal and slowest animal?

7. If a hummingbird travels at full speed, how many hours would it take for it to fly 120 miles?

8. If a greyhound travels at full speed, how many hours would it take for it to travel 120 miles?

9. How many more miles an hour can a cheetah travel than a greyhound?

10. What animal travels twice as fast as a man can run?

Think: $2 \times 20 = \square$.

11. A man can run how many times as fast as he can swim?

Think: $5 \times \triangle = 20$.

12. A racehorse can travel how many more miles an hour than a cat?

13. A golden eagle can fly how many times as fast as a snake can crawl?

14. A cheetah can travel how many miles an hour faster than a jack rabbit?

15. A snake travels how many miles an hour slower than a hummingbird?

16. A man can run how many times as fast as a snake can crawl?

USING FRACTIONS

1. What part of a dollar is 1 cent? How many cents in one dime? in ten dimes?

2. **a.** What part of a dollar is 10 cents?

   b. How many dimes make a dollar?

   c. One dime is what part of a dollar?

   d. $\frac{10}{100} = \frac{\triangle}{10}$

3. **a.** What part of a dollar is 25 cents?

   b. How many quarters make a dollar?

   c. One quarter is what part of a dollar?

   d. $\frac{25}{100} = \frac{\square}{4}$

4. What part of a dollar is 50 cents? 75 cents? Write two fractional numerals for each.

EXERCISES

This ruler is marked to show $\frac{1}{8}$ inches. Use it to help you make each sentence true.

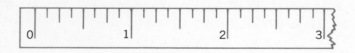

1. $\frac{8}{8} = \square$ 2. $\frac{2}{8} = \frac{\triangle}{4}$ 3. $\frac{4}{8} = \frac{\triangle}{2}$

4. $\frac{6}{8} = \frac{\triangle}{4}$ 5. $\frac{9}{8} = 1\frac{\triangle}{8}$ 6. $\frac{11}{8} = 1\frac{\triangle}{8}$

7. $\frac{16}{8} = \square$ 8. $\frac{19}{8} = 2\frac{\triangle}{8}$ 9. $\frac{24}{8} = \square$

PROBLEM SOLVING

Solve each problem.

1. The highest temperature recorded on earth is about 136° Fahrenheit. The temperature on the surface of the sun is about 74 times as great. About what is the temperature on the surface of the sun?

2. Stars vary in color and temperature. Some red stars have a temperature of 4,140°F. Blue stars have a temperature 15 times as great. What is the temperature of a blue star?

3. Right now you are moving about 60 miles a minute as the earth spins on its axis. How many miles do you move in one hour as the earth moves?

4. In order to escape the earth's gravity, a rocket must travel at least 7 miles in one second.

   a. How many miles must it travel in one minute?

   b. How many miles an hour is this?

5. Because of gravity you weigh less on the moon. The earth's gravity is 6 times as great as the moon's. If a computer weighs 18 pounds on the earth, how much would it weigh on the moon?

METERS AND CENTIMETERS

Many people around the world use the *metric* system.

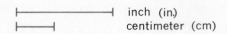

1. Which is longer?

   a. an inch or a centimeter

   b. 10 cm or 10 in.

2. Is a centimeter longer or shorter than a half inch? a quarter inch?

A **centimeter** (cm) is a little less than $\frac{1}{2}$ inch.

3. Measure to the nearest centimeter.

   a.   **b.**

   c.   **d.**

1 **meter** (m) is 100 centimeters.
A meter is a little longer than a yard.

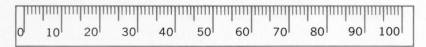

4. a. How many centimeters is 12 meters?

    b. How many meters is 400 centimeters?

5. 350 cm = 300 cm + 50 cm or 3 m 50 cm

    a. 842 cm = ___ m 42 cm

    b. 605 cm = ___ m ___ cm

    c. 964 cm = ___ m ___ cm

6. The distance between Peter's house and Karen's house is about 750 meters. Is this more or less than 750 yards?

1 **kilometer** (km) is 1,000 meters.

A kilometer is about $\frac{5}{8}$ of a mile.

7. How many kilometers is:

    a. 4,000 m   **b.** 10,000 m   **c.** 25,000 m

8. How many meters is:

    a. 4 km   **b.** 10 km   **c.** 25 km

9. It is about 850 miles from New York to Chicago. Is this more or less than 850 kilometers?

EXERCISES

1. A race is 100 meters long.

    a. Is it more or less than 100 yards?

    b. Is it more or less than 1 km?

Copy and complete.

2. 3 m is ___ cm   3. 250 cm is ___ m ___ cm

4. 100 m is ___ cm   5. 3,000 cm is ___ m

6. 4 km is ___ m   7. 100,000 m is ___ km

OUNCES, POUNDS, TONS

We measure the weight of candy bars in ounces.

1. What unit might we use to measure the weight of sugar?

1 pound (lb) is 16 ounces (oz)

2. How many ounces is
   a. 6 pounds
   b. 4 pounds
   c. 32 pounds
   d. 102 pounds

3. a. 19 oz = 1 lb + ___ oz
   b. 47 oz = ___ lb + ___ oz
   c. 96 oz = ___ lb + ___ oz

4. Would we measure the weight of a truck in pounds? What other unit could we use?

1 ton is 2,000 pounds

5. How many pounds is
   a. 2 tons
   b. 7 tons
   c. 16 tons
   d. 58 tons

6. 2,500 lb = 1 ton + ___ lb

7. A notice on a small bridge says: No Vehicles Over $2\frac{1}{2}$ Tons. A truck weighs 2,900 pounds. May it cross the bridge? Explain your answer.

8. How much do you weigh in pounds to the nearest pound? How many ounces is this?

EXERCISES

1. Copy and complete.

Tons	$\frac{1}{2}$		3
Pounds		4,000	

2. 27 oz = ___ lb + ___ oz

3. 4,000 lb = ___ tons + ___ lb

4. 8,242 lb = ___ tons + ___ lb

5. 4,720 lb = ___ tons + ___ lb

6. 38,242 lb = ___ tons + ___ lb

Solve each problem.

7. A delivery van weighs $1\frac{1}{2}$ tons empty. It can carry 1,280 pounds of newspapers. How many pounds does the van weigh when it is full?

8. Mr. Goetz bought $3\frac{1}{2}$ lbs of meat for hamburgers. How many ounces of meat did he buy?

GRAMS, KILOGRAMS

This is a cube 1 centimeter long on an edge. Imagine that it is filled with pure water. The water weighs 1 *gram*.

1 **kilogram** (kg) is 1,000 grams (gm)

1. How many grams is
   a. 4 kilograms   b. 9 kilograms
   c. 29 kilograms   d. 15 kilograms

Copy and complete.

2. a. 1,500 gm = 1 kg + ___ gm
   b. 2,700 gm = ___ kg + ___ gm
   c. 4,100 gm = ___ kg + ___ gm

A kilogram is a little more than two pounds.

3. Carlos bought 4 kilograms of meat.
   a. How many grams is this?
   b. About how many pounds is it?

EXERCISES

Copy and complete.

1. 2,000 gm = ___ kg   2. ___ gm = 6 kg

3. 4,965 gm = ___ kg ___ gm

4. Mrs. Olsen bought 6 kilograms of flour. Is this more or less than 12 pounds?

PARTS OF A GALLON

1. Is 2 quarts more or less than a gallon?

> 1 **pint** (pt) is 2 **cups**
> 1 **quart** (qt) is 2 pints
> 1 **gallon** (gal) is 4 quarts

2. Copy and complete.

    a. ___ cups = 1 pt   **b.** ___ pt = 1 qt

    c. ___ qt = $\frac{1}{4}$ gal   **d.** 2 qt = ___ gal

    e. 4 qt = ___ gal   **f.** 1 gal = ___ pt

> 1 pint is 16 **fluid ounces** (oz)

3. How many ounces is

    a. 1 quart   **b.** 1 gallon   **c.** 1 cup

4. **a.** How many ounces of soda are in six cans?

    b. Is this as much as two quarts?

    c. How many cans of soda are needed to make 1 gallon?

1. Copy and complete.

gallons	1		3	
quarts		8		
pints			24	
cups				64

2. The Acme Garage uses 20 quarts of oil a week for its delivery trucks.

   a. How many gallons is this?

   b. How many gallons do they use in 1 year?

Copy and complete.

   3. a. 15 qt = 3 gal + ___ qt

   b. 27 qt = ___ gal + ___ qt

Let's Practice

Solve each problem.

1. A gallon of water weighs about 8 pounds. About how much would 5 gallons weigh? 12 gallons?

2. A playing field is 100 yards long. How many feet long is the field?

3. Louise and Elena bought 6 yards of ribbon to share equally. How much ribbon did each girl receive?

4. Ruth can type 60 words in one minute. How many words can she type in $\frac{1}{2}$ minute?

USING MEASURES

1. A *fathom* is a unit that is often used in measuring the depth of water. A fathom is 6 feet. Change these depths to fathoms.

   a. 216 feet   **b.** 720 feet   **c.** 1,764 feet

2. **a.** How many feet are in 100 yards?

   b. How many fathoms are in 100 yards?

3. There are 5,280 feet in one mile. How many fathoms are in one mile?

4. A nautical mile is about 6,080 feet. It is a unit of measure for ships and aircraft. How much longer is a nautical mile than a statute mile?

5. The average depth of the Pacific Ocean is 13,215 feet. The average depth of the Atlantic Ocean is 12,880 feet. How much greater is the average depth of the Pacific Ocean than the Atlantic Ocean?

6. The greatest known depth of the Pacific Ocean is about 37,782 feet. The greatest known depth of the Atlantic Ocean is about 30,246 feet. How much deeper is the Pacific Ocean than the Atlantic Ocean?

UNEXPLORED TERRITORY

If a kilogram is 1,000 grams, what is a kiloton? What is a kilowatt?

CHAPTER REVIEW

1. **a.** What time is shown?

   b. What time will it be 2 hours and 20 minutes later?

   c. What time was it 2 hours and 20 minutes earlier?

2. $1\frac{1}{2}$ hours = _____ minutes

3. 4 hours 10 minutes = 3 hours _____ minutes

4. Tom left Syracuse at 4:35 pm. He rode on the train for 8 hours and 10 minutes. What time was it when he got off the train?

5. How many seconds are in three minutes?

6. Copy and complete.

Temperature	Temperature Rises	New Temperature
12°C	13°C	
0°C		14°C
	10°C	15°C

7. **a.** Measure $\overline{AB}$, $\overline{BC}$, and $\overline{CD}$ to the nearest $\frac{1}{8}$ inch.

   b. How far is it from A to D through B and C?

8. a. Find the perimeter.

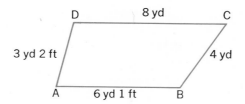

b. How much longer is $\overline{DC}$ than $\overline{BC}$?

9. A jet flies at a height of 6 miles. How many feet is this?

10. Is 10,000 yards more or less than 10 kilometers?

11. 7,523 m = ____ km ____ m ____ cm

12. Sue uses $\frac{1}{2}$ kilogram of butter in a week.

a. Is this more or less than a pound?

b. How many kilograms does she use in 10 weeks?

13. 4 kg + 25 gm = ____ gm

14. One can of syrup holds 16 fluid ounces. How many cans are needed to make 1 gallon?

Terms You Should Know

noon	Fahrenheit	centimeter	foot
midnight	Celsius	kilometer	yard
mile	fluid ounce	kilogram	pint
meter	ton	gram	cup
pound	quart	gallon	inch

CHAPTER TEST

1. **a.** What time is shown? It is morning.

   b. What time will it be in two hours and forty-five minutes?

2. Mary left New York City at 7:30 am. She arrived at camp at 4:45 pm on the same day. How long did the trip take?

3. In the morning the temperature was 26° C. At noon the temperature had risen 7° C. What was the temperature at noon?

Measure to the nearest $\frac{1}{8}$ in.

4. 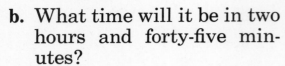   5.

6. **a.** Find the perimeter.

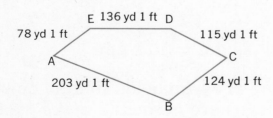

   b. How much longer is $\overline{DE}$ than $\overline{BC}$?

7. Is 100 kilometers more or less than 100 miles?

8. 1,795 m = ___ km ___ m

9. 5,642 gm = ___ kg ___ gm

370

Practice Exercises

Add.

0	8	6	3	4	1	5	2	9
6	0	2	4	4	0	3	0	0
3	7	0	5	3	1	6	7	1
5	2	1	4	3	8	1	3	9
4	5	1	2	1	8	0	2	8
6	5	1	1	7	1	5	4	2
2	4	3	5	3	4	7	9	0
3	5	2	2	6	3	1	1	9
3	4	0	6	6	2	2	5	1
1	2	2	3	4	5	2	0	3
1	1	5	2	0	6	2	0	3
2	4	1	8	8	0	6	4	7
4	0	1	2	1	4	0	0	7
1	3	5	7	6	0	7	0	0
2	7	8	6	3	7	6	9	5
9	4	8	5	8	5	7	4	7
8	5	9	6	8	4	7	5	9
9	9	3	6	3	7	6	6	5
5	8	3	7	6	9	8	9	7
8	4	9	7	8	9	5	6	9
7	6	8	4	9	4	9	8	9
8	9	6	9	7	8	8	7	2

Subtract.

1	6	4	5	9	2	7	3	9
0	5	2	4	1	0	0	1	2

8	9	6	7	2	6	4	9	10
6	6	4	4	1	1	4	9	2

4	6	9	9	3	5	7	10	6
1	6	5	0	2	5	3	1	0

2	8	4	5	3	6	3	10	8
2	1	0	3	0	3	3	9	2

10	5	7	8	5	8	9	1	7
4	2	6	8	0	4	3	1	2

10	7	5	8	7	6	10	7	9
5	1	1	0	5	2	3	7	4

9	10	10	8	4	8	10	9	8
8	6	8	5	3	3	0	7	7

15	16	18	12	16	12	15	12	17
9	7	9	9	8	4	6	5	9

12	17	15	11	12	14	12	14	13
8	8	8	9	6	8	3	6	9

14	11	14	12	13	15	14	13	11
5	5	9	7	7	7	7	4	6

13	16	11	13	11	12	11	13	11
5	9	8	8	4	3	7	6	3

Multiply.

1	2	5	4	0	1	4	3	0
1	8	5	0	0	2	3	1	6

8	4	1	0	4	3	9	1	9
1	1	6	1	8	9	8	0	2

2	5	3	2	7	2	7	0	3
1	4	0	7	8	0	9	9	3

0	5	0	3	0	5	8	3	9
2	3	8	8	5	0	5	5	3

1	2	9	0	1	3	9	1	4
5	9	4	3	3	2	1	7	6

4	5	1	2	4	7	7	8	6
5	2	4	6	7	1	7	4	8

7	0	4	6	1	3	8	0	2
3	4	9	2	9	4	2	7	4

8	6	2	4	6	5	7	8	7
6	7	5	2	1	6	6	7	4

2	8	9	1	8	9	8	2	9
2	9	5	8	8	6	3	3	7

3	6	5	9	3	6	5	5	6
6	5	1	9	7	3	8	9	9

6	7	4	5	6	7	7	9	8
6	2	4	7	4	0	5	0	0

Divide.

$6 \div 1$	$48 \div 6$	$6 \div 6$	$9 \div 3$	$14 \div 7$
$32 \div 8$	$10 \div 5$	$3 \div 1$	$18 \div 2$	$27 \div 3$
$21 \div 7$	$7 \div 1$	$15 \div 5$	$18 \div 9$	$25 \div 5$
$45 \div 9$	$28 \div 4$	$6 \div 2$	$10 \div 2$	$64 \div 8$
$2 \div 1$	$0 \div 1$	$24 \div 8$	$7 \div 7$	$32 \div 4$
$48 \div 8$	$6 \div 3$	$54 \div 6$	$72 \div 9$	$24 \div 4$
$40 \div 8$	$40 \div 5$	$81 \div 9$	$4 \div 1$	$2 \div 2$
$8 \div 1$	$16 \div 2$	$8 \div 4$	$0 \div 9$	$12 \div 6$
$18 \div 3$	$4 \div 2$	$4 \div 4$	$36 \div 9$	$56 \div 7$
$12 \div 3$	$24 \div 6$	$5 \div 1$	$1 \div 1$	$21 \div 3$
$72 \div 8$	$35 \div 5$	$36 \div 4$	$49 \div 7$	$0 \div 5$
$9 \div 1$	$20 \div 5$	$24 \div 3$	$45 \div 5$	$9 \div 9$
$42 \div 7$	$30 \div 6$	$35 \div 7$	$5 \div 5$	$27 \div 9$
$12 \div 4$	$54 \div 9$	$3 \div 3$	$8 \div 2$	$63 \div 7$
$15 \div 3$	$14 \div 2$	$16 \div 8$	$12 \div 2$	$18 \div 6$
$0 \div 4$	$20 \div 4$	$30 \div 5$	$28 \div 7$	$42 \div 6$
$36 \div 6$	$8 \div 8$	$56 \div 8$	$16 \div 4$	$0 \div 6$
$0 \div 8$	$63 \div 9$	$0 \div 7$	$0 \div 3$	$0 \div 2$

(10) Write standard numerals.

1. Thirty-eight   2. Seventy-five

3. Ninety-four   4. Forty-two

5. Sixty-three   6. Twenty-two

7. 6 tens + 7 ones   8. 5 tens + 0 ones

9. 8 tens + 6 ones   10. 4 tens + 9 ones

11. 3 tens + 5 ones   12. 3 tens + 4 ones

13. 9 tens + 3 ones   14. 9 tens + 6 ones

15. 20 + 6   16. 40 + 6   17. 10 + 7

18. 70 + 3   19. 90 + 1   20. 60 + 4

21. 50 + 5   22. 10 + 9   23. 70 + 7

24. $(7 \times 10) + (4 \times 1)$ 25. $(6 \times 10) + (0 \times 1)$

26. $(4 \times 10) + (7 \times 1)$ 27. $(5 \times 10) + (6 \times 1)$

28. $(5 \times 10) + (6 \times 2)$ 29. $(8 \times 10) + (9 \times 1)$

Write three expanded numerals for each.

30. 49   31. 68   32. 50   33. 33   34. 28

Make each sentence true.

35. $17 = 10 + \underline{\quad}$ 36. $83 = \underline{\quad} + 3$

37. $64 = 60 + \underline{\quad}$ 38. $34 = 30 + \underline{\quad}$

39. $33 = 30 + \underline{\quad}$ 40. $17 = \underline{\quad} + 7$

41. $89 = 80 + \underline{\quad}$ 42. $22 = 20 + \underline{\quad}$

(12) Write standard numerals.

1. Three hundred sixty-three

2. One hundred eighty-nine

3. Five hundred thirty

4. Two hundred forty-two

5. Seven hundred and thirty-six

6. 6 hundreds + 7 tens + 9 ones

7. 7 hundreds + 0 tens + 6 ones

8. 4 hundreds + 7 tens + 0 ones

9. 5 hundreds + 6 tens + 3 ones

10. $400 + 20 + 7$ 11. $600 + 50 + 4$

12. $600 + 10 + 4$ 13. $900 + 70 + 3$

14. $700 + 20 + 3$ 15. $600 + 30 + 6$

16. $200 + 50 + 2$ 17. $200 + 0 + 6$

Make each sentence true.

18. $347 = (3 \times 100) + (\underline{\quad} \times \underline{\quad}) + (7 \times 1)$

19. $489 = (\underline{\quad} \times \underline{\quad}) + (8 \times 10) + (9 \times 1)$

20. $893 = (8 \times 100) + (9 \times 10) + (\underline{\quad} \times \underline{\quad})$

21. $754 = (\underline{\quad} \times 100) + (5 \times 10) + (\underline{\quad} \times \underline{\quad})$

Write three expanded numerals for each.

22. 546   23. 789   24. 579   25. 987

376

(15) Write standard numerals.

1. Three thousand, nine hundred eight

2. Seven thousand, five hundred ninety

3. Five thousand, three hundred thirteen

4. 3 thousands + 4 hundreds + 6 tens + 4 ones

5. 2 thousands + 0 hundreds + 0 tens + 7 ones

6. 8 thousands + 6 hundreds + 5 tens + 0 ones

7. $5,000 + 200 + 70 + 3$

8. $4,000 + 300 + 70 + 6$

Make each sentence true.

9. $2,021 = (2 \times 1,000) + (0 \times 100)$
$$+ (\underline{} \times \underline{}) + (1 \times 1)$$

10. $5,873 = (5 \times 1,000) + (\underline{} \times \underline{})$
$$+ (7 \times 10) + (3 \times 1)$$

11. $3,456 = (\underline{} \times \underline{}) + (4 \times 100)$
$$+ (5 \times 10) + (\underline{} \times \underline{})$$

12. $4,376 = 4,000 + 300 + 70 + \underline{}$

13. $9,634 = 9,000 + 600 + \underline{} + 4$

14. $3,450 = 3,000 + \underline{} + 50 + \underline{}$

Write three expanded numerals for each.

15. 9,643   **16.** 9,873   **17.** 2,784   **18.** 7,066

(18)   Write standard numerals.

1. Two hundred forty-nine thousand, one hundred ten

2. Ten thousand

3. Sixty-eight thousand, ninety-four

4. Ninety-nine thousand, nine hundred seventy-nine

5. 3 ten thousands + 4 thousands + 6 hundreds + 8 tens + 5 ones

6. 5 ten thousands + 2 thousands + 4 hundreds + 7 tens + 7 ones

Make each sentence true.

7. $10,643 = (1 \times 10,000) + (0 \times 1,000) + (6 \times \underline{\quad}) + (4 \times 10) + (3 \times 1)$

8. $89,206 = (8 \times 10,000) + (\underline{\quad} \times 1,000) + (2 \times 100) + (0 \times 10) + (6 \times \underline{\quad})$

9. $15,767 = (1 \times 10,000) + (\underline{\quad} \times 1,000) + (7 \times 100) + (6 \times 10) + (7 \times \underline{\quad})$

10. $60,511 = 60,000 + 500 + 10 + \underline{\quad}$

11. $56,728 = 50,000 + 6,000 + \underline{\quad} + 20 + 8$

12. $74,432 = 70,000 + 4,000 + 400 + \underline{\quad} + 2$

Write three expanded numerals for each.

13. 64,338   14. 33,982   15. 44,652   16. 38,940

378

(47)   Add.

1. 30   60   50   23   63
       +4   +7   +40   +13   +34

2. 123   321   214   316   721
       +614   +461   +605   +142   +236

3. 3,547   7,849   8,212   2,458
       +1,152   +2,140   +1,140   +1,401

(50)   Add.

1. 23   46   37   64   26
       +7   +9   +9   +27   +26

2. 42   35   36   67   15
       +29   +25   +14   +29   +38

3. 25   42   16   67   22
       +56   +59   +67   +17   +39

(52)   Add.

1. 856   347   829   537   228
       +24   +43   +27   +453   +344

2. 546   171   131   742   493
       +161   +434   +786   +175   +165

3. 252   143   246   784   462
       +659   +257   +475   +149   +289

4. 566   652   215   152   538
       +74   +379   +198   +69   +169

379

(54) Add.

1.   7,646   6,536   3,946   1,752
      +1,875   +2,897   +1,497   +6,659

2.   7,688   1,236   2,826   6,688
      +1,653   +4,895   +6,385   +1,658

3.   936   765   446   874   836
       +697   +648   +749   +836   +176

(55) Add.

1. 674   989   6,048   9,657
         38   238   2,739   8,389
        389   676   8,454   1,073
         +6   +365   +6,593   +7,842

2.   63   973   4,683   7,489
        439   564   5,968   6,853
        +85   +683   +7,034   +7,989

3. 657   187   8,647   8,473
         83   943   5,309   5,814
        928   847   4,555   3,786
       +432   +356   +8,637   +9,594

(60) Add.

1. $2.78 $2.20 $9.07 $6.58
       +5.00   +8.51   +4.60   +.95

2. $4.62 $6.65 $1.92 $6.79
        +.50   +4.05   +7.56   +.77

3. $7.87 $7.54 $16.37 $70.99
       +3.89   +7.69   +6.93   +13.17

(67)   Make each sentence true.

1. $\Box + 7 = 13$ $13 - 7 = \Box$ $13 - 6 = \triangledown$

2. $\Box + 9 = 17$ $17 - 8 = \Box$ $17 - 9 = \Box$

3. $9 + 9 = \Box$ $18 - \Box = 9$ $\Box - 9 = 9$

4. $\Box + 6 = 12$ $12 - 6 = \Box$ $\triangle - 6 = 6$

5. $9 + 3 = \Box$ $12 - \Box = 3$ $12 - \Box = 9$

6. $\Box + 7 = 15$ $15 - \Box = 7$ $15 - \Box = 8$

7. $7 + \Box = 14$ $14 - \Box = 7$ $\Box - 7 = 7$

8. $14 = 9 + \Box$ $\Box - 9 = 3$ $\Box - 3 = 9$

9. $9 + \Box = 15$ $15 - \Box = 6$ $15 - 9 = \Box$

10. $6 + 5 = \triangle$ $11 - \triangle = 5$ $11 - 6 = \triangle$

(72)   Subtract.

1.
$$\begin{array}{r} 28 \\ -21 \\ \hline \end{array} \qquad \begin{array}{r} 27 \\ -13 \\ \hline \end{array} \qquad \begin{array}{r} 28 \\ -1 \\ \hline \end{array} \qquad \begin{array}{r} 38 \\ -24 \\ \hline \end{array} \qquad \begin{array}{r} 45 \\ -23 \\ \hline \end{array}$$

2.
$$\begin{array}{r} 27 \\ -14 \\ \hline \end{array} \qquad \begin{array}{r} 49 \\ -11 \\ \hline \end{array} \qquad \begin{array}{r} 76 \\ -16 \\ \hline \end{array} \qquad \begin{array}{r} 37 \\ -11 \\ \hline \end{array} \qquad \begin{array}{r} 28 \\ -27 \\ \hline \end{array}$$

3.
$$\begin{array}{r} 721 \\ -410 \\ \hline \end{array} \qquad \begin{array}{r} 497 \\ -346 \\ \hline \end{array} \qquad \begin{array}{r} 787 \\ -674 \\ \hline \end{array} \qquad \begin{array}{r} 534 \\ -203 \\ \hline \end{array} \qquad \begin{array}{r} 912 \\ -712 \\ \hline \end{array}$$

4.
$$\begin{array}{r} 172 \\ -62 \\ \hline \end{array} \qquad \begin{array}{r} 717 \\ -105 \\ \hline \end{array} \qquad \begin{array}{r} 425 \\ -105 \\ \hline \end{array} \qquad \begin{array}{r} 874 \\ -722 \\ \hline \end{array} \qquad \begin{array}{r} 666 \\ -135 \\ \hline \end{array}$$

5.
$$\begin{array}{r} 5,483 \\ -3,371 \\ \hline \end{array} \qquad \begin{array}{r} 6,804 \\ -5,201 \\ \hline \end{array} \qquad \begin{array}{r} 8,757 \\ -5,656 \\ \hline \end{array} \qquad \begin{array}{r} 8,556 \\ -3,253 \\ \hline \end{array} \qquad \begin{array}{r} 5,973 \\ -1,443 \\ \hline \end{array}$$

(74) Rename.

1. $422 = 400 + 10 + \triangle$ $788 = 700 + 70 + \triangle$

2. $336 = 300 + \triangle + 16$ $829 = 800 + \triangle + 19$

3. $238 = 200 + 30 + \triangle$ $943 = \triangle + 140 + 3$

4. $539 = 400 + \triangle + 9$ $632 = 500 + \triangle + 2$

5. $634 = 500 + \triangle + 14$ $811 = 700 + \triangle + 11$

(75) Subtract.

| 1. | 54 | 27 | 93 | 77 | 62 |
| | −9 | −8 | −8 | −9 | −7 |

| 2. | 73 | 62 | 65 | 47 | 50 |
| | −55 | −23 | −48 | −28 | −25 |

| 3. | 63 | 74 | 93 | 56 | 64 |
| | −45 | −8 | −47 | −39 | −25 |

| 4. | 495 | 274 | 982 | 283 | 444 |
| | −369 | −138 | −735 | −167 | −336 |

(77) Subtract.

| 1. | 654 | 926 | 444 | 536 | 684 |
| | −382 | −864 | −53 | −182 | −191 |

| 2. | 859 | 327 | 716 | 937 | 432 |
| | −273 | −184 | −236 | −684 | −168 |

| 3. | 735 | 842 | 561 | 385 | 635 |
| | −568 | −386 | −307 | −246 | −546 |

| 4. | 714 | 653 | 577 | 814 | 351 |
| | −263 | −186 | −383 | −552 | −196 |

5.	865	961	932	853	461
	−586	−582	−187	−468	−387

6.	8,347	56,535	8,453	7,767
	−7,291	−16,484	−2,991	−2,982

7.	6,456	7,382	8,436	5,246
	−5,182	−5,192	−1,582	−2,151

8.	7,214	9,871	5,624	5,231
	−3,895	−2,983	−1,983	−4,179

9.	6,426	9,842	6,341	6,841
	−3,598	−6,958	−5,987	−2,622

(80) Subtract.

1.	109	809	707	200	700
	−89	−482	−274	−136	−346

2.	603	400	706	909	405
	−571	−314	−352	−444	−314

3.	704	806	606	500	503
	−658	−329	−208	−306	−476

4.	400	508	700	601	603
	−307	−409	−365	−562	−123

5.	900	701	407	500	503
	−693	−155	−198	−162	−476

6.	7,004	6,003	5,005	9,009
	−1,789	−2,346	−2,587	−3,642

7.	8,001	3,200	5,003	1,403
	−5,668	−2,500	−4,886	−1,358

(84)   Make each sentence true.

1. $\square - 60 = 27$ $\square + 73 = 121$

2. $272 + \square = 307$ $334 - \square = 275$

3. $835 + \square = 1{,}479$ $793 + \square = 1{,}500$

4. $715 - \square = 682$ $\square + 78 = 176$

5. $443 + \square = 568$ $280 + \square = 307$

6. $602 + \square = 718$ $\square - 69 = 96$

(87)   Subtract.

1.	$5.86 $-.94$	$7.56 -4.87	$8.41 $-.97$	$11.43 -8.75
2.	$7.54 -3.39	$18.63 -14.56	$28.10 -19.39	$15.45 -7.73
3.	$6.65 $-.74$	$8.32 $-.98$	$5.07 -3.48	$10.32 -6.57
4.	$5.65 $-.93$	$13.05 $-.79$	$26.37 $-.69$	$29.76 -4.85
5.	$9.63 -4.58	$13.27 -8.65	$14.00 -6.39	$6.58 -1.96

(147)   Find the missing factor.

1. $\square \times 8 = 40$ $\square \times 5 = 5$ $\square \times 3 = 27$

2. $1 \times \square = 8$ $\square \times 3 = 24$ $5 \times \square = 35$

3. $\square \times 5 = 10$ $7 \times \square = 7$ $\square \times 6 = 30$

4. $36 = \square \times 6$ $\square \times 9 = 63$ $\square \times 9 = 72$

(174) Multiply.

1. 47×10 100×5 10×100

2. 189×10 34×100 100×69

3. 10×53 121×10 44×100

4. 10×70 76×100 100×11

5. 215×100 33×10 415×100

6. $6 \times 1,000$ $1,000 \times 37$ $58 \times 1,000$

7. $10 \times 1,000$ $11 \times 1,000$ $4 \times 1,000$

8. $1,000 \times 77$ $41 \times 1,000$ $99 \times 1,000$

(176) Multiply.

1. 4×20 5×60 7×20

2. 8×30 9×60 9×80

3. 7×40 5×90 3×70

4. 8×60 3×80 2×60

5. 6×90 6×40 7×30

(177) Multiply.

1. 6×200 4×300 7×400

2. 3×500 $7 \times 6,000$ 8×900

3. $9 \times 7,000$ $6 \times 8,000$ $8 \times 7,000$

4. $2 \times 4,000$ 5×400 2×100

5. 3×600 $8 \times 5,000$ 4×700

(179) Multiply.

1. 20 × 20   70 × 20   60 × 70

2. 40 × 60   50 × 30   40 × 20

3. 20 × 400   90 × 600   30 × 300

4. 40 × 300   50 × 700   70 × 400

(184) Multiply.

1. 2 × 53   2 × 432   4 × 511

2. 3 × 843   9 × 61   6 × 819

3. 60 × 48   80 × 421   90 × 632

(189) Multiply.

1. 24   122   432   233   124
       ×4   ×3   ×2   ×2   ×2

2. 46   625   134   43   334
       ×3   ×5   ×8   ×6   ×2

3. 2,312   7,322   4,312   6,124
        ×2   ×2   ×3   ×2

(191) Multiply.

1. 16   17   18   25   37
       ×7   ×3   ×7   ×2   ×2

2. 116   212   317   415   308
       ×4   ×5   ×4   ×3   ×4

3. 219   2,116   1,234   1,219   1,229
       ×7   ×3   ×3   ×2   ×2

4. 343   481   762   860   742
    ×3   ×8   ×3   ×4   ×4

5. 1,382   851   791   291   172
    ×2   ×7   ×8   ×7   ×3

(193)   Multiply.

1. 234   323   567   298   778
    ×5   ×8   ×9   ×6   ×7

2. 5,962   1,237   2,967   1,467   1,762
    ×5   ×7   ×4   ×6   ×6

3. 5,769   5,673   9,183   9,710   4,928
    ×8   ×9   ×6   ×4   ×4

(197)   Multiply.

1.   53   69   64   63   920
    ×40   ×50   ×30   ×60   ×70

2.   52   42   607   171   300
    ×70   ×30   ×40   ×80   ×30

(201)   Multiply.

1.   32   46   29   17   36
    ×45   ×96   ×18   ×82   ×89

2.   37   34   16   88   44
    ×56   ×89   ×55   ×48   ×67

3.   51   68   28   64   35
    ×29   ×34   ×35   ×45   ×48

(203) **Multiply.**

1. 536   943   725   565   798
    ×40   ×30   ×45   ×24   ×42

2. 679   153   258   258   337
    ×26   ×69   ×67   ×85   ×98

(206) **Multiply.**

1. $2.25 $7.82 $5.75 $7.38 $7.32
    ×84   ×53   ×63   ×25   ×48

2. $6.54 $8.97 $7.64 $5.53 $9.98
    ×38   ×43   ×21   ×94   ×76

(213) **Divide.**

1. $6\overline{)48}$ $6\overline{)30}$ $6\overline{)54}$ $4\overline{)24}$ $8\overline{)72}$ $4\overline{)36}$

2. $5\overline{)60}$ $3\overline{)18}$ $7\overline{)28}$ $9\overline{)63}$ $2\overline{)14}$ $9\overline{)72}$

Make each sentence true.

3. $27 \div 9 = \square$ $9 \div \square = 1$ $63 \div \square = 9$

4. $28 \div \square = 4$ $35 \div \square = 5$ $\square \div 6 = 5$

(221) **Divide.**

1. $8\overline{)80}$ $2\overline{)64}$ $3\overline{)45}$ $6\overline{)96}$ $5\overline{)65}$

2. $5\overline{)70}$ $2\overline{)62}$ $7\overline{)84}$ $3\overline{)93}$ $6\overline{)78}$

(223) **Divide.**

1. $7\overline{)462}$ $9\overline{)459}$ $8\overline{)544}$ $9\overline{)648}$ $7\overline{)644}$

2. $8\overline{)432}$ $5\overline{)355}$ $6\overline{)342}$ $4\overline{)272}$ $2\overline{)102}$

(224)   Divide.

1. 3)345   2)536   4)444   7)784   8)968

2. 6)684   2)254   8)944   4)652   3)672

(226)   Divide.

1. 4)832   3)921   2)618   3)315   3)606

2. 9)927   7)742   8)864   2)816   7)763

(230)   Divide.

1. 7)87   2)63   7)84   3)68   3)85

2. 6)48   3)26   7)46   7)37   9)67

(236)   Divide.

1. 7)441   4)197   2)157   6)148   5)347

2. 4)379   2)107   6)308   7)456   8)257

3. 9)586   8)569   5)338   7)473   6)469

4. 6)569   6)223   7)538   8)636   8)447

5. 8)335   4)394   7)457   3)178   5)483

(237)   Divide.

1. 40)334   90)361   80)325   60)562   70)358

2. 80)672   90)742   70)656   70)698   50)243

3. 60)459   70)572   90)649   70)572   60)342

4. 60)469   80)336   80)663   70)446   30)189

(238) Divide.

1. $90\overline{)992}$ $50\overline{)755}$ $60\overline{)943}$ $40\overline{)884}$

2. $70\overline{)885}$ $30\overline{)619}$ $20\overline{)414}$ $20\overline{)627}$

3. $60\overline{)548}$ $30\overline{)646}$ $80\overline{)984}$ $30\overline{)1,850}$

4. $20\overline{)620}$ $50\overline{)850}$ $80\overline{)4,640}$ $60\overline{)750}$

5. $70\overline{)970}$ $40\overline{)4,360}$ $30\overline{)540}$ $20\overline{)350}$

(240) Divide.

1. $\$9.92 \div 8$ $\$79.50 \div 8$ $\$65.45 \div 7$

2. $\$91.52 \div 9$ $\$6.54 \div 3$ $\$8.10 \div 5$

3. $\$6.44 \div 7$ $\$3.44 \div 4$ $\$14.30 \div 2$

(279) Write fractional numerals.

1. one-fourth   2. two-thirds

3. five-sixths   4. four-fifths

5. three-eighths   6. one-seventh

7. two-fifths   8. three-fourths

9. two-ninths   10. four-sevenths

(287) Make each sentence true.

1. $\frac{1}{8}$ of 64 = ____ $\frac{1}{3}$ of 12 = ____ $\frac{1}{7}$ of 42 = ____

2. $\frac{1}{6}$ of 36 = ____ $\frac{1}{7}$ of 49 = ____ $\frac{1}{5}$ of 45 = ____

3. $\frac{1}{3}$ of 24 = ____ $\frac{1}{5}$ of 40 = ____ $\frac{1}{4}$ of 20 = ____

(292) Make each sentence true. Use > or <.

1. $\frac{1}{3} \equiv \frac{2}{3}$ $\frac{2}{8} \equiv \frac{7}{8}$ $\frac{4}{5} \equiv \frac{1}{5}$ $\frac{1}{4} \equiv \frac{3}{4}$

2. $\frac{4}{8} \equiv \frac{3}{8}$ $\frac{3}{9} \equiv \frac{6}{9}$ $\frac{1}{8} \equiv \frac{2}{8}$ $\frac{5}{6} \equiv \frac{1}{6}$

(293) Make each sentence true. Use > or <.

1. $\frac{3}{5} \equiv \frac{3}{6}$ $\frac{4}{8} \equiv \frac{4}{9}$ $\frac{3}{8} \equiv \frac{3}{4}$ $\frac{6}{8} \equiv \frac{6}{7}$

2. $\frac{5}{6} \equiv \frac{5}{9}$ $\frac{1}{4} \equiv \frac{1}{2}$ $\frac{2}{3} \equiv \frac{2}{4}$ $\frac{7}{8} \equiv \frac{7}{9}$

(296) Write standard numerals.

1. $\frac{2}{2}$ $\frac{6}{3}$ $\frac{6}{6}$ $\frac{18}{9}$ $\frac{10}{5}$ $\frac{8}{4}$ $\frac{6}{2}$

2. $\frac{4}{4}$ $\frac{14}{2}$ $\frac{14}{7}$ $\frac{32}{8}$ $\frac{20}{4}$ $\frac{16}{8}$ $\frac{24}{3}$

(298) Make each sentence true. Use >, <, or =.

1. $1 \equiv \frac{3}{2}$ $1 \equiv \frac{2}{3}$ $\frac{1}{4} \equiv \frac{1}{6}$ $1 \equiv \frac{7}{8}$ $\frac{3}{9} \equiv 1$

2. $\frac{1}{2} \equiv \frac{1}{3}$ $\frac{4}{8} \equiv \frac{3}{8}$ $1 \equiv \frac{7}{8}$ $\frac{3}{2} \equiv \frac{2}{4}$ $1 \equiv \frac{5}{8}$

(306) Make each sentence true.

1. $\frac{8}{8} = \frac{1}{\triangle}$ $\frac{1}{6} = \frac{\triangle}{12}$ $\frac{4}{8} = \frac{\triangle}{16}$ $\frac{2}{2} = \frac{\triangle}{8}$

2. $\frac{3}{4} = \frac{\triangle}{20}$ $\frac{4}{9} = \frac{\triangle}{18}$ $\frac{3}{7} = \frac{\triangle}{14}$ $\frac{3}{5} = \frac{\triangle}{15}$

3. $\frac{4}{5} = \frac{\triangle}{20}$ $\frac{2}{3} = \frac{\triangle}{12}$ $\frac{5}{8} = \frac{\triangle}{24}$ $\frac{4}{7} = \frac{\triangle}{14}$

4. $\frac{1}{2} = \frac{\triangle}{4}$ $\frac{1}{5} = \frac{\triangle}{20}$ $\frac{3}{7} = \frac{\triangle}{21}$ $\frac{6}{6} = \frac{\triangle}{12}$

(309)   Which pairs of numerals are equivalent?

1. $\frac{4}{6}, \frac{8}{12}$ $\frac{1}{2}, \frac{3}{6}$ $\frac{7}{8}, \frac{4}{7}$ $\frac{5}{6}, \frac{8}{9}$ $\frac{3}{4}, \frac{6}{24}$

2. $\frac{1}{8}, \frac{3}{24}$ $\frac{2}{3}, \frac{4}{5}$ $\frac{6}{8}, \frac{9}{12}$ $\frac{1}{2}, \frac{4}{6}$ $\frac{6}{7}, \frac{7}{14}$

3. $\frac{1}{3}, \frac{8}{24}$ $\frac{2}{7}, \frac{3}{14}$ $\frac{2}{3}, \frac{6}{9}$ $\frac{3}{8}, \frac{6}{16}$ $\frac{5}{8}, \frac{10}{16}$

(317)   Add.

1. $\frac{1}{8} + \frac{2}{8}$ $\frac{4}{6} + \frac{1}{6}$ $\frac{5}{12} + \frac{6}{12}$ $\frac{7}{9} + \frac{1}{9}$ $\frac{1}{3} + \frac{1}{3}$

2. $\frac{2}{5} + \frac{1}{5}$ $\frac{3}{8} + \frac{1}{8}$ $\frac{3}{5} + \frac{1}{5}$ $\frac{3}{7} + \frac{2}{7}$ $\frac{1}{4} + \frac{2}{4}$

(320)   Subtract.

1. $\frac{7}{12} - \frac{6}{12}$ $\frac{10}{12} - \frac{7}{12}$ $\frac{4}{9} - \frac{2}{9}$ $\frac{7}{8} - \frac{5}{8}$ $\frac{3}{3} - \frac{1}{3}$

2. $\frac{3}{10} - \frac{1}{10}$ $\frac{7}{9} - \frac{2}{9}$ $\frac{4}{7} - \frac{3}{7}$ $\frac{6}{11} - \frac{5}{11}$ $\frac{3}{8} - \frac{1}{8}$

(326)   Add.

1. $\frac{1}{3} + \frac{2}{6}$ $\frac{1}{4} + \frac{2}{8}$ $\frac{5}{12} + \frac{1}{6}$ $\frac{1}{2} + \frac{2}{8}$ $\frac{2}{3} + \frac{1}{4}$

2. $\frac{1}{5} + \frac{1}{3}$ $\frac{1}{8} + \frac{1}{3}$ $\frac{2}{4} + \frac{1}{5}$ $\frac{1}{6} + \frac{1}{5}$ $\frac{2}{5} + \frac{1}{2}$

(329)   Subtract.

1. $\frac{2}{3} - \frac{1}{2}$ $\frac{4}{5} - \frac{1}{3}$ $\frac{3}{4} - \frac{1}{2}$ $\frac{5}{6} - \frac{1}{8}$ $\frac{2}{3} - \frac{1}{3}$

2. $\frac{6}{8} - \frac{1}{4}$ $\frac{4}{5} - \frac{1}{4}$ $\frac{6}{8} - \frac{1}{3}$ $\frac{7}{8} - \frac{1}{4}$ $\frac{3}{8} - \frac{1}{8}$

(332)　Write mixed numerals.

1. $\frac{4}{3}$　$\frac{9}{4}$　$\frac{9}{5}$　$\frac{5}{3}$　$\frac{7}{6}$　$\frac{8}{3}$　$\frac{9}{8}$　$\frac{10}{3}$

2. $\frac{5}{3}$　$\frac{6}{4}$　$\frac{7}{5}$　$\frac{6}{5}$　$\frac{7}{2}$　$\frac{11}{2}$　$\frac{13}{4}$　$\frac{14}{8}$

3. $\frac{8}{5}$　$\frac{9}{7}$　$\frac{3}{2}$　$\frac{7}{3}$　$\frac{9}{2}$　$\frac{12}{5}$　$\frac{12}{9}$　$\frac{13}{7}$

4. $\frac{8}{7}$　$\frac{5}{2}$　$\frac{8}{3}$　$\frac{5}{4}$　$\frac{7}{4}$　$\frac{12}{7}$　$\frac{16}{9}$　$\frac{16}{7}$

(336)　Add.

1. $2\frac{1}{8} + 4\frac{2}{8}$　　　　$8\frac{1}{4} + 7\frac{2}{4}$　　　　$3\frac{2}{4} + 4\frac{1}{4}$

2. $6\frac{1}{2} + 4\frac{1}{4}$　　　　$9\frac{1}{2} + 1\frac{2}{8}$　　　　$8\frac{1}{2} + 6\frac{1}{8}$

3. $7\frac{1}{3} + 1\frac{1}{2}$　　　　$7\frac{1}{5} + 6\frac{1}{4}$　　　　$9\frac{1}{5} + 6\frac{1}{3}$

4. $8\frac{1}{8} + 2\frac{3}{4}$　　　　$5\frac{1}{6} + 2\frac{2}{3}$　　　　$6\frac{1}{5} + 7\frac{1}{2}$

(338)　Subtract.

1. $9\frac{1}{2} - 4\frac{1}{4}$　　　　$10\frac{7}{8} - 1\frac{5}{8}$　　　　$7\frac{5}{6} - 7\frac{2}{3}$

2. $12\frac{9}{12} - 4\frac{8}{12}$　　　$15\frac{5}{6} - 1\frac{2}{3}$　　　$6\frac{7}{8} - 1\frac{1}{2}$

3. $7\frac{3}{5} - 6\frac{1}{4}$　　　　$4\frac{3}{4} - 1\frac{1}{6}$　　　　$6\frac{2}{5} - 1\frac{1}{7}$

4. $7\frac{4}{5} - 2\frac{1}{8}$　　　　$9\frac{5}{6} - 2\frac{3}{12}$　　　$6\frac{2}{9} - 5\frac{1}{9}$

(90)   Solve each problem.

1. John ate 8 pancakes for breakfast. His brother ate 5 pancakes. How many pancakes did they eat altogether?

2. Gerald bought a small toy for 13 cents. He gave the clerk a quarter. How much change did he receive?

3. There were 49 boys and 23 girls on the bus. How many children were on the bus?

4. Mrs. Jones planted 16 rose bushes. Four of them did not grow. How many bushes grew?

5. The class had cupcakes for a party. There were 16 with white frosting, 7 with blue frosting, and 12 with pink frosting. How many cupcakes were there?

6. Mother baked 95 cookies. She gave 16 cookies to David and 17 cookies to Kathy. How many cookies does she have left?

7. Jane had 25 cents. Her mother gave her 5 cents more. She then spent 10 cents. How much does she have now?

8. If you had 50 cents and spent 10 cents for candy and 15 cents for pop, how much would you have left?

9. Henry had 75 cents. He earned 20 cents more. If he spent 45 cents, how much did he have left?

394

(169)   Solve each problem.

1. John has 3 cents. Mike has 5 times as much money. How much money does Mike have?

2. There are 3 feet in a yard. How many yards are in 24 feet?

3. Jerry practices his guitar one hour a day. If he practices 25 minutes before school, how long must he practice after school?

4. Carlos bought a coat for $35.95 and a hat for $6.98. How much did he spend?

5. How many baseball teams of 9 players each can be formed with 45 boys?

6. A businessman had $3,000 in his bank account. He deposited $283 more. He wrote a check for $987. How much does he now have in his bank account?

7. Harold mows 8 lawns each week. How many lawns will he mow in 8 weeks?

8. Charles puts 8 books in one box. How many boxes does he need to pack 72 books?

9. Mr. Davis wants to buy a television set that costs $189. He has $132. How much more money does he need?

10. Mary and Pat were given $10.50 each by their father. How much money did the girls receive altogether?

(209) Solve each problem.

1. George mowed 8 lawns. He received $2.25 for each lawn. How much money did he earn?

2. The highest point in the state of Wyoming is 13,785 feet above sea level. The lowest point is 3,100 feet. What is the difference in height between these two points?

3. Boston scored 112 points in a basketball game. Detroit scored 109 points. What was the total number of points scored in the game?

4. If 32 pretzels are shared equally by 4 people, how many pretzels should each person receive?

5. If pumpkins cost 7 cents a pound, how much would a 13-pound pumpkin cost?

6. A dog eats 4 pounds of food each day. How many days will 28 pounds of food last?

7. Alma bought 3 pounds of apples for 33 cents a pound and 4 pounds of oranges for 39 cents a pound. How much money did she spend?

8. Ted had $10. He spent $3.75 for a bike light and $1.49 for handle grips. How much money does he have left?

9. Al washed 4 cars for $1.75 each. Every customer tipped him 50 cents. How much money did he receive?

(250)   Solve each problem.

1. A newspaper costs $2.75 a month. How much does it cost for a year?

2. There are 52 cards in a deck. Four people share the cards equally. How many cards will each person have?

3. Jerry spends 6 hours a day at school. There are 180 school days in a year. How many hours does he spend in school each year?

4. Marie had $38.65. She earned $49.67 more. How much money does she have now?

5. a. Spencer had $100. He bought 2 presents for Christmas. Each one cost $7.95. How much money does he have left?

   b. Spencer then bought a guitar for $24.95, a toy boat for $8.98, a toy airplane for $11.98. How much money did he spend for these items? How much does he have left?

6. Charles earns $8 a week. He saves $5 and spends $3 each week. How long will it take Charles to save $50?

7. Charles bought 3 toy cars at $3.95 each. He also bought an airplane for $7.98. How much money did he spend?

8. David's vacation was 7 weeks and 3 days long. How many days was this?

9. Find the perimeter and the area of a room that is 12 feet long and 8 feet wide.

(341)   Solve each problem.

1. Kari left her house at 6 pm to visit a friend. Her friend lived 9 blocks away. She returned at 9 pm. How long was Kari gone?

2. Mr. Jones caught 4 fish that weighed $3\frac{3}{8}$ pounds in all. Mr. Smith caught 6 fish that weighed $5\frac{1}{2}$ pounds. How much did all the fish weigh?

3. Doug bought 15 toy cars for 75 cents each. How much money did he spend?

4. **a.** Mike caught 8 fish. He gave half of them to a friend. How many did he give to his friend?

   b. Mike ate 2 of the fish he had left. How many fish did he have then?

5. Mr. Dale bought 2 steaks. Together they weighed $4\frac{1}{2}$ pounds. One steak weighed $1\frac{1}{4}$ pounds. How much did the other steak weigh?

6. Joe had $2\frac{3}{4}$ pounds of feed. After he fed his turkeys, he had $\frac{1}{2}$ pound of feed left. How much feed was used?

7. **a.** A dime weighs $\frac{1}{4}$ ounce. How much do 2 dimes weigh?

   b. A nickel weighs $\frac{5}{8}$ ounce. How much heavier is a nickel than a dime?

398

Tables of Measure

LENGTH

12 inches (in.) = 1 foot (ft)
3 feet = 1 yard (yd)
5,280 feet = 1 mile (mi)
1,760 yards = 1 mile

WEIGHT

16 ounces (oz) = 1 pound (lb)
2,000 pounds = 1 ton

LIQUID

16 fluid ounces (oz) = 1 pint (pt)
2 cups (c) = 1 pint
2 pints = 1 quart (qt)
4 quarts = 1 gallon (gal)

LENGTH

100 centimeters (cm) = 1 meter (m)
1,000 meters = 1 kilometer (km)

WEIGHT

1,000 grams (gm) = 1 kilogram (kg)

TIME

60 seconds (sec) = 1 minute (min)
60 minutes = 1 hour (hr)
24 hours = 1 day

Glossary

This glossary contains an illustration or a brief description of important terms used in this book.

Addends   Numbers to be added.

   Example Addends

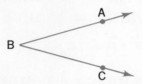

Angle (∠)   A geometric shape formed by two rays with a common endpoint. This is ∠ *ABC*, also named ∠ *CBA*.

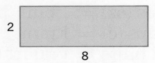

Area   The measure of a region. The area of this rectangle is 16 square units.

Array   An arrangement of the members of a set into equal rows and columns.

Circle   A geometric figure. All points of the circle are the same distance from the center.

Counting numbers   The numbers 1, 2, 3, 4, ...

Cube   A three-dimensional shape with square faces.

Diameter   A line segment through the center of a circle, with both endpoints on the circle.

Difference   The answer in subtraction. In $7 - 2 = 5$, the difference is 5.

Digit   Any of the whole numbers 0, 1, 2, 3, 4, 5, 6, 7, 8, 9.

Digit symbol   A name for a digit.

Empty set   A set with no members. The number of the empty set is 0.

Equilateral triangle   A triangle whose three sides are the same length.

Expanded numeral   A name for a number which explains the meaning of a standard numeral.

Example $43 = 40 + 3$ or $(4 \times 10) + (3 \times 1)$

Fraction   Numbers like $\frac{6}{7}$ and $\frac{11}{5}$ are fractions. We use fractions to tell about parts of things.

Intersect   When two sets of points have one or more points in common, we say they intersect.

Intersecting lines Two lines that cross each other. They have one point in common.

Isosceles triangle A triangle with two sides the same length.

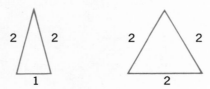

Length The measure of a line segment.

Line A straight path that goes on forever in both directions. This is line $\overleftrightarrow{BA}$ or $\overleftrightarrow{AB}$.

Line segment A straight path between two points. This is line segment $\overline{BA}$ or $\overline{AB}$.

Metric system A system of measures. The meter and gram are basic units.

Multiple A multiple of a number is the product of that number and some whole number.

Number line A line on which numbers are matched with points.

Number sentence A number sentence tells about numbers and their relations.
Examples $3 + 2 = 5$, $3 + 2 > 4$, $3 + 2 < 6$.

Parallel lines   Lines are parallel if they are on the same surface and do not meet. Segments and rays are parallel if they lie on parallel lines.

Perimeter   The distance around a figure.
Perpendicular lines   Lines which form right angles.

Quadrilateral   A four-sided geometric shape.

Radius   A line segment with one endpoint at the center of a circle and the other endpoint on the circle. $\overline{AB}$ is a radius.

Ray   A straight path that goes on forever in one direction. Ray $\overrightarrow{AC}$.

Rectangle   A four-sided figure with four square corners (right angles).

Related sentences   Sentences like $3 + \triangle = 5$, $5 - \triangle = 3$, and $5 - 3 = \triangle$ are related sentences.

Right angle An angle that looks like a square corner.

Square A rectangle with all sides the same length.

Standard numeral The usual name of a number. 23 is the standard numeral for twenty-three.

Triangle A three-sided figure.

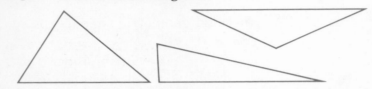

Vertex A corner point of a figure.

Whole numbers The numbers 0, 1, 2, 3, ...

Symbol List

$>$	is greater than	24
$<$	is less than	24
$=$	equals or is equal to	37
$\overrightarrow{AB}$	ray from A through B	93
$\overleftrightarrow{AB}$	line through A and B	94
$\overline{AB}$	line segment from A to B	95
$\angle A$	angle A	99
$80°$	80 degrees	337

404

Index

meaning of, 279–280, 284
mixed, 332–333
one named as, 296–297
problems with, 289
whole numbers named as,
296–297

Fractional parts of an inch,
352–353

Fractions
addition of with different
denominators, 324–327,
334–337
addition of with like
denominators, 317–318,
334–337
comparing, 292–295
of a dollar, 358
greater than one, 298–299,
332–335
less than one, 299
meaning of, 278
subtraction of with different
denominators, 329–330
subtraction of with like
denominators, 320

Geometric figures, 93–119
Graph
bar, 246–247
picture, 244–245
Gravity, 359
Greater than, 24, 292
Grouping
of addends, 44–45, 328
of factors, 168, 176–180

Hundreds
division of, 224–225
grouped as tens, 12–14
regrouping in addition, 54
renaming in subtraction,
77–78, 80–82
Hundred thousand, 18

Intersection
of lines, 102
of segments, 102

Large numbers
addition of, 52–54
reading and writing, 18–21
subtraction of, 77–78
Length, 255, 352–353, 360–361
Less than, 24, 295
Lines
intersecting, 102
meaning of, 94
parallel, 102
perpendicular, 104
reflection of, 114–115
segment, 95
symmetry of, 112–115
Liquid measure, 365

Matching figures, 117, 271
Measurement
of length, 352–353, 360–361
of liquids, 365
problems with, 367
of temperature, 350–351
of time, 345–349
of weight, 362–364
Metric system, 360–361, 364
Millions, 20–21
Missing addend, 68
Missing factor, 149, 183, 213
Mixed numerals
addition of, 336–337
meaning of, 332–333
subtraction of, 338–339
Multiple(s)
of one hundred, 179–180,
226–227
of ten, 176–180, 197–198,
237–238
Multiplication
addition and, 125–126
associative property of, 168,
176–180
commutative property of,
128–129
distributive property over
addition, 136–137, 184–187

Order
of addends, 39–40
of factors, 128–129
of numbers, 34–35

Parallel
lines, 102
segments, 102, 107
Partial product, 187–194
Partial quotient, 219, 221–227
Partial sums, 50, 52
Perimeter
meaning of, 110–111
of a rectangle, 258–261
of a square, 258–261
Periods in a numeral, 18
Perpendicular
lines, 104
segments, 104, 108
Picture graph, 244–245
Place value of numerals, 9–21
Point(s)
meaning of, 93
on a number line, 34–35
reflection of, 114–115
Product
estimating, 195–196
meaning of, 126
partial, 187–194

Quadrilateral, 108–109
Quotient
estimating, 221–227
meaning of, 149, 166, 183, 213
partial, 219, 221–227

Radius, 264
Ray, 93, 99, 100
Rectangle
area of, 253–261
diagonal of, 108–109
meaning of, 106–111
perimeter of, 110–111,
258–261
Rectangular box, 262–263
Reflection, 114–115

**Regrouping in multiplica-
tion,** 191–194
Related number sentences
addition and multiplication,
125–126
addition and subtraction,
67–68, 84–85
division and subtraction,
151–152, 215–216
multiplication and division,
149–150, 153–154, 183, 213,
217–218, 229
Remainder, 230–231, 235–236
Renaming
addends, 44–45, 49–51
factors in multiplication, 137
fractions in addition, 326–327
in subtraction, 74–82
Right angle, 96, 99, 104, 106
Roman numeral, 6–7
Rotation, 118–119
Rounding numbers
in estimating, 59, 86, 195–196
meaning of, 25–26

Segment(s)
intersecting, 102
meaning of, 95
measure of, 352–353, 360–361
parallel, 102
perpendicular, 104, 108
reflection of, 114–115
Sequences, 74
Sets
combining, 36
counting members of, 8, 34
dividing into groups, 151–152
empty, 33
fractional parts of, 278,
283–285, 287–288, 304
Square
area of, 253–261
diagonal of, 108–109
meaning of, 107
perimeter of, 110–111,
258–261